JUMP Math 8.2

Book 8 Part 2 of 2

Contents

jump math™

MULTIPLYING POTENTIAL.

JUMP Math
One Yonge Street, Suite 1014
Toronto, Ontario M5E 1E5
Canada
www.jumpmath.org

Writers: Dr. Anna Klebanov, Saverio Mercurio, Dr. Sohrab Rahbar, Kelly Young
Editors: Megan Burns, Liane Tsui, Natalie Francis, Julie Takasaki, Jackie Dulson, Janice Dyer,
          Laura Edlund, Rachelle Redford
Layout and Illustrations: Linh Lam, Fely Guinasao-Fernandes, Sawyer Paul, Marijke Friesen,
          Gabriella Kerr, Ilyana Martinez
Cover Design: Blakeley Words+Pictures
Cover Photograph: © NASA, ESA, S. Beckwith (STScI), and The Hubble Heritage Team (STScI/Aura)

ISBN 978-1-927457-53-5

First printing November 2015

Printed and bound in Canada

MIX
Paper from
responsible sources
FSC
www.fsc.org   FSC® C004071

Welcome to JUMP Math

Entering the world of JUMP Math means believing that every child has the capacity to be fully numerate and to love math. Founder and mathematician John Mighton has used this premise to develop his innovative teaching method. The resulting resources isolate and describe concepts so clearly and incrementally that everyone can understand them.

JUMP Math is comprised of teacher's guides (which are the heart of our program), interactive whiteboard lessons, student assessment & practice books, evaluation materials, outreach programs, and teacher training. The Common Core Editions of our resources have been carefully designed to cover the Common Core State Standards. All of this is presented on the JUMP Math website: **www.jumpmath.org**.

Teacher's guides are available on the website for free use. Read the introduction to the teacher's guides before you begin using these resources. This will ensure that you understand both the philosophy and the methodology of JUMP Math. The assessment & practice books are designed for use by students, with adult guidance. Each student will have unique needs and it is important to provide the student with the appropriate support and encouragement as he or she works through the material.

Allow students to discover the concepts by themselves as much as possible. Mathematical discoveries can be made in small, incremental steps. The discovery of a new step is like untangling the parts of a puzzle. It is exciting and rewarding.

Students will need to answer the questions marked with a ▯ in a notebook. Grid paper notebooks should always be on hand for answering extra questions or when additional room for calculation is needed.

Contents

PART 1

Unit 4: Expressions and Equations: Linear Equations

Unit 5: Expressions and Equations: Graphing Proportional Relationships

Unit 6: Functions: Defining, Evaluating, and Comparing Functions

Unit 7: Statistics and Probability: Patterns in Scatter Plots

PART 2

Unit 1: Functions: Modeling Linear Relationships Using Functions

Unit 2: Geometry: Transformations

Unit 3: The Number System: Real Numbers

Unit 4: Geometry: Pythagorean Theorem

Unit 5: Expressions and Equations: Systems of Equations

Unit 6: Geometry: Volume

Unit 7: Statistics and Probability: Line of Best Fit and Two-Way Tables

F8-13 Coordinate Plane—Four Quadrants

We can extend both axes on a coordinate grid to include negative numbers. The axes divide the grid into four **quadrants**. We use **Roman numerals** to number the quadrants: 1 = I, 2 = II, 3 = III, 4 = IV.

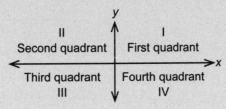

1. a) Label the origin (O) and the x- and y-axes.

   b) Label both axes with positive and negative integers. Count by 1s.

   c) Number the four quadrants (using I, II, III, IV).

   d) Which quadrants are these points in?

   A (3, 3) __*I*__   B (−3, −2) _____

   C (−3, 3) _____   D (3, −2) _____

   Bonus ▸ Point E has coordinates (−154, −238).

   Which quadrant is it in? _____

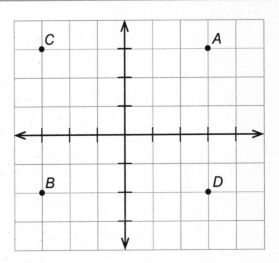

2. In Figure 1, point A (2, 3) is in the first quadrant. Its x- and y-coordinates are both positive.

   a) Find the coordinates of these points.

   P (,   )   Q (,   )

   R (,   )   S (,   )

   b) Plot and label these points.

   B (3, 2)   C (1, 4)   D (4, 1)

3. In Figure 1, point F (−2, 3) is in the second quadrant. Its x-coordinate is negative and its y-coordinate is positive.

   a) Find the coordinates of these points.

   K (,   )   L (,   )

   M (,   )   N (,   )

   b) Plot and label these points.

   G (−3, 2)   H (−1, 6)   I (−4, 1)

Figure 1

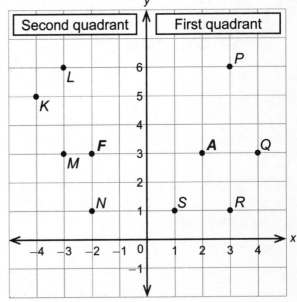

4. In Figure 2, point *A* (−2, −3) is in the third quadrant. Its *x*- and *y*-coordinates are both negative.

a) Find the coordinates of these points.

K (,   )   L (,   )

M (,   )   N (,   )

b) Plot and label these points.

B (−3, −4)   C (−2, −6)   D (−4, −3)

5. In Figure 2, point *F* (2, −3) is in the fourth quadrant. Its *x*-coordinate is positive and its *y*-coordinate is negative.

a) Find the coordinates of these points.

P (,   )   Q (,   )

R (,   )   S (,   )

b) Plot and label these points.

G (3, −4)   H (1, −6)

I (4, −1)   J (1, −2)

Figure 2

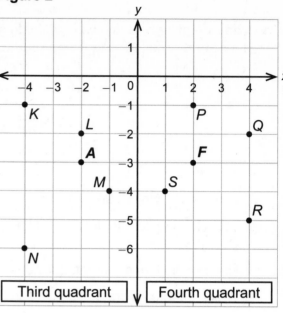

6. In Figure 3, points *B* (2, 0) and *C* (−4, 0) are both on the *x*-axis. The *y*-coordinate of any point on the *x*-axis is zero.

a) Find the coordinates of these points.

P (,   )   Q (,   )

b) Plot and label these points.

A (4, 0)   M (−2, 0)

7. In Figure 3, points *D* (0, 2) and *E* (0, −3) are both on the *y*-axis. The *x*-coordinate of any point on the *y*-axis is zero.

a) Plot and label these points.

G (0, 4)   H (0, −1)

b) Find the coordinates of these points.

K (,   )   L (,   )

Figure 3

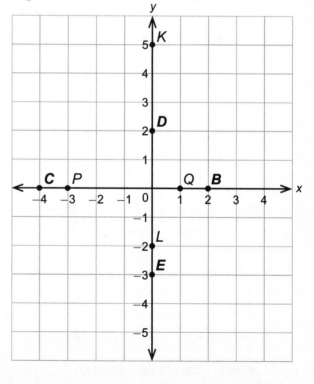

8. a) Find the coordinates of these points.

P (,   )   Q (,   )

R (,   )   S (,   )

T (,   )   U (,   )

V (,   )   W (,   )

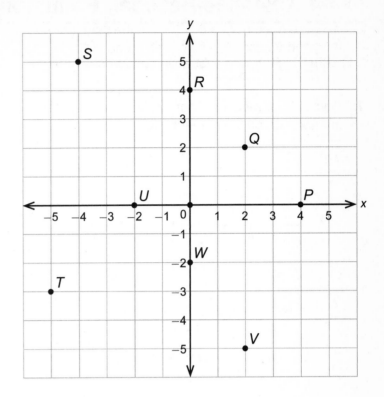

b) Plot and label these points.

A (3, 4)   B (5, −2)

C (−3, −2)   D (−4, 1)

E (3, 0)   F (0, 2)

G (0, −3)   H (−5, 0)

c) Plot and label these points. Hint: Use a ruler to estimate for decimals and fractions.

I (4.5, 2.5) $J\left(-2\frac{1}{2}, 3\frac{1}{2}\right)$

$K\left(-3.5, -4\frac{1}{4}\right)$ $L\left(3\frac{1}{3}, -3\frac{2}{3}\right)$

9. a) Plot the set of points.

   i) (6, −4), (6, −2), (6, 0), (6, 1), (6, 3)

  ii) (−3, −4), (−3, −2), (−3, 0), (−3, 2)

 iii) (−6, 5), (−3, 5), (0, 5), (5, 5)

b) Draw a line that joins the points in each set in part a). Label each line.

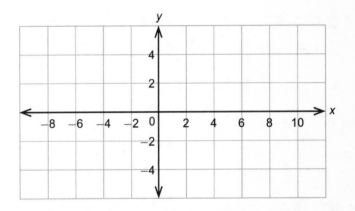

c) Fill in the table for each set of points and the line.

	i)	ii)	iii)
Which axis is the line parallel to?			
Which coordinate changes?			
Which coordinate stays the same?			
Write the coordinates for another point on the line where it extends beyond the grid.			
Bonus ▶ Write an equation for the line.	x = 6		

F8-14 Distance Between Points on a Vertical or Horizontal Line

> REMINDER: When subtracting integers, $2 - 3 = 2 + (-3)$ and $2 - (-3) = 2 + (+3)$.

1. Do both subtractions. Then circle the subtraction that tells you how far apart the integers are on the number line.

   a) $3 - 2 = $ ___1___

      $2 - 3 = $ ___-1___

      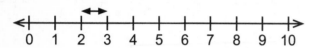

   b) $7 - 4 = $ _____

      $4 - 7 = $ _____

      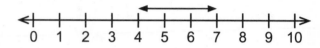

   c) $(+2) - (-4) = $ _____

      $(-4) - (+2) = $ _____

      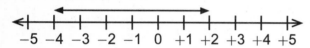

   d) $(-2) - (-5) = $ _____

      $(-5) - (-2) = $ _____

2. Which subtraction will give the distance between -3 and $+5$, $(+5) - (-3)$ or $(-3) - (+5)$?

   How do you know? _____

   _____

A distance is always positive. The **absolute value** of a number is its distance from zero.

The notation $|-3|$ is short for "the absolute value of -3." Examples: $|-3| = 3$ and $|+3| = 3$

---

3. Write the absolute value.

   a) $|-2| = $

   b) $|+4| = $

   c) $|-25| = $

   d) $|0| = $

   e) $\left|-\dfrac{3}{4}\right| = $

   f) $\left|+2\dfrac{1}{7}\right| = $

   g) $|+2.76| = $

   h) $|-0.6| = $

The distance between two integers is the absolute value of their difference. Examples:

4 and 7 are $|4 - 7| = |-3| = 3$ units apart.   2 and (-4) are $|-4 - 2| = |-6| = 6$ units apart.

---

4. Subtract. Then take the absolute value to find the distance apart.

   a) $|(-6) - (+3)| = |$ ___-9___ $| = $ ___9___ ,

      so -6 and $+3$ are ___9___ units apart.

   b) $|(-4) - (-1)| = |$ _____ $| = $ _____ ,

      so -4 and -1 are _____ units apart.

   c) $|(+16) - (-5)| = |$ _____ $| = $ _____ ,

      so $+16$ and -5 are _____ units apart.

   d) $|35 - 200| = |$ _____ $| = $ _____ ,

      so 35 and 200 are _____ units apart.

5. Use Figure 1 to find the distance between the points.

Figure 1

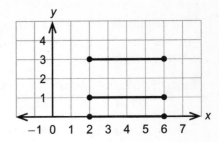

a) The distance between (2, 0) and (6, 0) is _____ units.

b) The distance between (2, 1) and (6, 1) is _____ units.

c) The distance between (2, 3) and (6, 3) is _____ units.

d) The distance between (2, y) and (6, y) is _____ units.

6. Use Figure 2 to find the distance between the points.

Figure 2

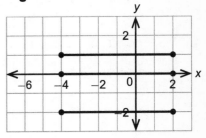

a) The distance between (−4, 0) and (2, 0) is _____ units.

b) The distance between (−4, 1) and (2, 1) is _____ units.

c) The distance between (−4, −2) and (2, −2) is _____ units.

d) The distance between (−4, y) and (2, y) is _____ units.

7. Look at your answers to Questions 5 and 6. Does the distance between two points on the same horizontal line depend on the x-coordinate or the y-coordinate?

_____

Points with the same x-coordinate are points on the same vertical line.
Points with the same y-coordinate are points on the same horizontal line.

8. Subtract the x-coordinates and take the absolute value to find the distance between the points.

a) (−3, 0) and (1, 0) _____ units

b) (5, 0) and (−2, 0) _____ units

c) (−1, −10) and (1, −10) _____ units

d) (−8, 6) and (−2, 6) _____ units

Figure 3

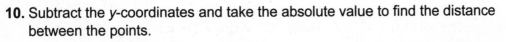

9. Use Figure 3 to find the distance between the points.

a) (0, −2) and (0, 5)

_____ units

b) (1, −2) and (1, 5)

_____ units

c) (−2, −2) and (−2, 5)

_____ units

d) (x, −2) and (x, 5)

_____ units

10. Subtract the y-coordinates and take the absolute value to find the distance between the points.

a) (1, −3) and (1, 2) _____ units

b) (1, −5) and (1, 2) _____ units

c) (−1, −2) and (−1, 2) _____ units

d) (−1, −5) and (−1, −2) _____ units

e) (184, −2) and (184, 7) _____ units

f) (−51, 2) and (−51, −5) _____ units

F8-15 Finding the y-intercept from a Graph

Remember, to find the rate of change for a line, you can find the slope between any two points, *A* and *B*, on the line.

Step 1: Choose two points. Use integer coordinates if possible.

Step 2: Label the point to the left *A* and find the slope from *A* to *B* so that the run will be positive.

Example: *A* (2, 3) and *B* (4, 2)

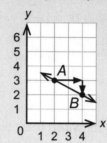

$$\text{run} = 4 - 2 = +2$$

$$\text{rise} = 2 - 3 = -1$$

$$\text{slope} = \frac{\text{rise}}{\text{run}} = \frac{-1}{+2} = -\frac{1}{2}$$

1. Mark points *A* and *B* on the line, then find the slope. Label the point to the left *A*.
   Hint: Use integer coordinates if possible.

a)

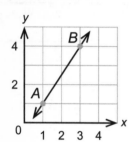

run = _____ rise = _____

$\text{slope} = \dfrac{\text{rise}}{\text{run}} =$ ——

b)

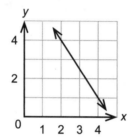

run = _____ rise = _____

$\text{slope} = \dfrac{\text{rise}}{\text{run}} =$ ——

c)

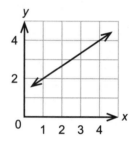

run = _____ rise = _____

$\text{slope} = \dfrac{\text{rise}}{\text{run}} =$ ——

d)

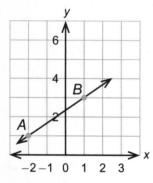

run = __3__ rise = __2__

$\text{slope} = \dfrac{\text{rise}}{\text{run}} =$ ——

e)

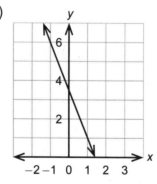

run = _____ rise = _____

$\text{slope} = \dfrac{\text{rise}}{\text{run}} =$ ——

f)

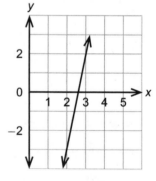

run = _____ rise = _____

$\text{slope} = \dfrac{\text{rise}}{\text{run}} =$ —— =

A line on a graph that goes from bottom left to top right shows an increasing function.
A line on a graph that goes from top left to bottom right shows a decreasing function.

2. a) Which linear functions in Question 1 are increasing?

   b) Which linear functions in Question 1 have a positive slope?

   c) How can you tell if a line is increasing or decreasing from its slope?

The **y-intercept** is where a line intersects the *y*-axis.

Examples:

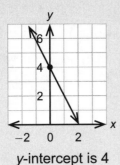

y-intercept is 4

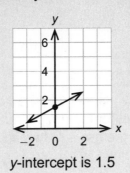

y-intercept is 1.5

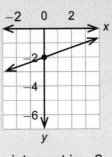

y-intercept is −2

3. a) Extend the line to find the *y*-intercept. Mark the *y*-intercept.

i)

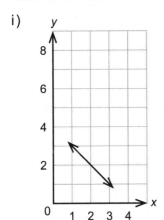

y-intercept: _____

ii)

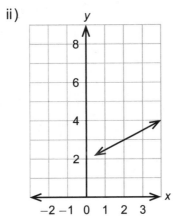

y-intercept: _____

iii)

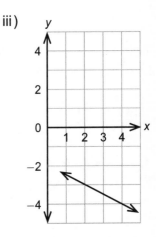

y-intercept: _____

iv)

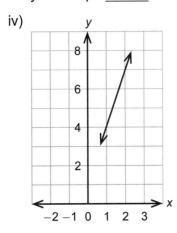

y-intercept: _____

v)

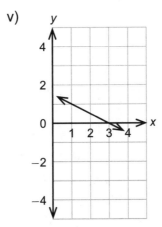

y-intercept: _____

vi)

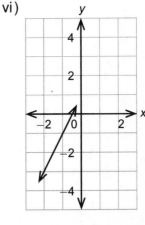

y-intercept: _____

b) Use two points with integer coordinates to find the slope of each line in part a). Do parts iv)
to vi) in your notebook. For vi), you will need to find two points with integer *x*-coordinates.

i) run = _____ rise = _____   ii) run = _____ rise = _____   iii) run = _____ rise = _____

slope = $\dfrac{\text{rise}}{\text{run}}$ = ___ =   slope = $\dfrac{\text{rise}}{\text{run}}$ = ___   slope = $\dfrac{\text{rise}}{\text{run}}$ = ___

c) Do you see any relationship between the slope and the *y*-intercept of a line? _____

Functions 8-15

To draw a line with y-intercept $= 3$ and slope $= \dfrac{-1}{2}$:

Step 1

Mark the y-intercept on the y-axis. y-intercept: 3

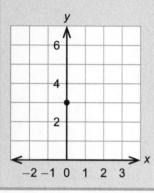

Step 2

slope $= \dfrac{\text{rise}}{\text{run}} = \dfrac{-1}{2}$

From the y-intercept, count 2 units to the right (for the run $+2$) and 1 unit down (for the rise -1) to mark the second point.

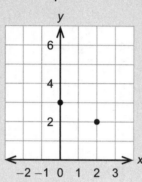

Step 3

Join the points with a straight line, then extend the line.

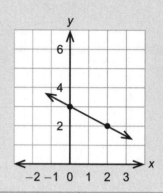

4. Mark the y-intercept, then draw a line with the given y-intercept and slope.

a)

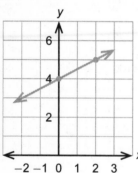

y-intercept $= 4$, slope $= \dfrac{1}{2}$

b)

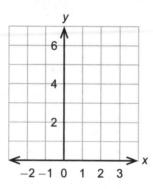

y-intercept $= 3$, slope $= \dfrac{-1}{3}$

c)

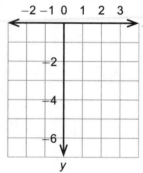

y-intercept $= -3$, slope $= \dfrac{-1}{2}$

d)

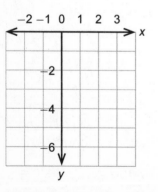

y-intercept $= -3$, slope $= 2$

Hint: Write the slope as $\dfrac{2}{1}$.

e)

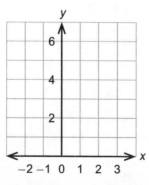

y-intercept $= 5$, slope $= -2$

Hint: Write the slope as $\dfrac{-2}{1}$.

f)

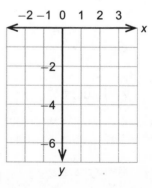

y-intercept $= -2$, slope $= -2$

1. a) Fill in the table using the equation, then plot the line. Extend the line to find the y-intercept.

i) $y = 2x - 1$

x	y
1	1
2	3

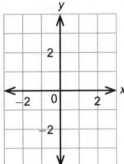

y-intercept: _____

ii) $y = -1.5x + 2$

x	y
1	
2	

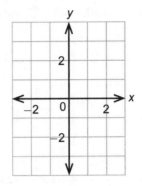

y-intercept: _____

iii) $y = -x - 0.5$

x	y
1	
2	

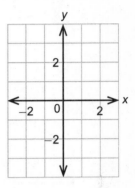

y-intercept: _____

iv) $y = \dfrac{1}{2}x - 3$

x	y
1	$-\dfrac{5}{2} = -2.5$
2	

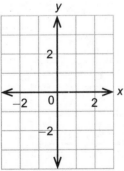

y-intercept: _____

v) $y = -2x + \dfrac{1}{2}$

x	y
1	
2	

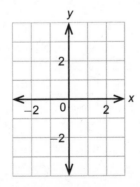

y-intercept: _____

vi) $y = \dfrac{1}{2}x - \dfrac{1}{2}$

x	y
1	
2	

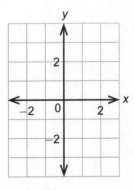

y-intercept: _____

b) Circle the y-intercept in each equation in part a). Remember to include the sign.

2. **a)** Fill in the table using the equation.

   i) $y = 2x + 3$

x	y
−1	1
0	3
1	

   ii) $y = 1.5x + 4$

x	y
−2	
0	
1	

   iii) $y = -2x - 3$

x	y
−1	
0	
2	

b) Plot the line for each equation in part a) and mark the *y*-intercept.

   i)
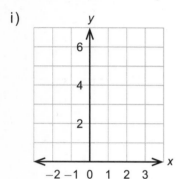
   y-intercept: _____

   ii)
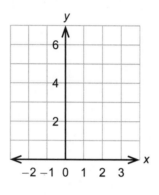
   y-intercept: _____

   iii)
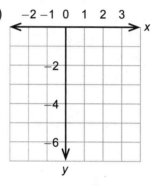
   y-intercept: _____

c) Where can you find the *y*-intercept in the table? _____

3. Find the value of *y* when $x = 0$.

   a) $y = 3x - 1$

   $= 3(0) - 1 = -1$

   b) $y = -0.5x + 2$

   $=$

   c) $y = 2x$

   $=$

   d) $y = -2x$

   $=$

   e) $y = 1.5x - 2$

   $=$

   f) $y = -2.5x + 1$

   $=$

4. Make a table for each function in Question 3.

   a) $y = 3x - 1$

x	y
1	
2	

   b) $y = -0.5x + 2$

x	y
1	
2	

   c) $y = 2x$

x	y
1	
2	

   d) $y = -2x$

   e) $y = 1.5x - 2$

   f) $y = -2.5x + 1$

5. **a)** Which functions in Question 4 would have a graph with a line that passes

   through (0, 0)? _____

   b) For lines that pass through (0, 0) in Question 4, the *y*-intercept is _____.

6. For each equation in Question 1.a), replace x with 0 to find y. If you don't get the y-intercept, find your mistake.

i) $y = 2x - 1$

$\quad = 2(0) - 1 = -1$ ✓

ii) $y = -1.5x + 2$

iii) $y = -x - 0.5$

iv) $y = \frac{1}{2}x - 3$

v) $y = -2x + \frac{1}{2}$

vi) $y = \frac{1}{2}x - \frac{1}{2}$

To find the y-intercept from the equation of a line, replace x with 0 and find y.

---

7. a) Fill in the table using the equation, then plot the line. Extend the line to find the y-intercept.

i) $y = 2x$

x	y
1	2
2	4

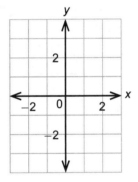

y-intercept: _____

ii) $y = 1.5x$

x	y
1	
2	

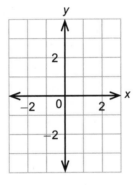

y-intercept: _____

iii) $y = -x$

x	y
1	
2	

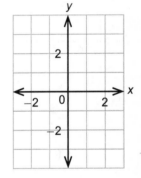

y-intercept: _____

b) Circle the graphs that go through the origin (0, 0).

Remember, lines that go through the origin represent a proportional relationship between x and y. The y-intercept for lines that go through the origin is 0.

---

8. Circle the tables in Question 7 that represent a proportional relationship between x and y.

9. Circle the equations that represent a proportional relationship.

A. $y = 3x - 2$

B. $y = 2.5x$

C. $y = -3x$

D. $y = \frac{1}{2}x$

E. $y = -1.5x + \frac{1}{2}$

F. $y = -\frac{3}{2}x$

F8-17 Finding the *y*-intercept from a Table

1. a) Use the run and rise to complete the table. Remember, change in *x* is run, and change in *y* is rise.

i)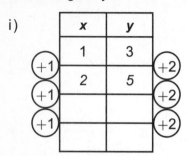

x	*y*
1	3
2	5

ii)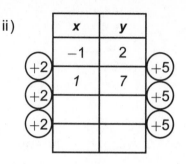

x	*y*
−1	2
1	7

iii)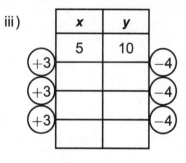

x	*y*
5	10

b) Find the slope for each table in part a) by finding the rise over run.

i) slope $= \dfrac{\text{rise}}{\text{run}} = \dfrac{2}{1} = 2$ ii) slope $= \dfrac{\text{rise}}{\text{run}} = \dfrac{\quad}{\quad} =$ iii) slope $= \dfrac{\text{rise}}{\text{run}} = \dfrac{\quad}{\quad} =$

2. a) Find the run and rise, then find the slope.

i)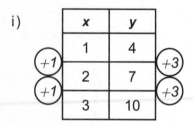

x	*y*
1	4
2	7
3	10

ii)

x	*y*
−3	−4
−1	0
1	4

iii)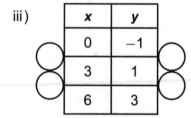

x	*y*
0	−1
3	1
6	3

slope $= \dfrac{\text{rise}}{\text{run}} = \dfrac{3}{1} = 3$ slope $= \dfrac{\text{rise}}{\text{run}} = \dfrac{\quad}{\quad} =$ slope $= \dfrac{\text{rise}}{\text{run}} = \dfrac{\quad}{\quad}$

b) Continue with the tables from part a). Multiply *x* by the slope. What must you add or subtract to each number in the second column to get *y*?

i)

x	slope × *x*	*y*
1	3 × 1 = 3	4
2	3 × 2 = 6	7
3		10

Add ___1___

ii)

x	slope × *x*	*y*
−3		−4
−1		0
1		4

Add _____

iii)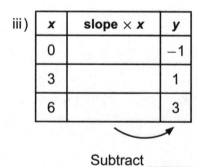

x	slope × *x*	*y*
0		−1
3		1
6		3

Subtract _____

c) Write an equation for each table in part b).

i) *y* = 3*x* + 1   ii) *y* =   iii) *y* =

d) Circle the *y*-intercept in each equation in part c).

To write the equation of a line and find the *y*-intercept from a table:

Step 1: Find the run and rise, then find the slope.

x	slope × x	y
1		2
3		8
5		14

+2 (between 1 and 3), +2 (between 3 and 5)
+6 (between 2 and 8), +6 (between 8 and 14)

$$\text{slope} = \frac{\text{rise}}{\text{run}} = \frac{6}{2} = 3$$

Step 2: Multiply each *x* by the slope.

x	slope × x	y
1	3	2
3	9	8
5	15	14

Step 3: What must you add (or subtract) to each number in the second column to get *y*?

x	slope × x	y
1	3	2
3	9	8
5	15	14

Subtract 1

Step 4: Write the equation for the table. Substitute *x* with 0 to find the *y*-intercept.

$$y = 3x - 1$$

$$y\text{-intercept} = 3(0) - 1 = -1$$

3. Find the slope to complete the table and write the equation. Circle the *y*-intercept.

a)
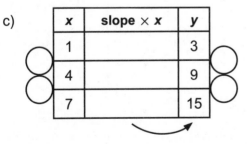

x	slope × x	y
1	−2	1
2	−4	−1
3	−6	−3

+1, +1 (left)   −2, −2 (right)
+ 3

$$\text{slope} = \frac{\text{rise}}{\text{run}} = \frac{-2}{1} = -2$$

equation: $y = -2x + 3$

b)
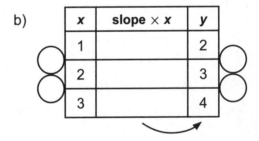

x	slope × x	y
1		2
2		3
3		4

$$\text{slope} = \frac{\text{rise}}{\text{run}} = \frac{\quad}{\quad} =$$

equation: _____

c)

x	slope × x	y
1		3
4		9
7		15

$$\text{slope} = \frac{\text{rise}}{\text{run}} = \frac{\quad}{\quad} =$$

equation: _____

d)
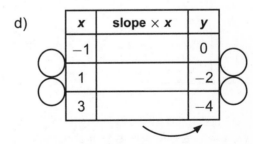

x	slope × x	y
−1		0
1		−2
3		−4

$$\text{slope} = \frac{\text{rise}}{\text{run}} = \frac{\quad}{\quad} =$$

equation: _____

4. a) Extend the line to find the *y*-intercept.

A.

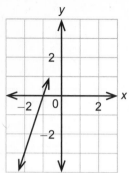

y-intercept: _____

B.

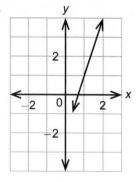

y-intercept: _____

C.

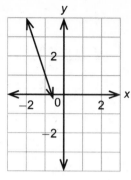

y-intercept: _____

b) Match the graph to the equation.

i) $y = 3x - 2$ _____   ii) $y = -3x - 2$ _____   iii) $y = 3x + 3$ _____

5. a) Match the table to the equation.

A.

x	y
−1	5
0	3
1	1

B.

x	y
−1	1
1	5
2	7

C.

x	y
−2	−7
−1	−5
1	−1

i) $y = 2x - 3$ _____   ii) $y = 2x + 3$ _____   iii) $y = -2x + 3$ _____

b) Circle the *y*-intercept in each equation.

c) Graph each table in part a), write the equation above the graph, and mark the *y*-intercept to check your answers to part b).

i) _____   ii) _____   iii) _____

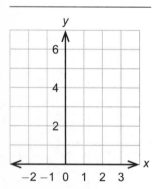

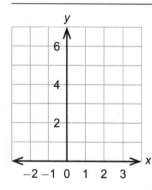

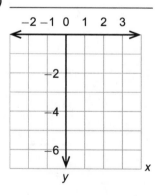

6. a) Finish writing five different equations with numbers of your choice.

$y = 2x +$ _____ $y = 2x -$ _____ $y = 3x +$ _____ $y = 3x -$ _____ $y = 2x +$ _____

b) Draw a graph for each of your five equations on grid paper, in random order.

c) Have a partner match the equations to the graphs.

1. a) Graph the list of ordered pairs and join them to make a line. Extend the line to find the *y*-intercept.

i) (1, 3), (2, 5)

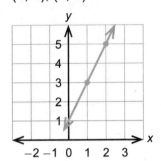

y-intercept: ___1___

ii) (−2, 4), (−1, 3)

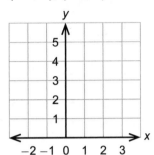

y-intercept: _____

iii) (1, 2), (3, 6)

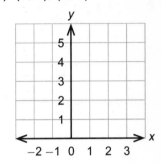

y-intercept: _____

iv) (−2, 2), (1, −4)

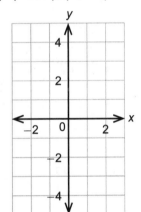

y-intercept: _____

v) (2, 4), (1, 1)

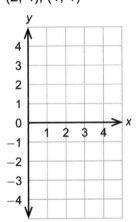

y-intercept: _____

vi) (−1, 3), (1, −3)

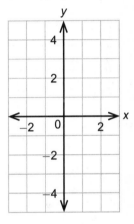

y-intercept: _____

b) Find the slope of each line in part a).

i) slope $= \dfrac{\text{rise}}{\text{run}} = \dfrac{2}{1} = 2$

ii) slope $= \dfrac{\text{rise}}{\text{run}} = \dfrac{\quad}{\quad} =$

iii) slope $= \dfrac{\text{rise}}{\text{run}} = \dfrac{\quad}{\quad} =$

iv) slope $= \dfrac{\text{rise}}{\text{run}} = \dfrac{\quad}{\quad} =$

v) slope $= \dfrac{\text{rise}}{\text{run}} = \dfrac{\quad}{\quad} =$

vi) slope $= \dfrac{\text{rise}}{\text{run}} = \dfrac{\quad}{\quad} =$

c) Make a table with the coordinates from part a). Use the slope to complete the table and write an equation. Circle the *y*-intercept. Do parts iv) to vi) in your notebook.

i)

x	slope × *x*	*y*
1	2	3
2	4	5

+ 1

equation: ___*y* = 2*x* (+ 1)___

ii)

x	slope × *x*	*y*
−2		4
−1		3

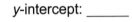

equation: _____

iii)

x	slope × *x*	*y*

equation: _____

To find the *y*-intercept from ordered pairs (1, 4), (3, 10) without graphing:

Step 1
Write the coordinates in a table, then find the run, rise, and slope.

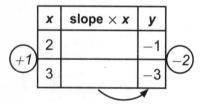

$$slope = \frac{rise}{run} = \frac{6}{2} = 3$$

Step 2
Multiply each *x* by the slope.

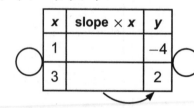

Step 3
What must you add (or subtract) to the second column to get *y*?

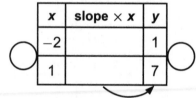

Add 1

The *y*-intercept is +1.

2. A line goes through the given points. Find the *y*-intercept without graphing.

a) (2, −1), (3, −3)

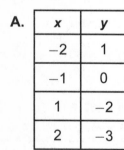

$$slope = \frac{rise}{run} = \frac{-2}{1} = -2$$

y-intercept: _____

b) (1, −4), (3, 2)

x	slope × *x*	*y*
1		−4
3		2

$$slope = \frac{rise}{run} = \text{——} =$$

y-intercept: _____

c) (−2, 1), (1, 7)

x	slope × *x*	*y*
−2		1
1		7

$$slope = \frac{rise}{run} = \text{——} =$$

y-intercept: _____

3. a) Four linear functions are represented in different ways below. Find the *y*-intercept for each.

A.

x	*y*
−2	1
−1	0
1	−2
2	−3

B.
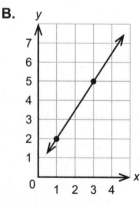

C. (−1, −2), (1, 2), (2, 4)   D. $y = -3x - 1$

b) Which function has the greatest *y*-intercept?

c) Which function has a negative *y*-intercept?

d) Which function goes through the origin?

e) Which function represents a proportional relationship between *x* and *y*?

Writing an Equation of a Line Using the Slope and *y*-intercept

> REMINDER: You can find the slope of a straight line from any two points on the line.

1. a) Find the slope of the line $y = 2x + 5$ using different pairs of points. Make sure you get the same slope each time.

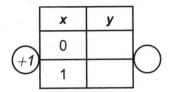

x	*y*
0	
1	

x	*y*
0	
2	

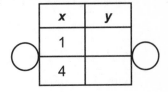

x	*y*
1	
4	

run = _____   rise = _____

$\text{slope} = \dfrac{\text{rise}}{\text{run}} = \dfrac{\quad}{\quad} =$

run = _____   rise = _____

$\text{slope} = \dfrac{\text{rise}}{\text{run}} = \dfrac{\quad}{\quad} =$

run = _____   rise = _____

$\text{slope} = \dfrac{\text{rise}}{\text{run}} = \dfrac{\quad}{\quad} =$

b) Which way of finding the slope was easiest? Using $x =$ _____ and $x =$ _____.

2. a) Fill in the table using the equation. Find the slope and *y*-intercept.

i) $y = 3x + 2$

x	*y*
0	2
1	5

y-intercept: __2__

run = 1   rise = __5 − 2 = 3__

$\text{slope} = \dfrac{\text{rise}}{\text{run}} = \dfrac{3}{1} = 3$

ii) $y = -1.5x + 2$

x	*y*
0	
1	

y-intercept: _____

run = 1   rise = _____

$\text{slope} = \dfrac{\text{rise}}{\text{run}} = \dfrac{\quad}{\quad} =$

iii) $y = -x - 0.5$

x	*y*
0	
1	

y-intercept: _____

run = 1   rise = _____

$\text{slope} = \dfrac{\text{rise}}{\text{run}} = \dfrac{\quad}{\quad} =$

b) Circle the *y*-intercept and underline the slope in each equation. Include the sign.

c) Where can you find the *y*-intercept in the equation? _____

d) Where can you find the slope in the equation? _____

3. Find the slope and the *y*-intercept of the line from the equation.

a) $y = 4x - 5$

slope: __4__

y-intercept: __−5__

b) $y = -1.5x + 2$

slope: _____

y-intercept: _____

c) $y = -x - 0.5$

slope: _____

y-intercept: _____

d) $y = \dfrac{1}{2}x - 3$

slope: _____

y-intercept: _____

e) $y = -2x + \dfrac{1}{2}$

slope: _____

y-intercept: _____

f) $y = \dfrac{1}{2}x - \dfrac{1}{2}$

slope: _____

y-intercept: _____

To write an equation for a line, multiply *x* by the slope, then add the *y*-intercept. Write the result equal to *y*.

If *m* is the slope of a line and *b* is the *y*-intercept, then $y = mx + b$ is called the **slope-intercept form** of the line.

Examples:

Slope	y-intercept	Equation of the Line
2	3	$y = 2x + 3$
1	−2	$y = x - 2$
−5	0	$y = -5x$
1.2	0.5	$y = 1.2x + 0.5$

4. For a line with the given slope and *y*-intercept, write the equation of the line in slope-intercept form.

   a) slope = 3, *y*-intercept = −3

   $\underline{\quad y = 3x - 3 \quad}$

   b) slope = −3, *y*-intercept = 3

   _____

   c) slope = 1.4, *y*-intercept = −1

   _____

   d) slope = $\frac{1}{2}$, *y*-intercept = −3

   _____

   e) slope = 2, *y*-intercept = $-\frac{2}{3}$

   _____

   f) slope = $\frac{1}{2}$, *y*-intercept = $\frac{3}{5}$

   _____

5. Find the slope and the *y*-intercept. Write the equation of the line. Hint: the *y*-intercept is the *y*-coordinate of a point that has *x*-coordinate equal to 0.

   a) *A* (2, −1), *B* (0, −3)

   y-intercept: *−3*

   run = 0 − 2 = −2

   rise = −3 − (−1) = −2

   slope = $\frac{\text{rise}}{\text{run}} = \frac{-2}{-2} = 1$

   equation: $\underline{\quad y = x - 3 \quad}$

   b) *A* (0, 2), *B* (1, 3)

   y-intercept: _____

   run = _____ − _____ = _____

   rise = _____ − _____ = _____

   slope = $\frac{\text{rise}}{\text{run}} = \underline{\quad} =$

   equation: _____

   c) *A* (−2, −1), *B* (0, −5)

   y-intercept: _____

   run = _____ − _____ = _____

   rise = _____ − _____ = _____

   slope = $\frac{\text{rise}}{\text{run}} = \underline{\quad} =$

   equation: _____

   d) *A* (1, −1), *B* (0, 1.5)

   y-intercept: *1.5*

   run = 0 − 1 = −1

   rise = 1.5 − (−1) = 2.5

   slope = $\frac{\text{rise}}{\text{run}} = \frac{2.5}{-1} = -2.5$

   equation: $\underline{\quad y = -2.5x + 1.5 \quad}$

   e) *A* (0, −2.5), *B* (1, −3.5)

   y-intercept: _____

   run = _____

   rise = _____

   slope = $\frac{\text{rise}}{\text{run}} = \underline{\quad} =$

   equation: _____

   f) *A* (−1, −1), *B* (0, −0.5)

   y-intercept: _____

   run = _____

   rise = _____

   slope = $\frac{\text{rise}}{\text{run}} = \underline{\quad} =$

   equation: _____

6. Check your answers to Question 5 by substituting.

   Example: a) $y = x - 3$, $y = 2 - 3 = -1$, *A* (2, −1) ✓

7. a) Extend the line to find the *y*-intercept. Mark two points with integer coordinates to find the slope of the line. Remember to mark the left point as *A* to have a positive run.

i)

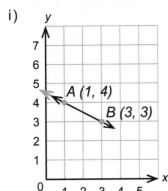

y-intercept: ___4.5___

run = ___3 − 1 = 2___

rise = ___3 − 4 = −1___

slope = $\dfrac{\text{rise}}{\text{run}} = \dfrac{-1}{2} = -0.5$

ii)

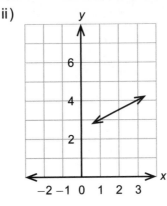

y-intercept: _____

run = _____

rise = _____

slope = $\dfrac{\text{rise}}{\text{run}} = \dfrac{}{} =$

iii)

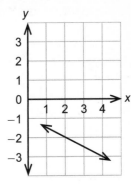

y-intercept: _____

run = _____

rise = _____

slope = $\dfrac{\text{rise}}{\text{run}} = \dfrac{}{} =$

iv)

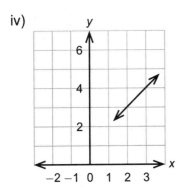

y-intercept: _____

run = _____

rise = _____

slope = $\dfrac{\text{rise}}{\text{run}} = \dfrac{}{} =$

v)

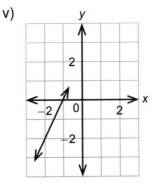

y-intercept: _____

run = _____

rise = _____

slope = $\dfrac{\text{rise}}{\text{run}} = \dfrac{}{} =$

vi)

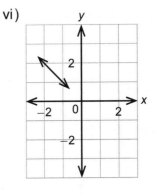

y-intercept: _____

run = _____

rise = _____

slope = $\dfrac{\text{rise}}{\text{run}} = \dfrac{}{} =$

b) Write the equation for each line in part a) in slope-intercept form.

i) *y* = ___−0.5x + 4.5___

ii) *y* = _____

iii) *y* = _____

iv) *y* = _____

v) *y* = _____

vi) *y* = _____

c) Which equation represents a proportional relationship between *x* and *y*? _____

1. a) Graph both functions on the same grid. Determine which function has the greater slope and which is steeper.

i) $y = x + 1$

$y = 2x - 3$

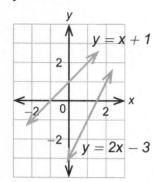

Greater slope: <u>$y = 2x - 3$</u>

Steeper: <u>$y = 2x - 3$</u>

ii) $y = 3x - 1$

$y = x + 2$

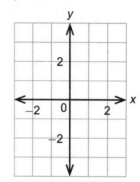

Greater slope: _____

Steeper: _____

iii) $y = 2x - 1$

$y = x - 2$

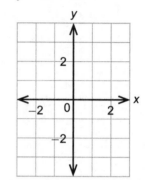

Greater slope: _____

Steeper: _____

iv) $y = -x - 1$

$y = -2x + 3$

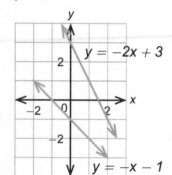

Greater slope: <u>$y = -x - 1$</u>

Steeper: <u>$y = -2x + 3$</u>

v) $y = -3x + 1$

$y = -2x - 2$

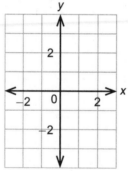

Greater slope: _____

Steeper: _____

Bonus ▶ $y = x + 1$

$y = -3x + 1$

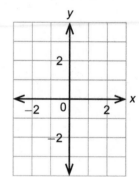

Greater slope: _____

Steeper: _____

b) Does a greater slope always mean a steeper slope? _____

c) Find the absolute value of the slopes for each part in a).

i) $|1| = 1, |2| = 2$

ii)

iii)

iv) $|-1| = 1, |-2| = 2$

v)

Bonus ▶

d) Does a greater absolute value slope always mean a steeper slope? _____

A greater slope does not always mean a steeper slope. You need to compare the absolute values of slopes to find out which is steeper.

Example: Line *AB* has a slope of 1 and *CD* has a slope of −3 so *AB* has a greater slope than *CD*. However, line *CD* has a steeper slope than *AB*.

Slope of *AB*: 1   Absolute value of slope of *AB*: 1

Slope of *CD*: −3   Absolute value of slope of *CD*: 3

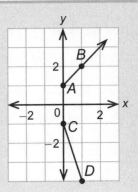

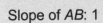
2. a) Four linear functions are represented in different ways below. Find the slope of each.

A.

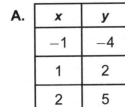

x	y
−1	−4
1	2
2	5
3	8

B.

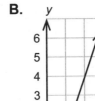

C. $(-2, 0), (0, 2), (3, 5)$

D. $y = -4x + 3$

b) Which two functions have the same slope? _____ and _____

c) Which function has the greatest slope? _____

d) Which function has the steepest slope? _____

3. The table shows the temperatures in the first week of May in Los Angeles, CA, at 8 a.m. and 4 p.m.

	Mon	Tue	Wed	Thu	Fri	Sat	Sun
Temperature at 8 a.m. (°F)	79	71	75	76	83	83	78
Temperature at 4 p.m. (°F)	74	71	78	84	85	77	75

a) Find the changes in temperature for each day.

	Mon	Tue	Wed	Thu	Fri	Sat	Sun
Change in Temperature	−5						

b) Which day had the greatest change in temperature? _____

c) Find the change in temperature per hour for each day.

d) Which day had the greatest change in temperature per hour? _____

e) Explain how you can use change in temperature to calculate change in temperature per hour.

_____

F8-21 Using the Equation of a Line to Solve Word Problems

1. A train is traveling at a constant speed of 50 mi/h.

   a) Write an equation for the distance the train traveled after x hours. $y = $ _____

   b) How far does the train travel in 3 hours? Hint: Replace x with 3. _____

   c) How far does the train travel in 4.5 hours? _____

   d) How long does it take for the train to travel 250 miles?
      Hint: Substitute $y = 250$ in the equation, then solve for x.

   e) How long does it take for the train to travel 425 miles?

2. To rent a pair of skates, you pay a $3 flat fee plus $2 per hour, as shown in the graph below.

   a) How much does it cost to rent a pair of skates for 1 hour? _____

   b) How much does it cost to rent a pair of skates for 3 hours? _____

   c) Julie paid $10 to rent a pair of skates. How many hours did she pay for?

      _____

   d) Find the y-intercept and the slope of the line.

      y-intercept: _____   slope $= \dfrac{\text{rise}}{\text{run}} = \underline{\quad} = $

   e) Write the equation of the line. $y = $ _____

   f) Substitute $x = 1$ in the equation to find the cost of renting skates

      for 1 hour. _____

   g) Where do you see the flat rate in the equation? _____

   h) How you can find the answer to part b) using the equation? _____

   i) Find the answer to part c) by replacing y with 10 in the equation and solving for x.

   j) Can you use the graph as is to find the cost of renting a pair of skates for 10 hours?

      Why or why not? _____

   k) How could you use the equation to find the cost of renting a pair of skates for 10 hours?

      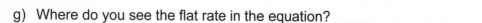

3. Kim has $10 and she saves $5 every week.

a) Create a table of values for Kim's savings after *x* weeks.

x weeks	$*y* in savings
0	10
1	15
2	
3	

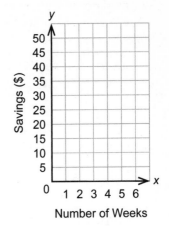

b) Plot the ordered pairs from the table of values above on the graph on the right.

c) Find the *y*-intercept and the slope of the line.

y-intercept: _____   slope $= \dfrac{\text{rise}}{\text{run}} = \dfrac{\quad}{\quad} =$

d) Write the equation of the line. *y* = _____

e) Kim plans to buy a skateboard for $85. How many weeks must she save to buy the skateboard?

f) Did you need the graph to answer parts c), d), and e)? _____

4. Tony has a $25.00 gift card for an online role-playing game. Subscribing to the game costs $4.25 per month.

a) How much money remains on the gift card after the first month? _____

b) Fill in the table of values for his remaining money after *x* months.

x months	$*y* on gift card
0	25.00
1	20.75
2	
3	

c) For the table above, find the *y*-intercept and the slope of a line that goes through all points.

d) Write the equation of the line. *y* = _____

e) How much money remains on the gift card after 5 months? _____

F8-22 Describing Graphs

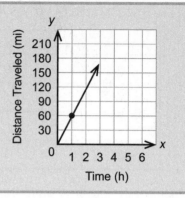

1. A group of Grade 8 students take a bike trip from their school.
   The graph shows the times and distances of their trip.

   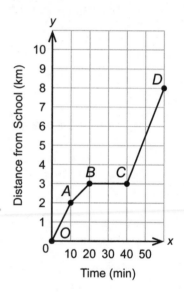

   a) How far did the students bike in 1 hour? _____

   b) Complete the table to find the slope between …

		Run (min)	Rise (km)	Slope (km/min)
i)	O and A	10 − 0 = 10	2 − 0 = 2	$\frac{rise}{run} = \frac{2}{10} = 0.2$
ii)	A and B			$\frac{rise}{run} = \frac{\quad}{\quad} =$
iii)	B and C			$\frac{rise}{run} = \frac{\quad}{\quad} =$
iv)	C and D			$\frac{rise}{run} = \frac{\quad}{\quad} =$

   c) Which line segment has the steepest slope? _____

   d) What was the maximum speed of the group during the trip? _____

   e) The maximum speed of the group happened in between _____ minutes

      and _____ minutes.

   f) The students stopped to have a rest. Which line segment shows the rest? _____
      Hint: During the rest, the distance from the school doesn't change.

   g) What is the students' speed during the rest? _____

2. Three students run 12 km in 60 minutes.

- Beth starts slowly and increases her speed as she warms up.
- John runs at a constant speed.
- Anna starts running fast, then she slows down.

a) Match the graph to the student by writing a name under each graph.

A.

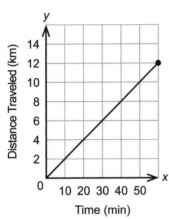

B.

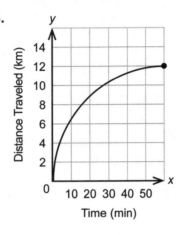

C.

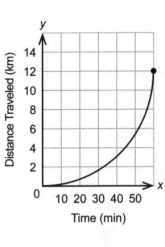

_____   _____   _____

b) Which graph represents a linear function? _____

3. May took a road trip to her aunt's house (500 miles away) and her grandmother's house (700 miles away). The graph shows how far from home she was during the last week.

a) How many miles did May drive in the first day? _____

b) How many days did she take to drive to her aunt's house?

_____

c) Which days did May not drive? _____

d) How many nights did May stay at her grandmother's house?

_____

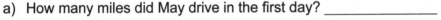

e) The nights that May didn't sleep at her relatives' homes, she stayed

in motels. How many nights did May stay in a motel? _____

f) Write a story about May's trip to describe all line segments of the graph.

_____

_____

_____

_____

4. The graph shows the number of gold medals won by the United States at each of the Summer Olympic Games from 1992 to 2012.

    a) Find the slope of each line segment.

    b) Which line segment has the greatest slope? _____

    c) In what year did the US have the best results compared

        with the previous Summer Olympic year's results? _____

    d) Which line segment has the smallest slope? _____

    e) In what year did the US have the worst results compared

        with the previous Summer Olympic year's results? _____

    f) Which line segment has the slope equal to 0? _____

    g) In what year did the results not change from the previous

        Summer Olympic year? _____

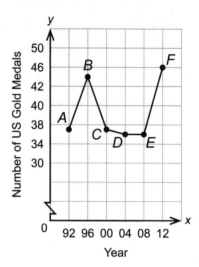

5. Sam lives 900 m from his school. Today, Sam:

    • walked 200 m in 4 minutes,
    • then ran 600 m in 3 minutes,
    • then rested for 1 minute, and
    • then walked the last 100 m in 2 minutes.

    a) How far did Sam go in the first 7 minutes? _____

    b) How far did Sam go in the first 8 minutes? _____

    c) Fill the table to find how far Sam went after t minutes. Then use the table to complete the graph at right.

Time (min)	4	7	8	10
Distance Traveled (m)	200			

    d) How long does it take Sam to get to school? _____

    e) Find the slope of each line segment to find Sam's speed during each part of his trip:

        i)   ii)   iii)   iv)

    f) In what period of time does the graph have the steepest slope? _____

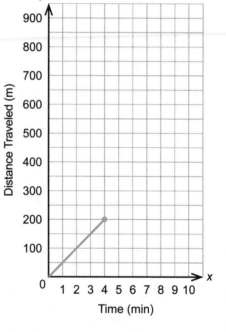

1. Test any input number to see if the picture shows a machine. Circle the machines.

a)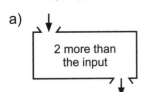

b)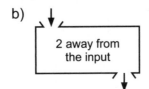

c)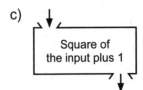

2. Circle the mapping diagrams that represent a function.

A.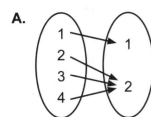
B.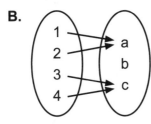
C.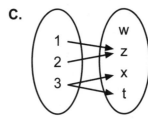
D.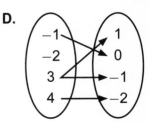

Bonus ▶ Draw a mapping diagram for the following set of ordered pairs. Does it represent a function? $(1, 1), (2, 4), (3, 4), (2, 2^2), (4, 2)$

3. Use the gap in the sequence to find the coefficient in the formula. Then complete the table to finish writing the formula.

a)

Input (*n*)	*n* × gap	Output
1		5
2		8
3		11

Bonus ▶

Input (*n*)	*n* × gap	Output
1		0
2		−2
3		−4

Formula: _____

Formula: _____

4. Match the graph to the equation.

A.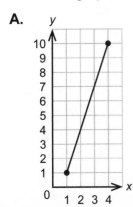

B.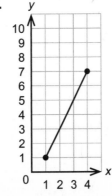

C.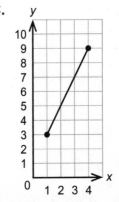

a) $y = 2x + 1$ _____

b) $y = 3x - 2$ _____

c) $y = 2x - 1$ _____

5. A ship is traveling across the ocean at a constant speed of 30 mi/h.

a) Create a table of values for the distance the ship traveled after t hours.

t (hours)	Distance Traveled (mi)
1	
2	
3	

b) Write the ordered pairs from the above table of values. Then plot the points on the graph on the right.

c) Join the points on the graph with a straight line. If the ship

traveled 3.5 hours, about how far would it go? _____

d) About how many hours would it take the ship to travel 195 miles?

Extend the line to find out. _____

e) Find the slope of the line using the table in part a). _____

f) Write the equation of the line. $y =$ _____

g) Answer parts c) and d) using the equation of the line.

h) Can you use the graph to find exactly how long it takes to go 160 miles? _____

i) Use the equation of the line to find exactly how long it takes to go 160 miles.

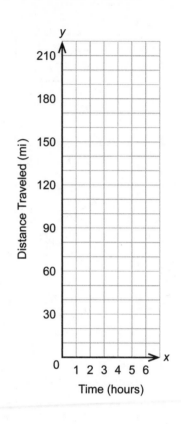

6. Kevin left his home to walk to school 500 m away. After a while, he realized he forgot something. The graph shows how far he was from home.

a) How far did Kevin walk before he noticed he forgot something?

_____

b) How many minutes did it take to walk back home? _____

c) How many minutes was Kevin at home again? _____

d) Find the slope of all four line segments.

e) When does Kevin walk faster toward the school: when he first

leaves home or after he gets what he forgot? _____

f) Write a story to describe the graph.

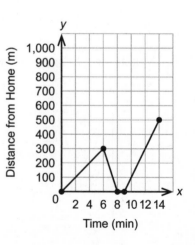

Functions 8-23

G8-17 Translations

1. How many units right or left did the dot slide from position *A* to position *B*?

a)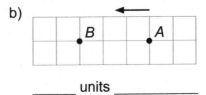

_____ units _right_

b)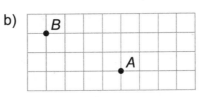

_____ units _____

c)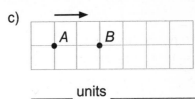

_____ units _____

2. How many units right or left and how many units up or down did the dot slide from position *A* to position *B*?

a)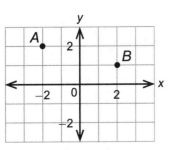

_____ units right

_____ units down

b)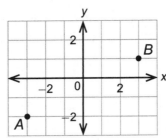

_____ units left

_____ units up

c)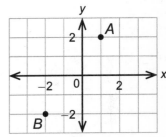

_____ units right

_____ unit down

3. How many units right or left and how many units up or down did the dot slide from position *A* to position *B*? Write the coordinates of both points.

a)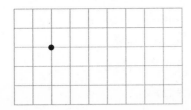

_____ units right

_____ unit down

A (,   )

B (,   )

b)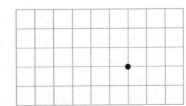

_____ units right

_____ units up

A (,   )

B (,   )

c)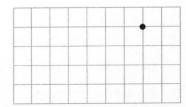

_____ units left

_____ units down

A (,   )

B (,   )

4. Slide the dot.

a) 5 units right, 2 units down

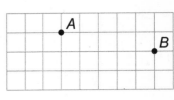

b) 6 units left, 3 units up

c) 3 units left, 4 units down

The mathematical term for a slide is **translation**. When we **translate** a point or a shape, the result is called the **image** of the original point or shape.

5. Translate the point by the given number of units. Write the coordinates of the original point and the image.

a) 5 units right, 2 units down

b) 6 units left, 3 units up

c) 5 units left, 4 units down

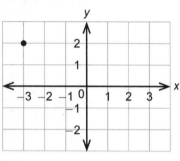

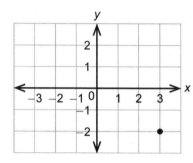

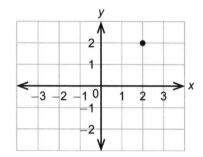

original point (,   )

original point (,   )

original point (,   )

image (,   )

image (,   )

image (,   )

To distinguish between the original point and the image, add a prime symbol (′) or a star (*) to the label of the image. You can write "to" or use an arrow to show a translation: A to A' or $B \rightarrow B^*$.

6. Translate each vertex 4 units to the right and 2 units down. Join the new vertices to draw the image of the triangle. Write the coordinates of the original vertices and images.

a)

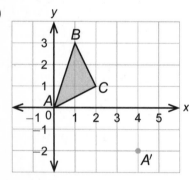

b)

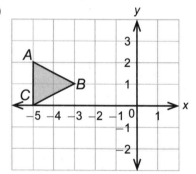

c)

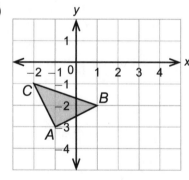

A (0 , 0) $\rightarrow$ A' (4 , -2)

B (,   ) $\rightarrow$ B' (,   )

C (,   ) $\rightarrow$ C' (,   )

A (,   ) $\rightarrow$ A' (,   )

B (,   ) $\rightarrow$ B' (,   )

C (,   ) $\rightarrow$ C' (,   )

A (,   ) $\rightarrow$ A^* (,   )

B (,   ) $\rightarrow$ B^* (,   )

C (,   ) $\rightarrow$ C^* (,   )

7. Draw the shape on a coordinate grid, translate the shape's vertices, and join them to draw the image of the shape. For the image, write the coordinates of its vertices.

a) square with vertices A (1, 1), B (1, 3), C (3, 3), D (3, 1)—3 units right, 4 units up

b) triangle with vertices A (3, 7), B (2, 5), C (5, 4)—4 units left, 3 units down

Geometry 8-17

G8-18 Describing Translations

1. a) A point is translated 3 units down. Find the coordinates of the image.

    i) $(2, 3) \rightarrow ($, $)$ ii) $(3, 2) \rightarrow ($, $)$ iii) $(-4, 1) \rightarrow ($, $)$

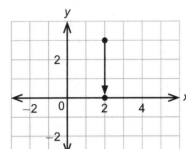 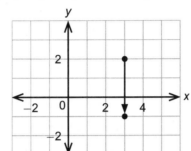 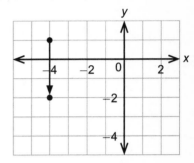

  b) Which coordinate changed during the translation? _____

  c) Look for a pattern and describe it: The _____-coordinate decreased by _____.
     Write an algebraic expression describing the change in the y-coordinate.

     Use y as a variable. $y \rightarrow$ _____

  d) Use the expression in part c) to predict the coordinates of the point after it slides
     3 units down.

    i) $(-1, 2) \rightarrow ($, $)$ ii) $(0, 3) \rightarrow ($, $)$ iii) $(-1, 0) \rightarrow ($, $)$

  e) Plot the points from d) and their images on the grids above to check your predictions.

2. a) A point is translated 4 units to the right. Find the coordinates of the image.

    i) $(-1, 3) \rightarrow ($, $)$ ii) $(0, 1) \rightarrow ($, $)$ iii) $(-3, -2) \rightarrow ($, $)$

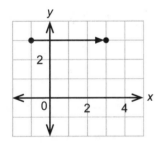 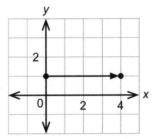 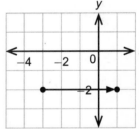

  b) Which coordinate changed during the translation? _____

  c) Look for a pattern and describe it: The _____-coordinate increased by _____.
     Write an algebraic expression describing the change in the x-coordinate.

     Use x as a variable. $x \rightarrow$ _____

  d) Use the expression in part c) to predict the coordinates of the point after it slides
     4 units to the right.

    i) $(-1, -1) \rightarrow ($, $)$ ii) $(1, 3) \rightarrow ($, $)$ iii) $(-4, 1) \rightarrow ($, $)$

  e) Plot the points and their images from d) on the grids above to check your predictions.

3. Translate point *P* two units in the given direction. Write the coordinates of the image. Which coordinate changed and by how much?

a) 2 units up

b) 2 units down

c) 2 units left

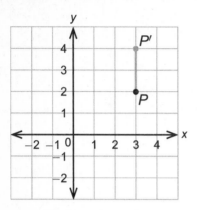

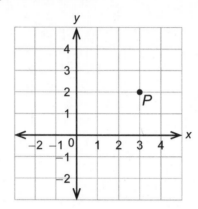

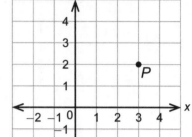

$P(3, 2) \rightarrow P'(\quad, \quad)$

$P(3, 2) \rightarrow P'(\quad, \quad)$

$P(3, 2) \rightarrow P'(\quad, \quad)$

The __*y*__-coordinate

The ____-coordinate

The ____-coordinate

__*increased by 2*__.

_____.

_____.

4. Point $Q(x, y)$ is translated to point Q'. Match the coordinates of Q' to the description of the translation.

A. 4 units up   **B.** 4 units down   **C.** 4 units left   **D.** 4 units right

a) $Q'(x + 4, y)$ __D__   b) $Q'(x, y - 4)$ ____   c) $Q'(x, y + 4)$ ____   d) $Q'(x - 4, y)$ ____

5. Write an algebraic expression for the change in each coordinate after the translation.

a) 5 units right, 2 units down

b) 6 units left, 3 units up

c) 3 units left, 4 units down

$(x, y) \rightarrow$ __$(x + 5, y - 2)$__

$(x, y) \rightarrow$ _____

$(x, y) \rightarrow$ _____

When a shape is translated, all points of the shape move the same way.

6. Draw arrows from each vertex of the shape to its image. Are the arrows parallel and the same length? Is this a translation?

a)

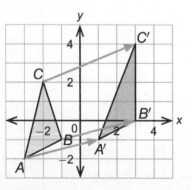

____*no*____

b)

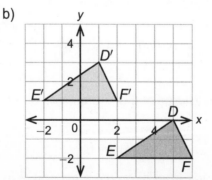

_____

c)

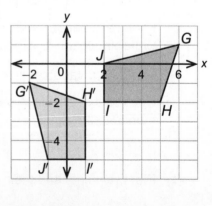

_____

Mathematicians say that A' is the "image of A under translation."

To describe a translation:

Step 1: Draw arrows from each vertex of the shape to its image. Check that the arrows are parallel and of the same length.

Step 2: Check the arrows to see how many units up or down, and left or right, the vertices of the shape moved. Describe the translation with the number of units and directions.

7. Describe the translation.

a)

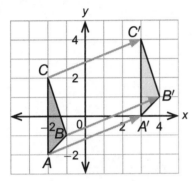

5 units right, 2 units up

b)

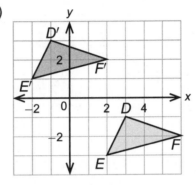

_____

c)

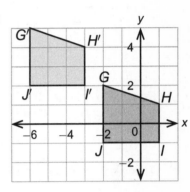

_____

d)

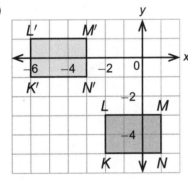

_____

e)

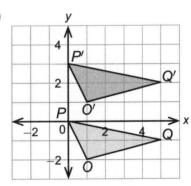

_____

Bonus ▶

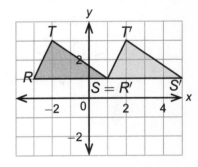

_____

8. For each translation in Question 7, write an algebraic expression for the changes in the coordinates.

a) $(x, y) \rightarrow$ ___$(x + 5, y + 2)$___

b) $(x, y) \rightarrow$ _____

c) $(x, y) \rightarrow$ _____

d) $(x, y) \rightarrow$ _____

e) $(x, y) \rightarrow$ _____

Bonus ▶ $(x, y) \rightarrow$ _____

9. Alice thinks that she can write an algebraic expression for the change of the coordinates under translation using addition only and no subtraction. Is she correct? If yes, write the expressions from Question 8 using only addition. If no, explain why this is impossible. Use examples, such as from Question 8, in your answer.

10. Draw a polygon on a coordinate grid. Translate the polygon and describe the translation.

G8-19 Properties of Translations

1. a) Translate points *A* and *C* to the right 2 units and up 3 units. Label their images *A'* and *C'*. Draw line *A'C'*.

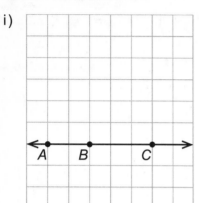

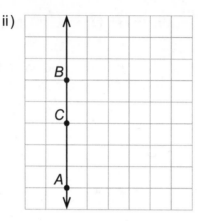

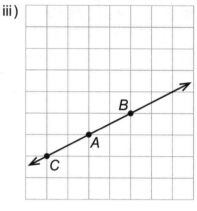

b) Point *B* is on line *AC*. Translate point *B* to the right 2 units and up 3 units. Label the image *B'*. Is *B'* on line *A'C'*?

i) _____   ii) _____   iii) _____

c) Translate points *E* and *F* as given. Label their images *E'* and *F'*. Draw line *E'F'*.

   i) 4 units down   ii) 3 units left   iii) 2 units left, 3 units up

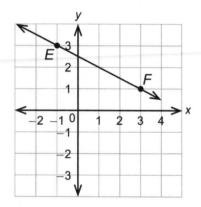

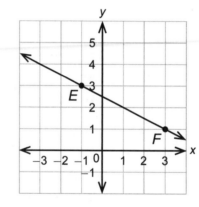

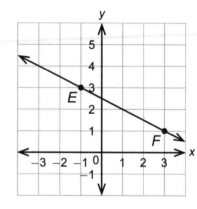

d) Choose a point *G* on line *EF*. The coordinates of *G* are (,   ). Mark and label point *G* on each grid in part c).

e) Translate point *G* as given in part c). What are the coordinates of the image?

   i) *G'* (,   )   ii) *G'* (,   )   iii) *G'* (,   )

f) Is point *G'* on line *E'F'*?

   i) _____   ii) _____   iii) _____

Mathematicians say that translations "take" lines to lines.

Translations preserve the order of points on a line. If point *B* is between points *A* and *C*, then point *B'* is between points *A'* and *C'*.

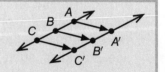

2. a) Use a ruler to measure the sides of each triangle.

i)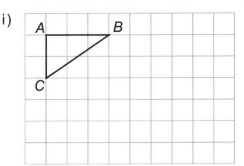

ii)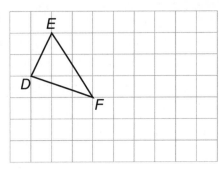

AB = _____

AC = _____

BC = _____

DE = _____

EF = _____

DF = _____

b) Translate each triangle 6 units to the right and 2 units down. Use ′ to label the images of the vertices.

c) Measure the sides of the image.

i) $A'B'$ = _____

$A'C'$ = _____

$B'C'$ = _____

ii) $D'E'$ = _____

$E'F'$ = _____

$D'F'$ = _____

d) Sides of triangles are line segments. Does this translation preserve the length of

line segments? _____

Bonus ▶ What can you say about the triangle and its image under translation? Explain using a congruence rule.

_____

_____

> REMINDER: If opposite sides in a quadrilateral are parallel and equal, then the other pair of sides are also parallel and equal, so the shape is a parallelogram.
>
> 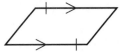 means

3. a) Write a description of a translation of your choice.

b) Draw a line segment PQ on a coordinate grid. Translate PQ using the translation from part a). Label the image $P'Q'$.

c) Draw the line segments PP' and QQ'.

d) All points of PQ move the same way. What does this mean about PP' and QQ'? Use the quadrilateral $PP'Q'Q$ to explain why $PQ = P'Q'$.

4. a) Describe a translation of your choice:

_____ units _____, _____ units _____

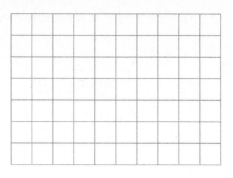

b) Draw a line *MN* on the grid. Translate *MN* using the translation in part a). Label the image *M'N'*.

c) Draw the line segments *MM'* and *NN'*.

d) What do know about *MM'* and *NN'*? Use the quadrilateral *MM'N'N* to explain why *MN* ∥ *M'N'*.

_____

_____

5. a) Measure the angles of each triangle.

i)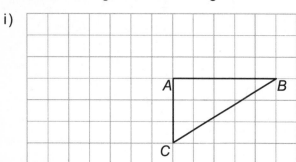

ii)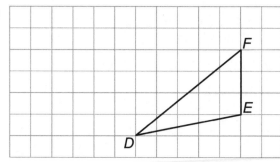

∠A = _____   ∠D = _____

∠B = _____   ∠E = _____

∠C = _____   ∠F = _____

b) Translate each triangle 5 units to the left and 2 units up. Use ′ to label the vertices of the images.

c) Measure the angles of each image.

i) ∠A' = _____   ii) ∠D' = _____

∠B' = _____   ∠E' = _____

∠C' = _____   ∠F' = _____

d) What do you notice about the angles of each triangle and its image?

_____

Does translation preserve angle sizes? _____

6. True or false? If the statement is true, explain why. If the statement is false, draw a counterexample.

a) A triangle and its image under translation are congruent.

Bonus ▶ Does this work the other way around? If two triangles are congruent, is there a translation that takes one of them onto the other?

Geometry 8-19

G8-20 Parallel Lines and Translations

REMINDER: Side-Angle-Side (SAS) Congruence Rule

If ABC and $A'B'C'$ are triangles with
$AB = A'B'$, $\angle B = \angle B'$, and $BC = B'C'$,
then $\triangle ABC \cong \triangle A'B'C'$.

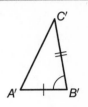

1. Are triangles ABC and $A'B'C'$ congruent?

a)

b)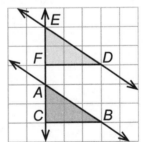

c)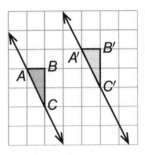

_____

_____

_____

REMINDER: Corresponding angles at parallel lines are equal.

If the corresponding angles are equal, the lines
are parallel.

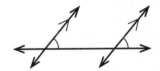

2. a) Can you apply the SAS rule to triangles ABC and DEF? If yes, write the two pairs
        of equal sides and the equal angles for the pair. If no, write "no."

i)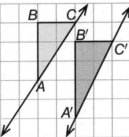

ii)

iii)

$\underline{AC = DF, \angle C = \angle F,}$

$\underline{CB = FE}$

_____

_____

b) Mark a pair of angles in triangles ABC and DEF that are corresponding angles at
    lines AB and DE.

c) Are the angles you marked in part b) equal?

i) _____yes_____   ii) _____   iii) _____

d) Are lines AB and DE parallel?

i) _____yes_____   ii) _____   iii) _____

3. Find the run, rise, and slope of the line.

a)

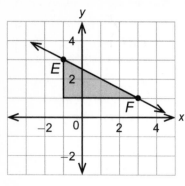

run = __3 − (−1) = 4__

rise = __1 − 3 = −2__

slope = $\dfrac{-2}{4} = -\dfrac{1}{2}$

b)

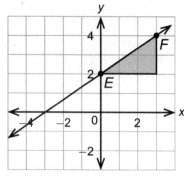

run = _____

rise = _____

slope =

c)

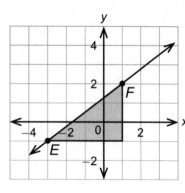

run = _____

rise = _____

slope =

4. a) Find the slope of each line in Question 2.

i)   slope $AB =$

slope $DE =$

ii) slope $AB =$

slope $DE =$

iii) slope $AB =$

slope $DE =$

b) What do you notice about the slopes of parallel lines? _____

5. For the given line, draw a triangle and a congruent triangle to draw a parallel line.

a)

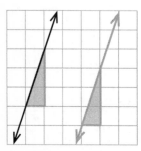

b)

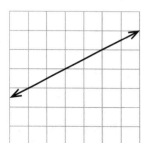

c)

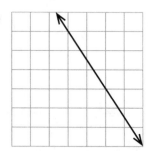

To translate a line, choose two points on the line and translate them.
Then draw a new line through the images of the points.

6. a) Translate the line as given. Find the slope of the line and its images.

i) $\ell \rightarrow \ell'$

3 units right, 1 unit up

ii) $\ell \rightarrow \ell^*$

2 units down, 2 units left

slope $\ell =$ slope $\ell' =$ slope $\ell^* =$

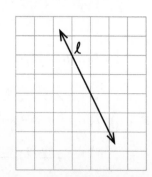

b) Do translations change the slope of a line? _____

Parallel lines have the same slope.

7. Line *n* is translated 27 units up and 72 units left to get line *n′*. Line *n* is translated 13 units down and 6 units right to get line *n**. Are lines *n′* and *n** parallel? Explain.

REMINDER: You can use any two points on a straight line to find the run, rise, and slope.
To make the calculation easy, choose points with integer coordinates.

8. a) Find the slopes of the lines and see if they are parallel. Label parallel lines with arrows.

i)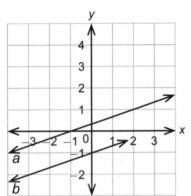

ii)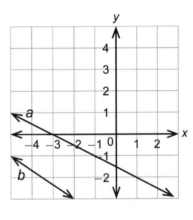

iii)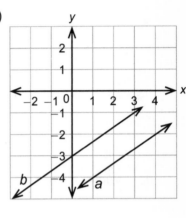

slope *a* =   slope *a* =   slope *a* =

slope *b* =   slope *b* =   slope *b* =

b) Translate the lines 3 units up and 2 units right. Label the images *a′* and *b′*.

c) Use the slope to say if *a′* and *b′* are parallel. Label parallel lines with arrows.

i) slope *a′* =   ii) slope *a′* =   iii) slope *a′* =

slope *b′* =   slope *b′* =   slope *b′* =

d) Does this translation take parallel lines to parallel lines? _____

9. a) Draw two congruent triangles anywhere on the grid.

b) Can you move from one triangle to the other using a translation? If yes, describe the translation. If no, explain why not.

c) Draw two congruent triangles so that there is no translation that takes one triangle to the other. Use the slope of one of the sides to explain why there is no translation.

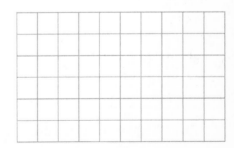

Bonus ▶ Translations take congruent triangles to congruent triangles. Use right triangles as in Question 2 to explain why translations take parallel lines to parallel lines.

To **reflect** a point *P* in a **mirror line** *m*:

Step 1: Draw a line through *P* perpendicular to *m*. Extend it beyond *m*.

Step 2: Measure the distance from *P* to *m* along the perpendicular.

Step 3: Mark the point *P′* on the perpendicular on the other side of *m* so that *P* and *P′* are the same distance from the mirror line *m*.

Point *P′* is the **mirror image** of *P*. Mathematicians say that *P′* is the image of *P* "under **reflection**" in the line *m*.

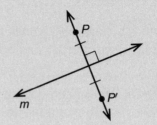

1. Use a ruler and a protractor. Reflect point *P* in the given mirror line.

   a)   •*P*

   b)

   c)   •*P*

2. Count the grid squares to reflect point *A* in the given line.

   a)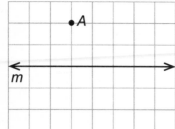

   b)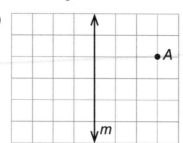

   c)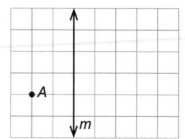

3. a) Reflect points *A* and *C* in line *m*. Label their images *A′* and *C′*. Draw line *A′C′*.

   i)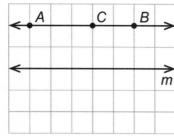

   ii)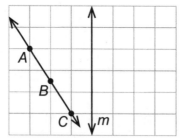

   iii)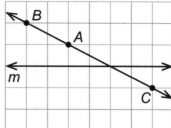

   b) In part a), point *B* is on line *AC*. In each case, reflect point *B* in line *m*. Label the image *B′*. Is *B′* on line *A′C′*?

   i) _____   ii) _____   iii) _____

   c) Do reflections take lines to lines? _____

   d) Compare the order of points *A*, *B*, and *C* on line *AC* to the order of points *A′*, *B′*, and *C′* on line *A′C′*. Does the order of the points stay the same in a reflected line? _____

To reflect a shape in a mirror line, reflect the shape's vertices and then join the images of the vertices.

4. a) Use a ruler to measure the sides of each triangle.

i)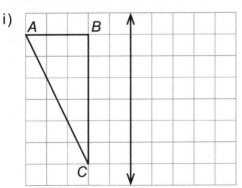

ii)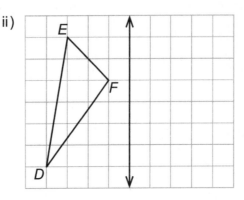

$AB =$ _____

$AC =$ _____

$BC =$ _____

$DE =$ _____

$EF =$ _____

$DF =$ _____

b) Reflect each triangle in the given line. Use ′ to label the images of the vertices.

c) Measure the sides of each image.

i) $A'B' =$ _____

  $A'C' =$ _____

  $B'C' =$ _____

ii) $D'E' =$ _____

  $E'F' =$ _____

  $D'F' =$ _____

d) Sides of triangles are line segments. Does reflection preserve the length of

line segments? _____

e) Measure the angles of the triangles above.

i) $\angle A =$ _____, $\angle B =$ _____, $\angle C =$ _____

  $\angle A' =$ _____, $\angle B' =$ _____, $\angle C' =$ _____

ii) $\angle D =$ _____, $\angle E =$ _____, $\angle F =$ _____

  $\angle D' =$ _____, $\angle E' =$ _____, $\angle F' =$ _____

f) What do you notice about the angles of each triangle and its image? _____

Does reflection preserve angle sizes? _____

5. True or false? If the statement is true, explain why. If the statement is false, draw a counterexample.

a) A triangle and its mirror image are congruent.

b) If two triangles are congruent, they are mirror images of each other.

6. Draw a scalene triangle XYZ on a grid. Draw a horizontal line. Reflect $\triangle XYZ$ in the line. Label the image $X'Y'Z'$. Translate $\triangle XYZ$ 6 units to the right and label the image $X*Y*Z*$. How are $\triangle X'Y'Z'$ and $\triangle X*Y*Z*$ the same? How are they different?

1. Reflect points *P*, *Q*, and *R* in the *x*-axis. Label the image points and write the coordinates of the original points and the images.

a)

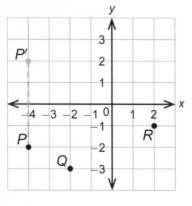

b)

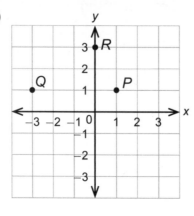

c)

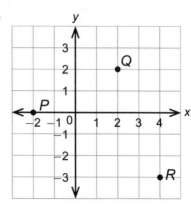

P (,   ) ➔ P′ (,   )   P (,   ) ➔ P′ (,   )   P (,   ) ➔ P′ (,   )

Q (,   ) ➔ Q′ (,   )   Q (,   ) ➔ Q′ (,   )   Q (,   ) ➔ Q′ (,   )

R (,   ) ➔ R′ (,   )   R (,   ) ➔ R′ (,   )   R (,   ) ➔ R′ (,   )

2. Look at your answers in Question 1.

   a) Which coordinate stayed the same after the reflection in the *x*-axis? _____

   b) Write "horizontal" or "vertical" to explain your answer in part a):

   A point and its reflection in the *x*-axis are on the same _____ line.

   Points on the same _____ line have the same *x*-coordinate.

   c) Which coordinate changed after the reflection in the *x*-axis? How did it change?

   _____

   d) Use your answers from parts a) and c) to predict the coordinates of the points after reflection in the *x*-axis.

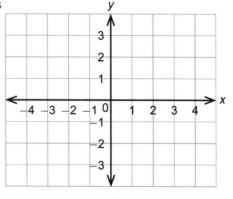

   D (0, −3) ➔ *D*′ (,   )   *E* (−3, −2) ➔ *E*′ (,   )

   F (−1, 3) ➔ *F*′ (,   )   *G* (3.5, 2) ➔ *G*′ (,   )

   H (2, −2.5) ➔ *H*′ (,   )   *I* (1, 0) ➔ *I*′ (,   )

   e) Plot the points from part d) to check your predictions.

   f) Use your answers from parts a) and c) to explain why a point on the *x*-axis does not move when reflected in the *x*-axis.

   _____

   _____

   _____

3. Reflect points *A*, *B*, and *C* in the *y*-axis. Label the image points *A'*, *B'*, and *C'*. Write the coordinates of the original points and the images.

a)

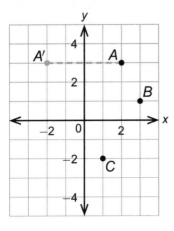

b)

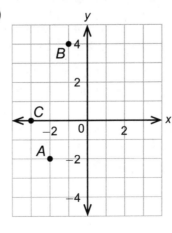

c)

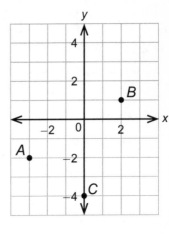

A (2 , 3) → *A'* (−2 , 3)   *A* (,   ) → *A'* (,   )   *A* (,   ) → *A'* (,   )

B (,   ) → *B'* (,   )   *B* (,   ) → *B'* (,   )   *B* (,   ) → *B'* (,   )

C (,   ) → *C'* (,   )   *C* (,   ) → *C'* (,   )   *C* (,   ) → *C'* (,   )

4. Look at your answers in Question 3.

   a) Which coordinate stayed the same after the reflection in the *y*-axis? _____

   b) Write "horizontal" or "vertical" to explain your answer in part a):

   A point and its reflection in the *y*-axis are on the same _____ line.

   Points on the same _____ line have the same *y*-coordinate.

   c) Which coordinate changed after the reflection in the *y*-axis? How did it change?

   _____

   d) Use your answers from parts a) and c) to predict the coordinates of the points after reflection in the *y*-axis.

   J (1, 2) → *J'* (,   )   *K* (3, −3) → *K'* (,   )

   L (2, 0) → *L'* (,   )   *M* (−2, −1) → *M'* (,   )

   $N\left(0, \frac{1}{2}\right)$ → *N'* (,   ) $O\left(-3, 2\frac{1}{2}\right)$ → *O'* (,   )

   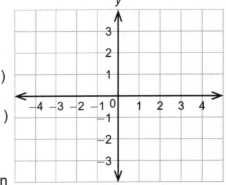

   e) Plot the points from part d) to check your predictions.

   f) Use your answers from parts a) and c) to explain why a point on the *y*-axis does not move when reflected in the *y*-axis.

   g) Tom thinks that when a point is reflected in an axis, the absolute values of the coordinates do not change. Is he correct? Explain. Use the word "distance" in your explanation.

Reflections and translations are examples of **transformations**.

5. A reflection in the *x*-axis, a reflection in the *y*-axis, or a translation was performed on Triangle 1 to get Triangle 2. Mathematicians say we "obtain" Triangle 2.

a) Without plotting the triangles, say which transformation was used. Say what the mirror line is, or what the direction and the distance of the translation are.

i) Triangle 1: △*ABC*, *A* (3, 1), *B* (3, 4), *C* (5, 2)

Triangle 2: △*A'B'C'*, *A'* (−3, 1), *B'* (−3, 4), *C'* (−5, 2)

△*A'B'C'* was obtained from △*ABC* by

_____.

ii) Triangle 1: △*DEF*, *D* (3, −1), *E* (3, −4), *F* (5, −2)

Triangle 2: △*D'E'F'*, *D'* (−3, −1), *E'* (−3, −4), *F'* (−1, −2)

△*D'E'F'* was obtained from △*DEF* by

_____.

iii) Triangle 1: △*ABC* in part i), above

Triangle 2: △*DEF* in part ii), above

△*ABC* was obtained from △*DEF* by

_____.

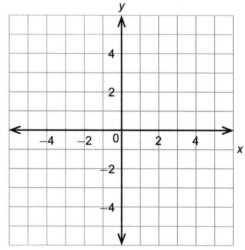

b) Plot the triangles on the same grid to check your answers in part a).

6. a) Reflect △*ABC* in the *x*-axis. Label the image △*A'B'C'*.

b) Reflect △*A'B'C'* in the *y*-axis. Label the image △*A*B*C**.

c) Jake thinks that △*A*B*C** is obtained from △*ABC* by a translation. Is he correct? Explain why or why not.

_____

_____

_____

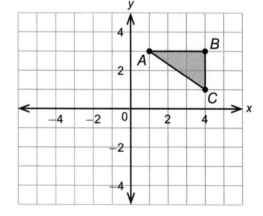

7. a) Reflect *ABCD* first in the *x*-axis, then in the *y*-axis.

b) Reflect *ABCD* first in the *y*-axis, then in the *x*-axis.

c) Did you get the same answer in parts a) and b)? Explain your answer using the predictions about the change in coordinates for reflections that you developed in Questions 2 and 4.

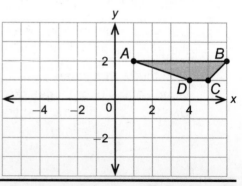

G8-23 Reflecting Lines

REMINDER: Run is the change in *x*. Rise is the change in *y*.

The slope of a line is $\dfrac{\text{rise}}{\text{run}}$. The slope of line ℓ is $\dfrac{4}{3}$.

Parallel lines have the same slope, so the slope of

line *n* is also $\dfrac{4}{3}$.

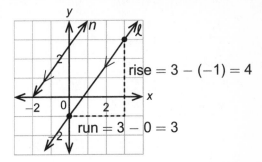

rise $= 3 - (-1) = 4$

run $= 3 - 0 = 3$

1. a) Find the slope of each line. If the lines are parallel, label them with arrows.

i)
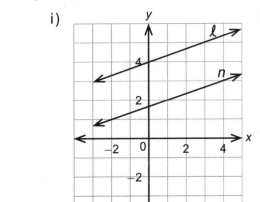

slope $\ell =$

slope $n =$

ii)
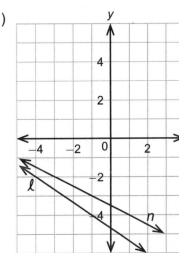

slope $\ell =$

slope $n =$

iii)
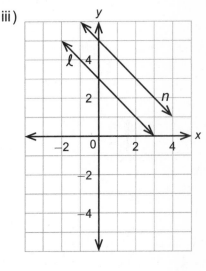

slope $\ell =$

slope $n =$

REMINDER: To reflect a line, select two points on the line and reflect the points. Then draw a new line through the mirror images of the points.

b) Reflect the lines in part a) in the *x*-axis. Label the images ℓ' and n'.

c) Find the slopes of the reflected lines. If the reflected lines are parallel, label them with arrows.

i) slope $\ell' =$ ii) slope $\ell' =$ iii) slope $\ell' =$

slope $n' =$ slope $n' =$ slope $n' =$

d) Does reflection in the *x*-axis take parallel lines to parallel lines? _____

Does reflection in the *x*-axis take lines that are not parallel to parallel lines? _____

e) How does reflection in the *x*-axis change the slope of a line? _____

f) Use your answer in e) to explain your answer in d).

2. a) Find the rise, run, and slope of lines *AB* and *CD*.

        A (4, −1), *B* (1, 3)   *C* (−2, 0), *D* (−5, 4)

        rise = _____ = _____   rise = _____ = _____

        run = _____ = _____   run = _____ = _____

        slope =   slope =

b) Are the lines *AB* and *CD* parallel? _____

> REMINDER: When a line is reflected in the *y*-axis, the *x*-coordinate changes sign (+ or −), and the *y*-coordinate stays the same.

c) Find the coordinates of the images of *A*, *B*, *C*, and *D* when reflected in the *y*-axis.

        A′ (,   ), *B′* (,   )   *C′* (,   ), *D′* (,   )

d) Find the rise, run, and slope of lines *A′B′* and *C′D′*.

        rise *A′B′* = _____ = _____   rise *C′D′* = _____ = _____

        run *A′B′* = _____ = _____   run *C′D′* = _____ = _____

        slope *A′B′* =   slope *C′D′* =

e) Are lines *A′B′* and *C′D′* parallel? _____

f) Plot lines *AB*, *CD*, *A′B′*, and *C′D′*. Then check your work.

g) Does reflection in the *y*-axis take parallel lines to parallel lines? _____

 Bonus ▶ Can reflection in the *y*-axis take a pair of lines that are not parallel to a pair of parallel lines? How do you know?

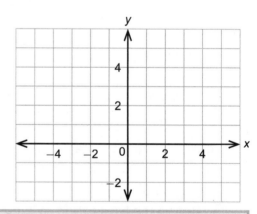

> A line through points all with the *y*-coordinate equal to 2 has the equation $y = 2$. It is a horizontal line.

3. a) Write the coordinates of two points on the line $y = 3$.

b) Use the points from part a) to find the slope of the line $y = 3$.

c) If you reflect the line in the *y*-axis, how will the coordinates of the two points change? How will the slope of the line change?

d) Predict the equation of the image of the line $y = 3$ when you reflect it in the *y*-axis.

e) Predict the equation of the image of the line $y = 3$ when you reflect it in the *x*-axis.

f) Draw a coordinate grid and check your predictions.

G8-24 Reflections in Lines That Are Not Axes

1. Draw a ray with endpoint *P* so that the ray is perpendicular to the line *m*.

a) 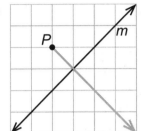   b) 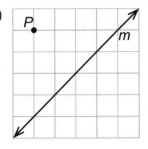   c) 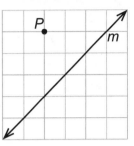   d)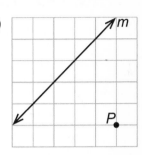

> The points $(-1, -1)$, $(0, 0)$, $(1, 1)$, and $(2, 2)$ all have the *x*-coordinate equal to the *y*-coordinate. They are all on the same line. This line has the equation $y = x$.

2. a) Plot the points $(-1, -1)$, $(0, 0)$, $(1, 1)$, and $(2, 2)$. Draw a line through the points and extend it across the grid.

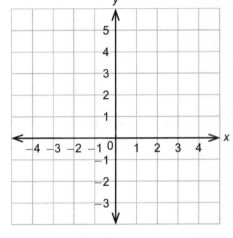

b) Write the coordinates of two more points on the line $y = x$.

(,   )   (,   )

Plot the points to check your prediction.

c) Plot the points on the grid.

$A\ (4, -1)$, $B\ (1, 3)$, $C\ (-2, 0)$, $D\ (-1, -3)$, $E\ (4, 2)$

d) Reflect the points from part c) in the line $y = x$. Write the coordinates of the mirror images in the table.

Point	$A\ (4, -1)$	$B\ (1, 3)$	$C\ (-2, 0)$	$D\ (-1, -3)$	$E\ (4, 2)$
Image					

e) Describe how coordinates of a point change after a reflection in the line $y = x$.

_____

f) Use your answer from part e) to explain why a point on the line $y = x$ does not change when reflected in the line $y = x$.

Bonus ▶ Use your answer from part e) to explain why a point in the second quadrant of the grid is reflected into the fourth quadrant. Why do the points in the first and third quadrant stay in the first and third quadrant?

Bonus ▶ Plot $A\ (-4, 3)$, $B\ (-2, 4)$, and $C\ (-1, 1)$ on a coordinate grid to make a triangle.

a) Reflect $\triangle ABC$ in the *x*-axis. Label the image $\triangle A'B'C'$.

b) Reflect $\triangle A'B'C'$ in the *y*-axis. Label the image $\triangle A*B*C*$.

c) May thinks that we get $\triangle A*B*C*$ from $\triangle ABC$ by reflecting in the line $y = x$. Is she correct? Explain why or why not using your answer from Question 2.e).

3. a) Find the coordinates of the vertices of the shapes below.

b) Predict the coordinates of the vertices after a reflection in the line $y = x$.

i)

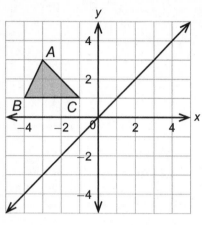

$A (\quad , \quad) \rightarrow A' (\quad , \quad)$

$B (\quad , \quad) \rightarrow B' (\quad , \quad)$

$C (\quad , \quad) \rightarrow C' (\quad , \quad)$

ii)

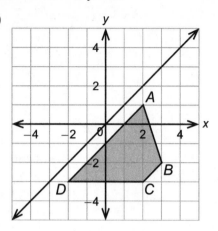

$A (\quad , \quad) \rightarrow A' (\quad , \quad)$

$B (\quad , \quad) \rightarrow B' (\quad , \quad)$

$C (\quad , \quad) \rightarrow C' (\quad , \quad)$

$D (\quad , \quad) \rightarrow D' (\quad , \quad)$

c) Reflect the shapes above by first reflecting the vertices in the line $y = x$, and check your answers from b).

4. a) Reflect the triangles in the vertical line $x = 2$. Write the coordinates of the vertices.

i)

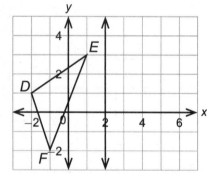

$D (\quad , \quad) \rightarrow D' (\quad , \quad)$

$E (\quad , \quad) \rightarrow E' (\quad , \quad)$

$F (\quad , \quad) \rightarrow F' (\quad , \quad)$

ii)

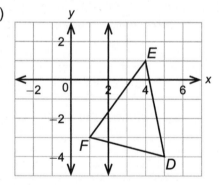

$D (\quad , \quad) \rightarrow D' (\quad , \quad)$

$E (\quad , \quad) \rightarrow E' (\quad , \quad)$

$F (\quad , \quad) \rightarrow F' (\quad , \quad)$

b) Draw a line segment between each vertex in part a) and its image. What do you notice about the line segments? _____

The **midpoint** of a line segment is the point halfway between the endpoints of the line segment.

midpoint

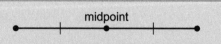

c) On the grids above, mark the midpoints of the line segments you drew in part b).

The shapes ABC and $A'B'C'$ are mirror images of each other when
• line segments between each vertex and its possible image are parallel; and
• all the midpoints of these line segments fall on the same perpendicular line.
Note: The line segments between the vertices have different lengths.

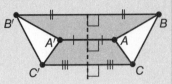

5. a) Draw line segments between the vertices of the shape and its images.

i) 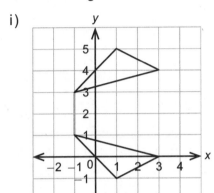   ii) 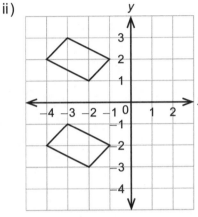   iii)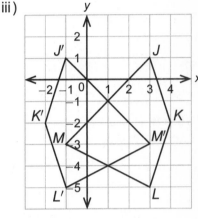

b) Find the midpoint of each line segment you drew in part a). Are the midpoints on the same line?

c) Are the shapes reflections of each other? If yes, write the equation of the mirror line. If no, write "no."

Bonus ▶ For the pair of shapes where your answer was "no" in part c), identify the transformation that takes one shape into the other.

6. Fill in the table to summarize what happens to a shape that is reflected. What happens when a shape is translated?

Transformation	Lengths of sides	Sizes of angles	Orientation
Reflection			
Translation			

7. The shapes are reflections of each other. Use a ruler and a protractor to find the mirror line.

a) 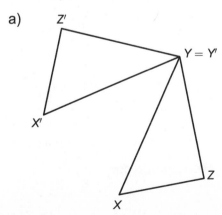   b) 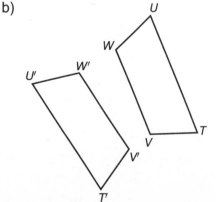   c)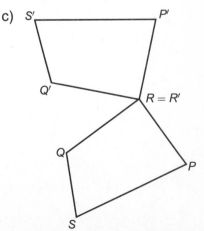

G8-25 Rotations

1. From the dark arrow, draw an arc showing the given turn. Draw the arrow after turning.

   a) 90° clockwise   b) 90° counterclockwise c) 90° clockwise   d) 90° counterclockwise

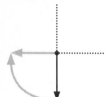 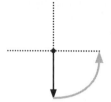 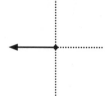 

To **rotate** point P around point O 60° clockwise:

Step 1: Draw line segment OP. Measure its length.

Step 2: Draw an arrow clockwise from P.

Step 3: Place the protractor so that the origin is at point O and the base line aligns with OP.

Step 4: Does the scale that counts clockwise have a 0 on the line segment? If not, turn the protractor upside-down.

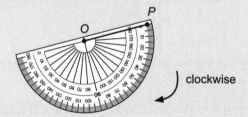

clockwise

Step 5: Make a mark at 60° on the scale that counts clockwise. Remove the protractor and draw a ray through the mark, starting at O.

Step 6: On the new ray, measure and mark the image point P' so that OP' = OP.

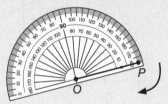 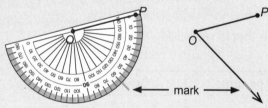 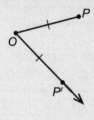

mark

---

2. Rotate point P around point O by the given angle and direction.

   a) 60° clockwise   b) 20° counterclockwise c) 150° counterclockwise   d) 180° clockwise

   P •   P   •P
                          O •   •

   O •   P •   O•   •O

3. For points O and P in Question 2, what rotation in the opposite direction around point O will take point P to the same image?

   a) _____   b) _____   c) _____   d) _____

4. a) Rotate points A and C around point O clockwise (CW) or counterclockwise (CCW), as given. Label their images A' and C'. Draw line $A'C'$.

i) 170° CW ii) 25° CCW iii) 90° CW

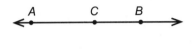

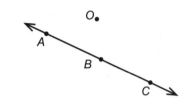

b) In part a), point B is on line AC. In each case, rotate point B around point O as you did for points A and C. Label the images B'. Is B' on line $A'C'$?

i) _____   ii) _____   iii) _____

c) Do rotations take lines to lines? _____

d) Compare the order of points A, B, and C on line AC to the order of points A', B', and C' on line $A'C'$. Do rotations preserve the order of the points on a line? _____

> To rotate a shape around point O, rotate the shape's vertices and join the images of the vertices.
>
> The point O is called the **center of rotation**. The center of rotation can be outside, inside, or on the side of the shape. The center of rotation is the only **fixed point** during a rotation; it does not move.

5. a) Rotate the triangle below 90° clockwise around the given point.

i) point O; use $'$ to label the image

ii) point B; use * to label the image

b) Do $\triangle A'B'C'$ and $\triangle A^*B^*C^*$ seem congruent? _____

c) What is different about $\triangle A'B'C'$ and $\triangle A^*B^*C^*$: the location, orientation, or both?

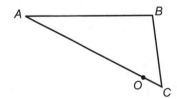

_____

d) Which transformation takes $\triangle A'B'C'$ to $\triangle A^*B^*C^*$? Draw the mirror line or the translation arrow.

_____

Bonus ▶ Mark any point inside $\triangle ABC$ and label it P. Rotate $\triangle ABC$ 90° clockwise around point P to get $\triangle A''B''C''$. Is $\triangle A''B''C''$ congruent to $\triangle A'B'C'$ and to $\triangle A^*B^*C^*$? What transformation will take $\triangle A''B''C''$ to each of the other two triangles?

6. a) Measure the sides of the triangle.

i)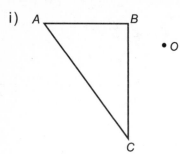

ii)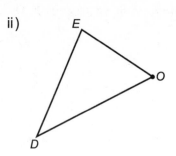

AB = _____   DE = _____

AC = _____   EO = _____

BC = _____   DO = _____

b) Rotate each triangle 120° counterclockwise around point O. Use ′ to label the vertices of the image.

c) Measure the sides of the images.

i) $A'B'$ = _____   ii) $D'E'$ = _____

$A'C'$ = _____ $E'O'$ = _____

$B'C'$ = _____ $D'O'$ = _____

d) Sides of triangles are line segments. Does rotation preserve the length of

line segments? _____

e) Measure the angles of the triangles.

i) $\angle A$ = _____, $\angle B$ = _____, $\angle C$ = _____   ii) $\angle D$ = _____, $\angle E$ = _____, $\angle O$ = _____

$\angle A'$ = _____, $\angle B'$ = _____, $\angle C'$ = _____ $\angle D'$ = _____, $\angle E'$ = _____, $\angle O'$ = _____

f) What do you notice about the angles of each triangle and its image? _____

Does rotation preserve angle sizes? _____

7. True or false? If the statement is true, explain why. If the statement is false, draw a counterexample.

a) A triangle and its image under rotation are congruent.

b) If two triangles are congruent, there is always a rotation that takes one triangle onto the other.

Bonus ▶ Use a ruler to draw a triangle ABC. Find the midpoint of side AC and label it M. Rotate △ABC 180° clockwise around point M. What type of quadrilateral do △ABC and its image make together? Explain.

G8-26 Rotations of 90° on a Grid

1. a) Which sides and angle in △OA'B' are equal to these sides and angle in △OAB?

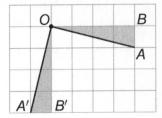

OB = _____   AB = _____   ∠ABO = _____

What can you say about △OA'B' and △OAB? _____

b) What can you say about ∠AOB and ∠A'OB'? _____

c) What is the degree measure of ∠BOB'? ∠BOB' = _____

d) Use the diagram and your answers in parts b) and c) to fill in the blanks.

∠A'OA = ∠_____ + ∠_____

= ∠AOB + ∠_____

= ∠_____ = _____°

e) What transformation takes △OAB to △OA'B'? _____

You can rotate a triangle 90° using a grid instead of a protractor.

Triangle *OCD* has sides: 2 units long horizontal, 3 units vertical.
Rotations take triangles to congruent triangles. A rotation of 90° takes horizontal lines to vertical lines and vertical lines to horizontal lines.

Triangle *OC'D'* has sides: 2 units long vertical, 3 units long horizontal.

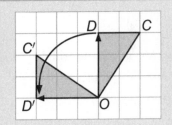

---

2. Rotate the triangle 90° counterclockwise around point *O*. Start with the side marked by an arrow. Hint: Note the direction first.

a)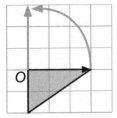

b)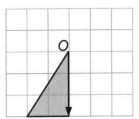

c)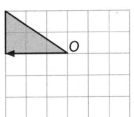

d)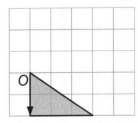

3. Rotate the triangle 90° clockwise around point *O*. Start with the horizontal or vertical side adjacent to point *O*.

a)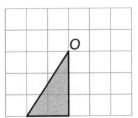

b)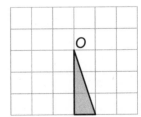

c)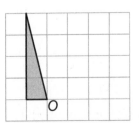

d)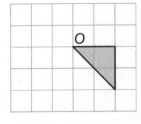

To rotate a slanted line segment *OP* on a grid 90° clockwise around the endpoint *O*:

Step 1: Shade a right triangle with *OP* as one side.

Step 2: Rotate the triangle 90° clockwise around *O*.

Step 3: Mark the image line segment *OP'*.

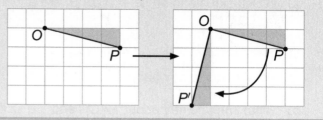

4. Mona wants to rotate point *P* (2, 3) 90° clockwise around the origin.

    a) Which quadrant of the grid is *P* in? _____

    b) Which quadrant do you predict the image *P'* will be in? _____

    c) Mona draws line segment *OP* and shades a right triangle as shown. Rotate *OP* 90° clockwise around the origin. Label *P'*.

    d) *OP* has run 2 and rise 3. *OP'* has run _____ and rise _____.

    e) The coordinates of *P'* are (,   ).

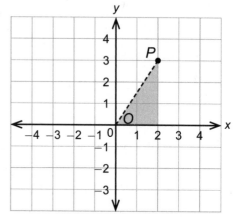

5. Use Mona's method from Question 4 to rotate the vertices of the polygon around the origin. Join the vertices to create the image of the polygon.

    a) 90° counterclockwise

    b) 90° clockwise

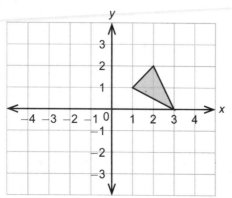

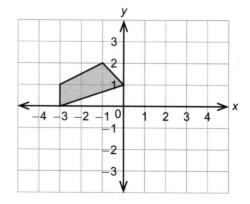

6. a) Predict the coordinates of points *L* (−3, −3), *M* (2, −1), and *N* (−3, 1) under the given rotation around the origin.

    i) 90° CW: *L'* (,   ), *M'* (,   ), *N'* (,   )

    ii) 90° CCW: *L** (,   ), *M** (,   ), *N** (,   )

    b) Plot the points, rotate them, and check your predictions.

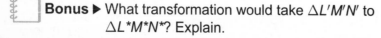

    Bonus ▶ What transformation would take △*L'M'N'* to △*L*M*N**? Explain.

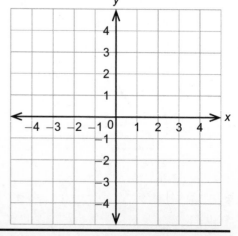

G8-27 More Rotations on a Grid

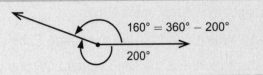

A full rotation is 360°. A clockwise (CW) rotation of 200° has the same image as a counterclockwise (CCW) rotation of 160° around the same point.

$160° = 360° - 200°$

200°

1. Point *P* is rotated counterclockwise around point *O*. What clockwise rotation around *O* has the same image as this rotation?

   a) 240° CCW _____   b) 180° CCW _____   c) 25° CCW _____   d) 359° CCW _____

2. Plot point *Q* (−2, −3) and then rotate *Q* around the origin as given. Write the coordinates of the image.

   a) 270° clockwise; *Q′* (,   )

   b) 270° counterclockwise; *Q** (,   )

   c) Which rotation around the origin will take point *Q′*

   to point *Q**? _____

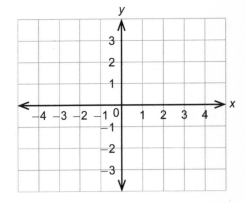

3. Triangle *A′OB′* is the image of △*AOB* under a rotation around point *O*.

   a) What is the degree measure of ∠*BOB′*? ∠*BOB′* = _____

   b) What is the degree measure of ∠*AOA′*? ∠*AOA′* = _____

   c) Which rotation takes △*AOB* to △*A′OB′*? _____

   d) △*AOB* has a horizontal side _____ units long and a vertical side _____ units long.

   △*A′OB′* has horizontal side _____ units long and vertical side _____ units long.

   e) Write "horizontal" or "vertical" to complete the sentence:

   A 180° rotation clockwise or counterclockwise takes horizontal lines to

   _____ lines and vertical lines to _____ lines.

   f) Explain why a rotation of 180° clockwise produces the same result as a rotation 180° counterclockwise around the same center.

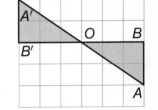

4. Rotate the triangle 180° clockwise or counterclockwise around point *O*. Start with a horizontal or a vertical side.

   a) 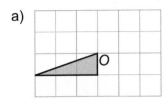   b) 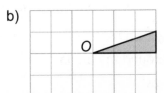   c) 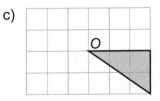   d)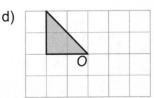

5. Alex wants to rotate point P (2, 3) 180° clockwise around the origin O.

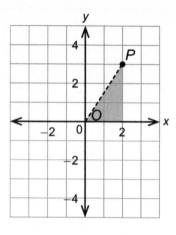

a) Which quadrant is P in? _____

b) Which quadrant will the image P' be in? _____

c) Alex draws the line segment OP and shades a right triangle as shown. Rotate OP 180° CW around the origin. Label the image P'.

d) OP has run = 2 and rise = 3. OP' has run = _____ and rise = _____.

e) The coordinates of P' are (,).

6. a) Plot the point on the grid and then rotate it around the origin as given. Write the coordinates of the image.

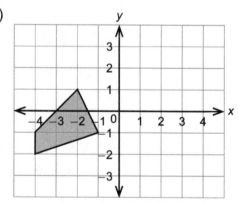

i) P (−3, 1), 180° clockwise; P' (,)

ii) Q (4, −2), 180° counterclockwise; Q' (,)

b) Predict the coordinates of the images of the points after a 180° rotation around the origin. Plot the points and the images and check your prediction.

R (−2, 0), R' (,) S (4, 0.5), S' (,)

7. Use Alex's method from Question 5 to rotate the vertices of the polygon 180° clockwise around the origin. Join the vertices to create the image of the polygon.

a)

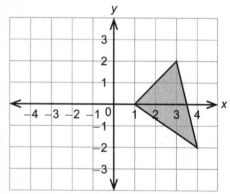

b)

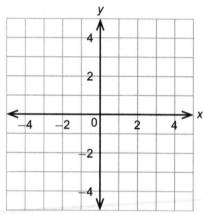

8. a) Plot point P (4, 2) on a coordinate grid.

b) Rotate the point around the origin as given. Write the coordinates of the image.

i) $P \rightarrow P'$: 90° clockwise   ii) $P' \rightarrow P''$: 180° clockwise   iii) $P'' \rightarrow P*$: 270° clockwise

c) Point P'' can be obtained by rotating point P _____° clockwise around the origin.

d) Point $P*$ can be obtained by rotating point P around the origin

90° + 180° + 270° − 360° = _____° clockwise.

Explain where each number in this equation comes from.

REMINDER: In the diagram:

- Points *P* (3, 1) and *P′* (3, −1) are reflections of each other in the *x*-axis.
  They have the same *x*-coordinates and opposite *y*-coordinates.

- Points *Q* (1, 3) and *Q′* (−1, 3) are reflections of each other in the *y*-axis.
  They have opposite *x*-coordinates and the same *y*-coordinates.

- Points *P* and *Q* are reflections of each other in the line *y* = *x*.
  They have *x*- and *y*-coordinates that switch from one point to the other.

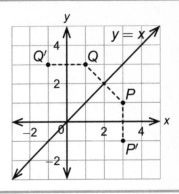

9. a) Reflect △*UVW* in the *x*-axis. Write the coordinates of the
   vertices of the image.

   U′ (,   ), *V′* (,   ), *W′* (,   )

   b) Reflect △*U′V′W′* in the *y*-axis. Write the coordinates of the
   vertices of the image.

   U* (,   ), *V** (,   ), *W** (,   )

   c) Which transformation takes △*UVW* to △*U*V*W**?

   _____

   d) Reflect △*UVW* in the *y*-axis and then reflect the image in

   the *x*-axis. Did you get △*U*V*W**? _____

   Bonus ▶ Use the changes in coordinates to explain
   your answers in parts c) and d).

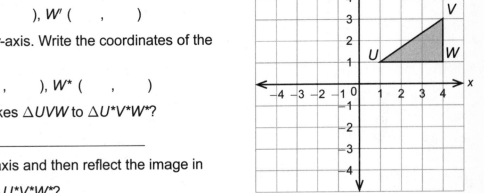

10. a) Reflect △*RST* in the *x*-axis. Write the coordinates of the
    vertices of the image.

    R′ (,   ), *S′* (,   ), *T′* (,   )

    b) Reflect △*R′S′T′* in the line *y* = *x*. Write the coordinates
    of the vertices of the image.

    R″ (,   ), *S″* (,   ), *T″* (,   )

    c) Which transformation takes △*RST* to △*R″S″T″*?

    _____

    d) Reflect △*RST* in the line *y* = *x* and mark the image
    points with *. Then reflect the image in the *x*-axis.
    Mark the image points with **. Write the coordinates
    of the vertices:

    R** (,   ), *S*** (,   ), *T*** (,   )

    Does it equal △*R″S″T″*? _____

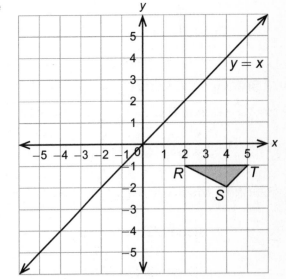

G8-28 Rotating Lines

1. a) Plot the points on the grid, then draw the lines *PQ* and *ST*.

   i) *P* (−3, 2), *Q* (−1, 3), *S* (0, −3), *T* (4, −1)   ii) *P* (2, −3), *Q* (−4, −1), *S* (−1, 0), *T* (2, −1)

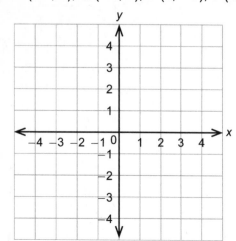   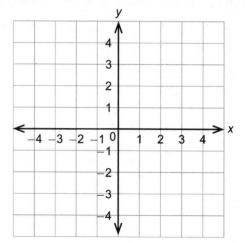

   b) Find the slope of lines *PQ* and *ST*. Reduce your answers to lowest terms.

   i) rise *PQ* = _____   run *PQ* = _____   ii) rise *PQ* = _____   run *PQ* = _____

   slope *PQ* =   slope *PQ* =

   rise *ST* = _____   run *ST* = _____   rise *ST* = _____   run *ST* = _____

   slope *ST* =   slope *ST* =

   c) Is *PQ* parallel to *ST*?

   i) _____   ii) _____

   d) Rotate lines *PQ* and *ST* around the origin as given. Mark each image with ʹ.

   i) 90° clockwise   ii) 180° counterclockwise

   e) Find the slope of lines *P'Q'* and *S'T'*. Reduce your answers to lowest terms.

   i) rise *P'Q'* = _____   run *P'Q'* = _____   ii) rise *P'Q'* = _____   run *P'Q'* = _____

   slope *P'Q'* =   slope *P'Q'* =

   rise *S'T'* = _____   run *S'T'* = _____   rise *S'T'* = _____   run *S'T'* = _____

   slope *S'T'* =   slope *S'T'* =

   f) Is *P'Q'* parallel to *S'T'*?

   i) _____   ii) _____

   g) Do rotations around the origin take parallel lines to parallel lines? _____

REMINDER: Corresponding angles and alternate angles at parallel lines are equal.
When corresponding angles or alternate angles are equal, the lines are parallel.

To check that lines *m* and *n* are parallel:

Step 1: Draw a line across *m* and *n*.

Step 2: Identify a pair of corresponding (*a*) or alternate (*b*) angles.

Step 3: Measure the angles from Step 2. If the angles are equal,
the lines are parallel. If not, the lines are not parallel.

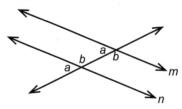

2. a) Draw line *AC* and use the steps above to check if lines *AB* and *CD* are parallel.
Label parallel lines with arrows.

i)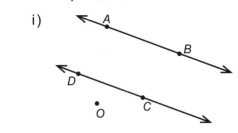

ii)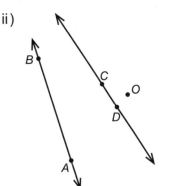

iii)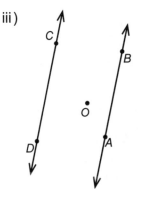

b) Rotate the lines around point *O* as given below. Use points *A, B, C,* and *D*.
Use ′ to label the images.

i) 160° clockwise ii) 75° counterclockwise iii) 35° clockwise

c) Draw line *A′C′*. Check if lines *A′B′* and *C′D′* are parallel. Label parallel lines
with arrows.

d) Do rotations take parallel lines to parallel lines? _____

Do rotations take lines that are not parallel to parallel lines? _____

e) Does rotation preserve angle sizes? _____

Does rotation preserve alternate angles? _____

f) Use your answers from part e) to explain your answers from part d).

Bonus ▶ Two lines, *AB* and *CD*, intersect at *O*. If the two lines are rotated
180° clockwise around point *O*, what happens? Use what you
know about rotations to explain why vertical angles *AOD* and *BOC*
are equal.

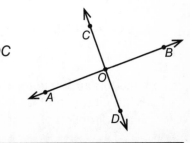

3. **a)** Rotate the line segment 90° clockwise around the origin. Use ′ to label the image.

i)	ii)	iii)	iv)
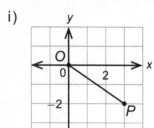	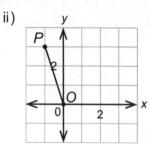	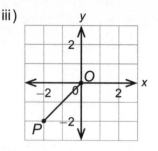	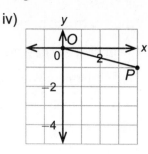

b) Use a protractor to check that the angle between *OP* and its image *OP′* is 90°.

c) Find the absolute value of the run, rise, and slope for each line segment in part a).

i) |run *OP*| = 3

|rise *OP*| = 2

|slope *OP*| = $\dfrac{2}{3}$

|run *OP′*| =

|rise *OP′*| =

|slope *OP′*| =

ii) |run *OP*| =

|rise *OP*| =

|slope *OP*| =

|run *OP′*| =

|rise *OP′*| =

|slope *OP′*| =

iii) |run *OP*| =

|rise *OP*| =

|slope *OP*| =

|run *OP′*| =

|rise *OP′*| =

|slope *OP′*| =

iv) |run *OP*| =

|rise *OP*| =

|slope *OP*| =

|run *OP′*| =

|rise *OP′*| =

|slope *OP′*| =

d) Compare the absolute values of the slopes of *OP* and *OP′*. What do you notice?

_____

4. Plot point *Q* (−4, −2) on the coordinate grid.

a) Rotate point *Q* 90° clockwise around the origin *O*. Label the image *Q′*.

i) *Q* is in quadrant _____. *Q′* is in quadrant _____.

ii) *OQ* has |run| = _____ and |rise| = _____.

   OQ′ has |run| = _____ and |rise| = _____.

iii) Point *Q′* has coordinates (,).

b) Rotate point *Q* (−4, −2) 90° counterclockwise around the origin. Label the image *Q″*.

i) *Q″* is in quadrant _____.

ii) *OQ″* has |run| = _____ and |rise| = _____.

iii) Point *Q″* has coordinates (,).

c) Compare the |rise| and |run| for *OQ′* and *OQ″*. Do they differ depending on the direction of rotation? For the coordinates of *Q′* and *Q″*, what impact does the direction of rotation have on them?

G8-29 Identifying Rotations

1. Triangle *ABC* was rotated around point *O*.

    a) Label the vertices of the image. Use *A′*, *B′*, *C′*.

    b) Draw line segments *OA* and *OA′*.

    c) Measure the angle *AOA′*. ∠*AOA′* = _____

    d) Predict the size of ∠*BOB′*. _____
    Draw the angle and measure it to check your prediction.

    e) Triangle *ABC* was rotated around the point *O* _____° clockwise

    or _____° counterclockwise to get △*A′B′C′*.

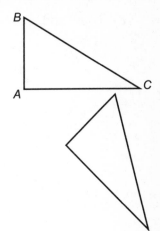

O•

2. Join a vertex and its image to point *O*. Identify the angle of rotation around point *O*.

    a)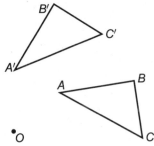

    b)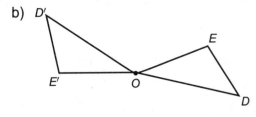

    _____° clockwise or _____° counterclockwise   _____° clockwise or _____° counterclockwise

---

REMINDER: When a shape is rotated around point *O*, all points on the shape move the same way.

For any point *A* on the shape and its image *A′*, ∠*AOA′* equals the angle of rotation and *OA* = *OA′*.

---

3. Triangle *DEF* was rotated around point *O* or point *P*.

    a) Draw line segments and measure angles to points *O* and *P* to compare.

    i)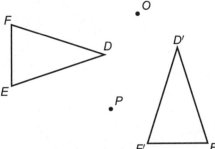

    Is ∠*DOD′* = ∠*EOE′*? _____

    Is ∠*DPD′* = ∠*EPE′*? _____

    ii)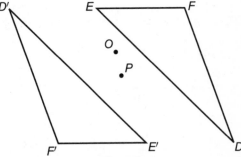

    Is ∠*DOD′* = ∠*EOE′*? _____

    Is ∠*DPD′* = ∠*EPE′*? _____

    b) Which point is the center of rotation, *O* or *P*?

    i) _____   ii) _____

4. Triangle *ABC* was rotated around point *O* or point *P*.

a) Draw and measure line segments *OA*, *OA'*, *OB*, and *OB'*.

i)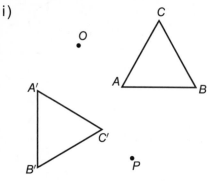

ii)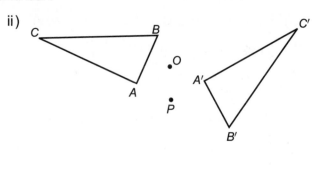

Is *OA* = *OA'*? _____ Is *OB* = *OB'*? _____   Is *OA* = *OA'*? _____ Is *OB* = *OB'*? _____

b) Draw and measure line segments *PA*, *PA'*, *PB*, and *PB'*.

i) Is *PA* = *PA'*? _____ Is *PB* = *PB'*? _____   ii) Is *PA* = *PA'*? _____ Is *PB* = *PB'*? _____

c) Which point is the center of rotation, *O* or *P*?   i) _____   ii) _____

5. For the rotation at right, which point is the center of rotation, *O*, *P*, or *Q*? What is the angle of rotation? Explain your answer.

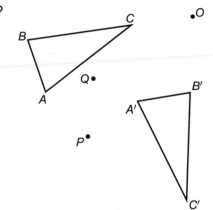

6. Fill in the table to summarize. What happens to a shape that is reflected? translated? rotated?

Transformation	Lengths of Sides	Sizes of Angles	Orientation
Reflection			
Translation			
Rotation			

7. a) Predict what type of transformation—translation, reflection, or rotation—takes *KLM* to *K'L'M'*.

i) 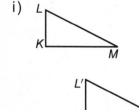   ii) 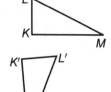   iii) 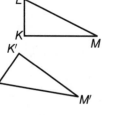   iv)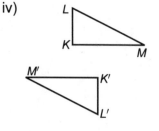

b) Join each vertex to its image. Are the line segments you drew parallel?

c) Are the line segments you drew in part b) equal?

d) How can the answers in parts b) and c) help you to confirm your predictions?

       Geometry 8-29

Combining Transformations

1. a) Translate triangle T as given. Label the image T'. Then translate the image again from T' to T*.

   i) 2 units up and 3 units left, then
      1 unit up and 4 units right

   ii) 4 units down and 3 units right, then
       3 units up and 4 units left

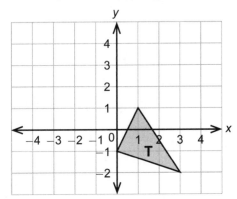

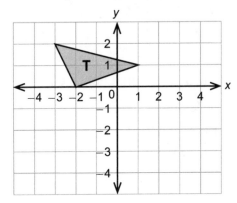

   b) Write the coordinates of the vertices of the original shape and its images.

   i)

T	(,)	(,)	(,)
T'	(,)	(,)	(,)
T*	(,)	(,)	(,)

   ii)

T	(,)	(,)	(,)
T'	(,)	(,)	(,)
T*	(,)	(,)	(,)

   c) What single transformation—translation, reflection, or rotation—takes triangle T to

      triangle T*? _____

REMINDER: You can use integers to write a formula for the
coordinates that describe a translation.

Examples: The formula for a translation 2 units right and
3 units up is $(x, y) \rightarrow (x + 2, y + 3)$
The formula for a translation 2 units left and
3 units down is $(x, y) \rightarrow (x + (-2), y + (-3))$

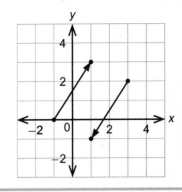

---

   d) Write a formula that describes each transformation in part a).

   i) T → T': $(x, y) \rightarrow (x + $ _____ $, y + $ _____ $)$ ii) T → T': $(x, y) \rightarrow (x + $ _____ $, y + $ _____ $)$

      T' → T*: $(x, y) \rightarrow (x + $ _____ $, y + $ _____ $)$ T' → T*: $(x, y) \rightarrow (x + $ _____ $, y + $ _____ $)$

      T → T*: $(x, y) \rightarrow (x + $ _____ $, y + $ _____ $)$ T → T*: $(x, y) \rightarrow (x + $ _____ $, y + $ _____ $)$

   e) If a polygon P is taken to polygon P' by a sequence of translations, is polygon P'
      congruent to polygon P? Explain.

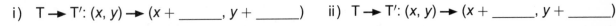

Geometry 8-30

2. a) Reflect triangle T in the mirror line. Label the image T′.

i)
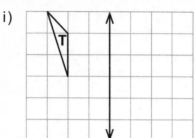

ii)
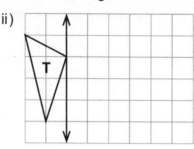

iii)
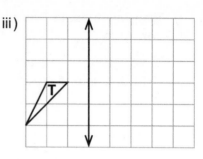

b) Translate T′ as given. Label the image T*.

    i) 3 units down   ii) 4 units right   iii) 3 units up and 2 units right

c) Draw the line segments joining each vertex in T to its image in T*. Are the line segments parallel?

    i) _____   ii) _____   iii) _____

d) Are the line segments you drew in part c) equal?

    i) _____   ii) _____   iii) _____

e) Is there a single transformation that takes T to T*? If yes, what transformation is that? Draw the translation arrow, the mirror line, or the center of rotation.

    i) _____   ii) _____   iii) _____

f) Are triangles T and T* congruent? How do you know?

3. a) Perform the transformations and label each image.

    i) T → T′: Rotate 45° clockwise around *P*.   ii) T → T′: Rotate 90° counterclockwise around *P*.

        T′ → T*: Rotate 90° clockwise around *Q*.   T′ → T*: Translate 2 units right and 3 units up.

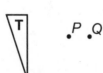

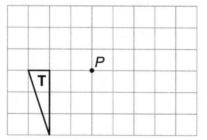

b) Is there a single translation or reflection that takes T to T*? If yes, draw the translation arrow or the mirror line.

    i) _____   ii) _____

c) Are triangles T and T* congruent? How do you know?

4. Carlos drew a polygon on a coordinate grid. He performed 10 different transformations (translations, reflections, and rotations) on it. Is the image of the polygon after the 10 transformations congruent to the original polygon? Explain.

G8-31 Congruent Polygons and Transformations

1. a) Reflect △ABC in the x-axis. Label the image using '.
   Write a congruence statement for the triangles.

   △ABC ≅ _____

   b) Rotate △ABC 180° around the origin. Label the image using *.
   Write a congruence statement for the triangles.

   △ABC ≅ _____

   c) In each triangle, draw a curved arrow showing the direction in
   which you read the name of the triangle. Is the arrow pointing
   clockwise (CW) or counterclockwise (CCW)?

   △ABC _____   △A'B'C' _____   △A*B*C* _____

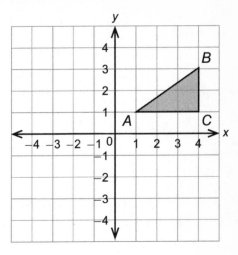

   d) Which transformation keeps the direction of the arrow the same? _____

   Which transformation changes the direction of the arrow? _____

2. a) Are the triangles congruent? If yes, write a congruence statement.

   i)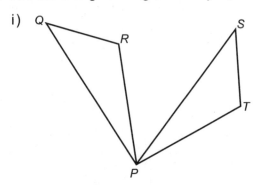   ii)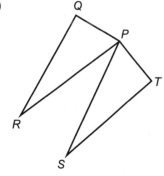

   _____   _____

   b) In each triangle, draw a curved arrow showing the direction in which you read
   the name of the triangle in the congruence statement. Is the direction the same
   or opposite?

   i) _____   ii) _____

   c) Which type of transformation—a rotation or a reflection—takes PQR to PST?

   i) _____   ii) _____

   d) In the reflection in part a), draw the line segments joining the corresponding vertices.
   Remember, the mirror line is perpendicular to these line segments and intersects
   them at each midpoint. Draw the mirror line.

   e) In the rotation in part a), what is the center of rotation? _____

   Measure the angle of rotation. Describe the rotation. _____

3. a) Are the triangles congruent? If yes, write a congruence statement.

i)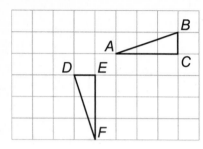

ii)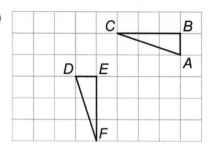

_____   _____

b) In the congruence statement, what vertex corresponds to vertex *A*? Draw an arrow on the grid to take vertex *A* to the corresponding vertex. Describe the translation.

i) _____   ii) _____

c) Translate triangle *ABC* with the same translation as in part b). Label the image vertices using ′.

d) What transformation performed on △*A′B′C′* will give you △*DEF*? Draw the mirror line or write the angle and the direction of rotation. Hint: The center of rotation is the common vertex of the triangles.

i) _____   ii) _____

4. a) Write a congruence statement for the polygons.

i)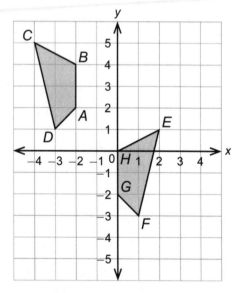

ii)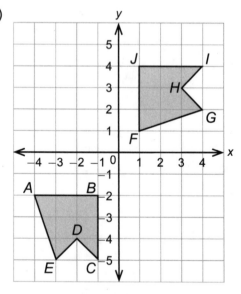

_____   _____

b) Describe a sequence of transformations to get from one shape to the other. Remember to describe in detail—the direction and the amount of translation, the mirror line, or the angle, direction, and center of rotation.

Bonus ▶ Describe another sequence of transformations that takes *ABCD* from to *GHEF* in part a) i).

G8-32 Similarity

In math, we say two shapes are **similar** if the lengths of their corresponding sides show a proportional relationship and their corresponding angles are equal.

Each side length in $\triangle DEF$ is twice the length in $\triangle ABC$.

$AB : DE = BC : EF = AC : DF = 1 : 2$

$\angle A = \angle D, \angle B = \angle E, \angle C = \angle F$

To show the correspondence, we write a **similarity statement**: $\triangle ABC \sim \triangle DEF$.

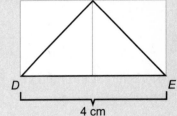
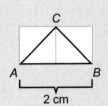

2 cm   4 cm

1. Each rectangle is made of 2 squares.

   a) Find the ratio of the corresponding sides of the rectangles.

   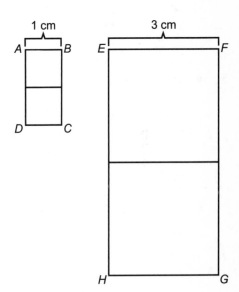

   $AB : EF =$ _____ : _____

   $BC : FG =$ _____ : _____

   $CD :$ _____ = _____ : _____

   $AD :$ _____ = _____ : _____

   b) Are these rectangles similar? _____

   c) Why is there no need to check equality between the angles to decide whether the rectangles are similar?

   _____

   d) Write the similarity statement. $ABCD \sim$ _____

2. Rectangles $ABCD$ and $EFGH$ are similar.

   a) Find $AB : EF$.

      i) $AB = 1$ cm, $BC = 2$ cm, $EF = 3$ cm

          $AB : EF = \underline{\quad 1 \quad} : \underline{\quad 3 \quad}$

      ii) $AB = 2$ cm, $BC = 6$ cm, $EF = 4$ cm

          $AB : EF =$ _____ : _____

      iii) $AB = 1$ cm, $BC = 3$ cm, $EF = 5$ cm

          $AB : EF =$ _____ : _____

      iv) $AB = 3$ cm, $BC = 2$ cm, $EF = 4$ cm

          $AB : EF =$ _____ : _____

   b) For the same rectangles, $AB : EF = BC : FG$. Find the length of FG.

      i) $1 : 3 = 2 : FG$ ii)   iii)   iv)

          $FG = 6$ cm

   c) Draw the rectangles $ABCD$ and $EFGH$.

3. a) A square and a rectangle have the same angles. Are they similar? Explain.

   b) Can a trapezoid and a square be similar? Explain.

4. Are the rectangles in the pair similar? Explain.

a)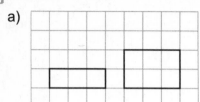

b)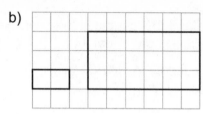

c)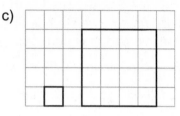

d) 2 in × 4 in and 3 in × 6 in   e) 1 m × 2 m and 2.5 m × 5.5 m   f) 5 ft × 4 ft and 4 ft × 3.2 ft

5. a) Which of these shapes are similar? _____

b) On the shape that is not similar to the other two, mark a side that is not proportional to the corresponding side in the other two shapes.

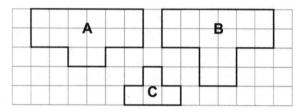

6. Which pairs of shapes are congruent? Which are similar? How do you know?

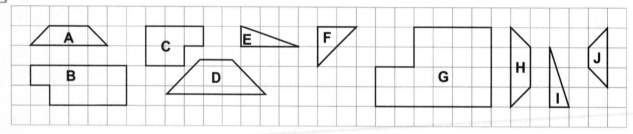

7. a) Measure all angles and all sides of the triangles.

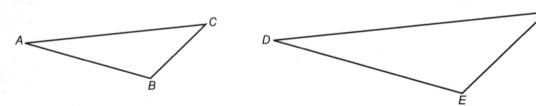

b) Are △ABC and △DEF similar? Explain using both angle measurements and ratios of sides.

8. In each pair, the triangles are similar. Measurements are in inches. Find x and y.

a)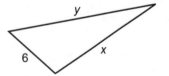

b)

9. a) △KLM has angles 30°, 60°, and 90°. △POR has angles 35°, 55°, and 90°. Are the triangles similar? Explain.

b) △GHI has sides 2 cm, 4 cm, and 5 cm. △UVW has sides 3 cm, 8 cm, and 10 cm. Are the triangles similar? Explain.

G8-33 Dilations

1. Find the ratio of the lengths of the line segments.

a)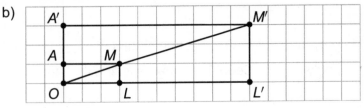

$OA' : OA = \underline{\ \ 3\ \ } : \underline{\ \ 1\ \ }$

$OB' : OB = \underline{\quad} : \underline{\quad}$

b)

$OA' : OA = \underline{\quad} : \underline{\quad}$ $A'M' : AM = \underline{\quad} : \underline{\quad}$

$OL' : OL = \underline{\quad} : \underline{\quad}$ $L'M' : LM = \underline{\quad} : \underline{\quad}$

2. Measure the line segments. Find the ratios of the lengths.
   Reduce your answers to lowest terms.

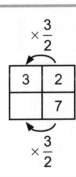

$OK' : OK = \underline{\quad} : \underline{\quad} = \underline{\quad} : \underline{\quad}$

$OM' : OM = \underline{\quad} : \underline{\quad} = \underline{\quad} : \underline{\quad}$

REMINDER: If you have a ratio and there is a number missing in an equivalent ratio,
you can use a ratio table to find the missing number.

Example: 3 : 2 = \underline{\quad} : 7

What number do you multiply the second term in the ratio by to get
the first term? In equivalent ratios, this number is the same.

The missing number is $7 \times \dfrac{3}{2} = \dfrac{21}{2}$.

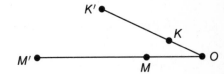

---

3. The ratio $OP^* : OP = 3 : 1$.

   a) Find the length of OP. Then find the length of OP^*.

   i)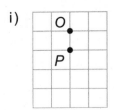

   ii)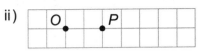

   iii)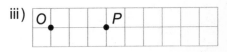

   $OP = \underline{\quad}$, $OP^* = \underline{\quad}$ $OP = \underline{\quad}$, $OP^* = \underline{\quad}$ $OP = \underline{\quad}$, $OP^* = \underline{\quad}$

   b) Draw the ray OP. Find the point P^* on OP so that $OP^* : OP = 3 : 1$.

4. Draw the ray OP. Find the point P^* on OP so that $OP^* : OP = 1 : 2$.

   a) 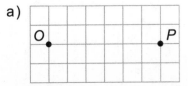   b) 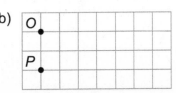   c)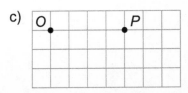

5. Zara thinks that $OP^* : OP = 3 : 1$.

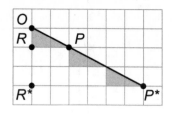

a) Measure the line segments. $OP = $ _____ $OP^* = $ _____

Is Zara correct? _____

b) Are the gray triangles in the picture congruent? _____

c) Draw triangle OP^*R^*. Count the squares to find the ratios.

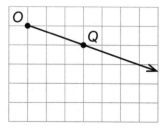

$OR^* : OR = $ _____ : _____ $\quad P^*R^* : PR = $ _____ : _____

d) Zara wants to draw a point Q^* on the ray OQ so that $OQ^* : OQ = 2 : 1$. How many triangles does she need to shade to find point Q^*? _____

e) Shade the triangles as in part c) and draw point Q^*.

f) A third point, S, helps form the right triangle OQS. Draw point S^* to form OQ^*S^*. Count squares to find the ratios.

$OS^* : OS = $ _____ : _____ $\quad Q^*S^* : QS = $ _____ : _____

g) How could you use counting squares to find point Q^*?

_____

_____

6. Draw the ray OP. Mark point P^* on the ray so that the lengths OP and OP^* have the given ratio.

a) $OP^* : OP = 3 : 1$

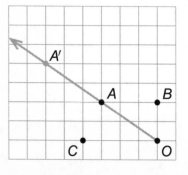

b) $OP^* : OP = 2 : 1$

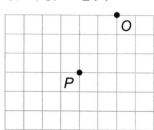

Bonus ▶ $OP^* : OP = 3 : 2$

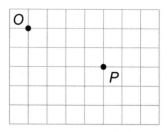

7. Find point A' on OA, point B' on OB, and point C' on OC, so that $OA' : OA = OB' : OB = OC' : OC$ are all equal to the given ratio.

a) $2 : 1$

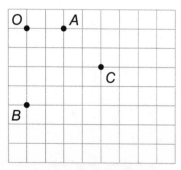

b) $3 : 2$

c) $1 : 3$

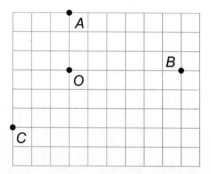

8. **a)** Draw rays from *O* through the vertices of △*ABC*. Extend the rays across the grid.

i)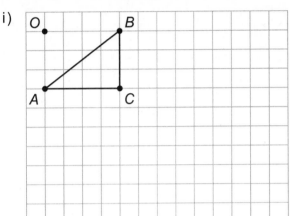

ii)

b) Find three points—*A′* on *OA*, *B′* on *OB*, and *C′* on *OC*—so that
 OA′ : *OA* = *OB′* : *OB* = *OC′* : *OC* are all equal to 3 : 1. Draw triangle *A′B′C′*.

c) Measure the angles of both triangles in the pair.

 i) ∠*A* = _____   ∠*A′* = _____   ii) ∠*A* = _____   ∠*A′* = _____

  ∠*B* = _____   ∠*B′* = _____   ∠*B* = _____   ∠*B′* = _____

  ∠*C* = _____   ∠*C′* = _____   ∠*C* = _____   ∠*C′* = _____

 What do you notice? _____

d) Measure the sides of both triangles in the pair.

 i) *AB* = _____   *A′B′* = _____   ii) *AB* = _____   *A′B′* = _____

  BC = _____   *B′C′* = _____   *BC* = _____   *B′C′* = _____

  AC = _____   *A′C′* = _____   *AC* = _____   *A′C′* = _____

e) Find the ratio of the lengths of the corresponding sides of △*ABC* and △*A′B′C′*.

 i) *A′B′* : *AB* = _____   ii) *A′B′* : *AB* = _____

  B′C′ : *BC* = _____   *B′C′* : *BC* = _____

  A′C′ : *AC* = _____   *A′C′* : *AC* = _____

f) Is the ratio in part e) the same as the ratio *OA′* : *OA* = *OB′* : *OB* = *OC′* : *OC*? _____

g) What can you say about △*ABC* and △*A′B′C′*? _____

The transformation you performed on △*ABC* is called a **dilation**. The point *O* is the **center of dilation**.

---

9. Is the statement true or false for dilations in Question 8?

 a) Dilations preserve the angles of shapes.   **b)** Dilations preserve the side lengths of shapes.

 c) Dilations take shapes to congruent shapes.   **d)** Dilations take shapes to similar shapes.

G8-34 Properties of Dilations

If *AB* is the side of the original shape and *A'B'* is the side image after dilation, the **scale factor of dilation** is the ratio *A'B'* : *AB*. The scale factor is usually written as a number equal to $\frac{A'B'}{AB}$.

1. The black dot marks the center of dilation. Label the vertices of the image after the dilation using ʹ. Then find the scale factor.

a)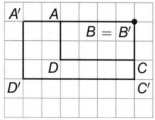

$$\frac{A'B'}{AB} = \frac{6}{4} = \frac{3}{2}$$

scale factor = ___1.5___

b)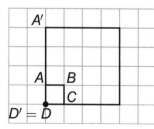

$$\frac{A'B'}{AB} =$$

scale factor = _____

c)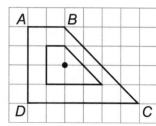

$$\frac{A'B'}{AB} =$$

scale factor = _____

d)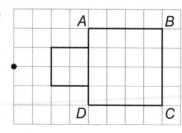

$$\frac{A'B'}{AB} =$$

scale factor = _____

e)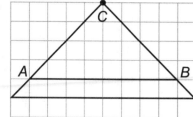

$$\frac{A'B'}{AB} =$$

scale factor = _____

f)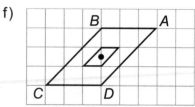

$$\frac{A'B'}{AB} =$$

scale factor = _____

A dilation is an **enlargement** if the image is larger than the original.
A dilation is a **reduction** if the image is smaller than the original.

2. a) Mark each dilation in Question 1 as an enlargement (E) or a reduction (R).

   b) Look at the scale factors of the dilations in Question 1. How can you tell by looking at the scale factor whether the dilation is an enlargement or reduction?

   _____

   c) In Questions 1.c) and f), label the center of dilation as *O*. Draw line segments *O'B'* and *OB* to the vertices of the original and the image.

   d) For Questions 1.c) and f), find the ratio $\frac{O'B'}{OB}$. What do you notice about this ratio

   and the scale factor of the dilation? _____

   e) How can you find the length of *O'B'* from the length of *OB* and the scale factor?

To perform a dilation with scale factor 2 and center *O*:

Step 1: Draw a ray from *O* through each vertex of the polygon *ABC*.
Find the distance from *O* to each vertex.

Step 2: Use the scale factor to find the distances from *O* to each vertex
of the image. For example, since the scale factor is 2, $OA' = 2OA$.

Step 3: Draw the vertices of the image on rays you drew in Step 1.
Join the vertices to form the image polygon $A'B'C'$.

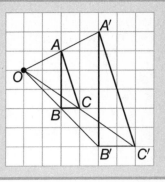

3. Perform a dilation with the given scale factor and center *O*. Identify the dilation as an
enlargement or a reduction.

a) scale factor = 2

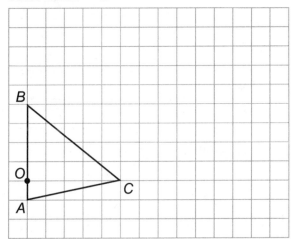

This is an _____.

b) scale factor = 0.6

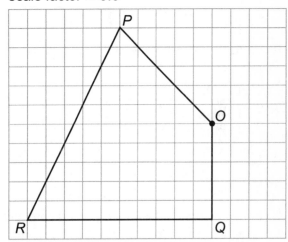

This is a _____.

4. a) Dilate △*KLM* using the given scale factor and center *O*. Label the image △*K'L'M'*.

i) scale factor = $\frac{3}{2}$

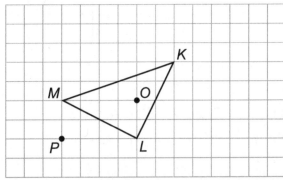

ii) scale factor = 0.25

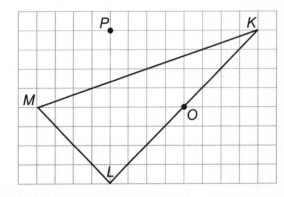

b) On the same grids, dilate △*KLM* using the same scale factors as in part a), but
with *P* as the center of dilation. Label each image △*K*L*M**.

c) What can you say about △*K'L'M'* and △*K*L*M**? _____

d) What transformation takes △*K'L'M'* to △*K*L*M**? Describe in detail.

5. a) Perform the dilations using the origin as the center.

    i)   scale factor = 3

    ii) scale factor = $\dfrac{1}{2}$

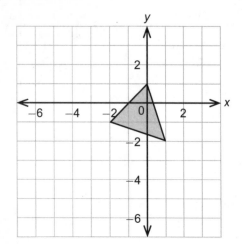
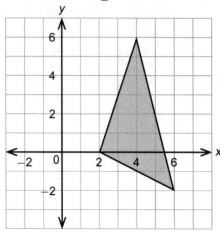

b) Write the coordinates of each original vertex and image.

i)

Original			
Image			

ii)

Original			
Image			

c) Write a formula for the change of the coordinates for each dilation in part a).

    i) $(x, y) \rightarrow ($, $)$

    ii) $(x, y) \rightarrow ($, $)$

d) For new dilations with the given scale factor and the origin as the center, write a formula for the change of coordinates.

    i)   scale factor = 1.5

    ii) scale factor = 0.25

    $(x, y) \rightarrow ($, $)$

    $(x, y) \rightarrow ($, $)$

e) Predict the coordinates of the vertices of each image using your formula in part d).

i)

Original	(2, 0)	(0, −4)	(6, −6)
Image			

ii)

Original	(0, 0)	(−4, 8)	(2, −2)
Image			

f) Draw a coordinate grid and check your predictions from part e).

6. a) Use a coordinate grid to plot a triangle with vertices A (2, 2), B (−6, 0), and C (0, −4).

b) Dilate $\triangle ABC$ by scale factor 2. Use the origin as the center of dilation. Label the image $\triangle A'B'C'$.

c) Dilate $\triangle A'B'C'$ by scale factor 0.5. Use the origin as the center of dilation.

    What triangle do you get as the image?

d) Repeat parts b) and c) using scale factors $\dfrac{3}{2}$ and $\dfrac{2}{3}$. Did you get the same result?

G8-35 Dilations and Other Transformations

1. Fill in the table to summarize. What happens to a shape that is reflected? translated? rotated? dilated?

Transformation	Lengths of Sides	Sizes of Angles	Orientation
Reflection			
Translation			
Rotation			
Dilation			

2. Write "similar" or "congruent" to make the statement true.

   a) Translations, reflections, and rotations each take polygons to _____ polygons.

   b) Dilations with a scale factor different from 1 take polygons to _____ polygons.

   c) A dilation with a scale factor different from 1 and another transformation will take

   a polygon to a _____ polygon.

   d) A combination of reflections, rotations, and translations takes any polygon to

   a _____ polygon.

3. a) Are triangles *ABC* and *DEF* congruent? _____

   b) What is the ratio $\dfrac{DE}{AB}$? _____

   c) Dilate $\triangle ABC$ using the origin as the center of dilation.

   Use $\dfrac{DE}{AB}$ as the scale factor. Label the image using '.

   d) Reflect $\triangle A'B'C'$ in the *x*-axis. Label the image using *.

   e) What can you say about $\triangle A*B*C*$ and $\triangle DEF$?

   _____

   f) What transformation will take $\triangle A*B*C*$ to $\triangle DEF$?

   _____

   g) What can you say about triangles *ABC* and *DEF*? Explain.

   h) Rani says that she can get $\triangle DEF$ from $\triangle A'B'C'$ by translating $\triangle A'B'C'$ 6 units down and 2 units left and then reflecting the image in the line $y = -4$. Is she correct? Explain.

   Bonus ▶ Write the formula for each transformation used. Use vertex *A* to check that your formulas are correct.

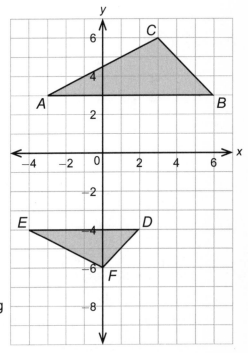

4. Plot points A (−4, −2), B (−4, 6), C (−6, 0), D (−2, −3), E (2, −3), and F (−1, −2).

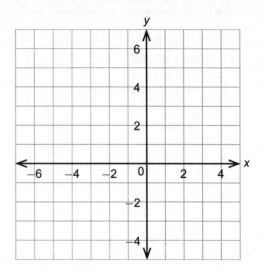

  a) Are triangles ABC and DEF congruent? _____

   Are they similar? _____

  b) Dilate $\triangle ABC$ using the origin as the center of dilation.

   Use $\dfrac{DE}{AB}$ as the scale factor. Label the image using ′.

  c) Rotate $\triangle A'B'C'$ 90° clockwise around the origin. Label the image using *.

  d) What can you say about $\triangle A*B*C*$ and $\triangle DEF$? What transformation will take $\triangle A*B*C*$ to $\triangle DEF$?

   _____

  e) Describe another sequence of transformations that will take $\triangle A'B'C'$ to $\triangle DEF$.

   Bonus ▶ Write the formula for each transformation used above. Use vertex A to check that your formulas are correct.

5. a) Write a similarity statement for the pair of polygons.

  i) 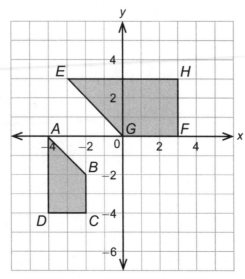 ii)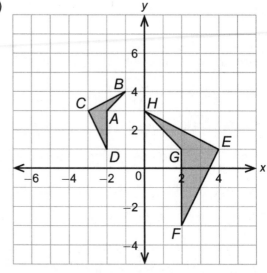

   _____   _____

  b) Describe a sequence of transformations to get from one shape to the other. Be as specific as possible in your description. Hint: The shapes are not congruent. Will the sequence involve a dilation?

   Bonus ▶ Describe another sequence of transformations for the same pair of shapes.

6. Triangle DEF has $DE = 3$ in, $EF = 4$ in, and $FD = 5$ in. Kim reflected the triangle in a vertical line, rotated the image by 50° clockwise around point E, and then dilated the result using scale factor 3 with point D as the center of dilation. What are the side lengths of the image triangle? Explain.

G8-36 Similarity Rules

1. a) Draw a scalene triangle *ABC* on the small grid. Measure sides *AB* and *AC*, plus ∠*A*.

   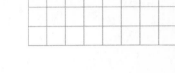

   $AB =$ _____ $AC =$ _____

   $∠A =$ _____

   b) Construct △*A′B′C′* with sides twice as long as △*ABC*, and ∠*A′* = ∠*A*. Use the large grid.

   $A′B′ = 2AB =$ _____

   $A′C′ = 2AC =$ _____

   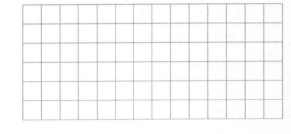

   c) Measure the rest of the sides and angles in both triangles.

   $BC =$ _____ $B′C′ =$ _____

   $∠B =$ _____ $∠B′ =$ _____

   $∠C =$ _____ $∠C′ =$ _____

   d) Find the ratios of the side lengths.

   $$\frac{A′B′}{AB} = \qquad\qquad \frac{A′C′}{AC} = \qquad\qquad \frac{B′C′}{BC} =$$

   Are the triangles similar? _____

   e) *Conjecture:* SAS is a similarity rule too:

   If ∠*A* = ∠*A′* and $\dfrac{A′B′}{AB} = \dfrac{A′C′}{AC}$, then △*ABC* is similar to △*A′B′C′*.

   Repeat parts a) to d) with an acute triangle and scale factor 0.25 to check the conjecture.

2. a) Draw a triangle *KLM*. Make *KL* a whole number of centimeters long.

   b) Measure the angles of △*KLM*.

   c) Draw a line segment *K′L′* that is a whole number of centimeters long, but different from *KL*. Use *K′L′* to construct a triangle with ∠*K′* = ∠*K* and ∠*L′* = ∠*L*.

   d) What do you know about the size of angle ∠*M′*? Explain.

   e) Measure the sides of both triangles and find the ratios of the side lengths.

   $$\frac{K′L′}{KL} = \qquad\qquad \frac{L′M′}{LM} = \qquad\qquad \frac{K′M′}{KM} =$$

   Are the triangles similar? _____

   f) *Conjecture:* AA is a similarity rule too:

   If ∠*K′* = ∠*K* and ∠*L′* = ∠*L*, then △*KLM* is similar to △*K′L′M′*.

   Repeat parts a) to d) with another triangle and scale factor 3 to check the conjecture.

3. Ron drew two triangles, ABC and $A'B'C'$. Triangles ABC and $A'B'C'$

have $\dfrac{A'B'}{AB} = \dfrac{B'C'}{BC} = \dfrac{A'C'}{AC} = 4$.

a) What does the equality mean about the side lengths?

$A'B' = $ _____ $\times AB$, $B'C' = $ _____, $A'C' = $ _____

b) Ron wants to prove that triangles ABC and $A'B'C'$ are similar. He performs a dilation on $\triangle ABC$ using scale factor 4. He labels the new triangle $A*B*C*$. What does he know about the sides of $\triangle A*B*C*$?

$A*B* = $ _____ $\times AB$, $B*C* = $ _____, $A*C* = $ _____

c) Compare the side lengths of $\triangle A'B'C'$ and $\triangle A*B*C*$.

$A*B* = $ _____, $B*C* = $ _____, $A*C* = $ _____

d) Write "similar," "congruent," or "neither."

Dilations take polygons to _____ polygons,

so $\triangle ABC$ and $\triangle A*B*C*$ are _____.

$\triangle A'B'C'$ and $\triangle A*B*C*$ are _____ by _____ congruence rule.

So $\triangle A'B'C'$ and $\triangle ABC$ are _____.

e) *Conjecture:* SSS is a similarity rule too:

If $\dfrac{A'B'}{AB} = \dfrac{B'C'}{BC} = \dfrac{A'C'}{AC}$, then $\triangle ABC$ is similar to $\triangle A'B'C'$.

Repeat parts a) to d) with $\dfrac{A'B'}{AB} = \dfrac{B'C'}{BC} = \dfrac{A'C'}{AC} = \dfrac{2}{3}$ to check the conjecture.

4. Does SSA (side-side-angle) work as a similarity rule? Check $\triangle A'B'C'$ and $\triangle ABC$.

a) Measure the sides and find the ratios:

$\dfrac{A'B'}{AB} = $ _____ $\dfrac{B'C'}{BC} = $

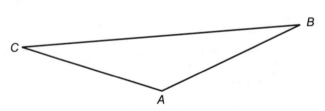

b) Measure the angles: $\angle C = $ _____, $\angle C' = $ _____

c) Do triangles $\triangle ABC$ and $\triangle A'B'C'$ look similar? _____

d) Does SSA (side-side-angle) work as a similarity rule? _____

5. a) Does AS (angle-side) work as a similarity rule? Explain using the example in Question 4.

b) Draw two triangles with $\dfrac{A'B'}{AB} = \dfrac{A'C'}{AC}$ to show that SS (side-side) is not a similarity rule.

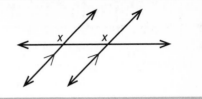

REMINDER: Corresponding angles at parallel lines are equal.

When corresponding angles are equal, the lines are parallel.

6. Lines *BD* and *CE* are parallel.

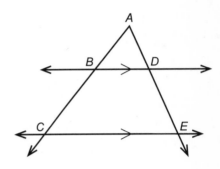

   a) Mark the angles you know are equal.

   b) Which angles are equal in △*ABD* and △*ACE*?

   c) What can you say about △*ABD* and △*ACE*? Explain.

   d) *AB* = 3 cm, *AC* = 9 cm, *AD* = 2.5 cm, and *BD* = 3.2 cm.
      Find the lengths of *AE* and *CE*. Explain how you know.

   e) What transformation will take △*ABD* to △*ACE*?

7. a) Which angle do △*KMN* and △*KLO* have in common? _____

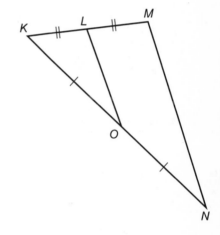

   b) *L* is the midpoint of *KM*, so *KM* = _____ × *KL*.

      O is the midpoint of *KN*, so *KN* = _____ × *KO*.

   c) $\dfrac{KM}{KL}$ = _____ and $\dfrac{KN}{KO}$ = _____

   d) What can you say about △*KMN* and △*KLO*? Explain.

   e) Note a pair of corresponding angles for lines *MN* and *LO*.
      What can you say about these angles? Explain.

   f) What does the relationship between the corresponding
      angles tell you about the lines *MN* and *LO*?

   g) What special quadrilateral is *LMNO*?

8. a) Which triangles in the diagram are congruent? Explain.

   b) Which triangles in the diagram are similar? Explain.

   c) What sequence of transformations will take one triangle to
      another? Remember to mention the mirror line; center,
      direction, and angle of rotation; center and scale factor of
      dilation; and the direction and amount of translation.

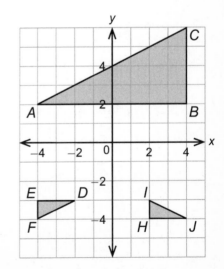

      i)   △*ABC* to △*EFD*

      ii) △*EFD* to △*HIJ*

      iii) △*HIJ* to △*ABC*

   Bonus ▶ Write the formulas for the change of coordinates
      for each transformation in part c).

G8-37 Similar Triangles and Slope of a Line

REMINDER: You can cross multiply to change an equation of fractions or ratios to a multiplication equation. Examples:

$$3x = 2 \times 5$$

$$ad = bc$$

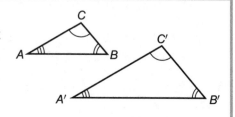

$$A'B' \times BC = B'C' \times AC$$

1. a) Cross multiply to rewrite the equation of ratios as an equality between two products.

   i) $\dfrac{3}{5} = \dfrac{6}{10}$

   ii) $\dfrac{6}{12} = \dfrac{7}{14}$

   iii) $\dfrac{6}{7} = \dfrac{12}{14}$

   _____ $3 \times 10 = 5 \times 6$ _____   _____   _____

   b) Circle the two multiplication equations above that are the same. Underline switched numbers.

2. a) Cross multiply to rewrite the equation of ratios as a multiplication equation.

   i) $\dfrac{A'B'}{AB} = \dfrac{B'C'}{BC}$

   ii) $\dfrac{A'B'}{B'C'} = \dfrac{AB}{BC}$

   iii) $\dfrac{A'B'}{AB} = \dfrac{A'C'}{AC}$

   _____   _____   _____

   b) Which two multiplication equations in part a) are the same? _____

   c) In triangles ABC and $A'B'C'$, $\dfrac{A'B'}{AB} = \dfrac{B'C'}{BC}$. So, $\dfrac{BC}{AB} =$ ———.

REMINDER: $\triangle ABC$ and $\triangle A'B'C'$ are similar.

The similarity statement $\triangle ABC \sim \triangle A'B'C'$ means that
$\angle A = \angle A'$, $\angle B = \angle B'$, $\angle C = \angle C'$

and $\dfrac{A'B'}{AB} = \dfrac{B'C'}{BC} = \dfrac{A'C'}{AC}$.

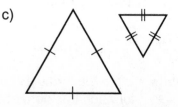

Similarity rules:

Angle-angle (AA) rule:

If $\angle A = \angle A'$ and $\angle B = \angle B'$, then $\triangle ABC \sim \triangle A'B'C'$.

Side-angle-side (SAS) rule:

If $\angle B = \angle B'$ and $\dfrac{A'B'}{AB} = \dfrac{B'C'}{BC}$, then $\triangle ABC \sim \triangle A'B'C'$.

Side-side-side (SSS) rule:

If $\dfrac{A'B'}{AB} = \dfrac{B'C'}{BC} = \dfrac{A'C'}{AC}$, then $\triangle ABC \sim \triangle A'B'C'$.

3. Which rule will you use to prove that the triangles are similar?

   a)

   b)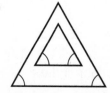

   c)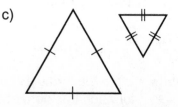

   similarity rule: _____   similarity rule: _____   similarity rule: _____

4. a) In triangle ABC, $\angle A = 60°$ and $AB = 2AC$. Find the ratio $\dfrac{AB}{AC} \cdot \dfrac{AB}{AC} = $ _____

b) In triangle $A'B'C'$, $\angle A = 60°$, $A'B' = 6$ cm, and $A'C' = 3$ cm. Find the ratio $\dfrac{A'B'}{A'C'} \cdot \dfrac{A'B'}{A'C'} = $ _____

c) What do you notice about the ratios $\dfrac{AB}{AC}$ and $\dfrac{A'B'}{A'C'}$? _____

d) Use cross multiplication to show $\dfrac{A'B'}{AB} = \dfrac{A'C'}{AC}$.

e) What do you know about $\triangle ABC$ and $\triangle A'B'C'$? _____

Which similarity rule can you use? _____

f) Do you know the side lengths of $\triangle ABC$? _____

REMINDER: Corresponding angles at parallel lines are equal.

When corresponding angles are equal, the lines are parallel.

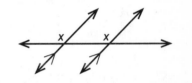

---

5. Grid lines are parallel and meet at right angles.

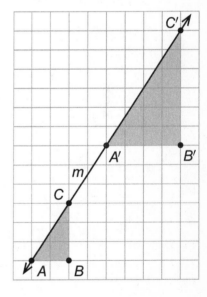

a) What can you say about the sides AB and $A'B'$ in triangles ABC and $A'B'C'$? _____

b) Name a pair of corresponding angles created when line m intersects lines AB and $A'B'$.

$\angle$_____ and $\angle$_____

What do you know about these angles? _____

c) Mark another pair of equal angles in $\triangle ABC$ and $\triangle A'B'C'$.

d) What similarity rule can you use to say that $\triangle ABC$ and $\triangle A'B'C'$ are similar? _____

e) What do you know about the ratios $\dfrac{C'B'}{CB}$ and $\dfrac{A'B'}{AB}$?

_____

f) What do you know about the ratios $\dfrac{CB}{AB}$ and $\dfrac{C'B'}{A'B'}$? Explain using cross multiplication.

6. a) Repeat the work in Question 5 for $\triangle PQR$ and $\triangle P'Q'R'$.

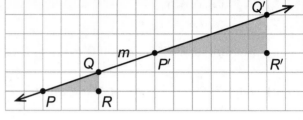

b) In Questions 5 and 6.a), did you ever use the exact side lengths of the triangles? _____

c) In Questions 5 and 6.a), did you ever use the exact size of the angles of the triangles? _____

d) Would the same method work for a pair of triangles with a different scale factor? _____

e) Write "rise," "run," or "slope" to make the sentence true.

   i) For points P and Q, the length of QR is the _____ of the line m.

   ii) For points P and Q, the length of PR is the _____ of the line m.

   iii) For points P' and Q', the length of $Q'R'$ is the _____ of the line m.

   iv) For points P' and Q', the length of $P'R'$ is the _____ of the line m.

   v) The ratio $\dfrac{Q'R'}{P'R'} = \dfrac{QR}{PR}$ is the _____ of the line m.

7. a) Find the run, rise, and slope using the given pair of points on the graph. Make sure that the run is positive.

   i) *A* and *B*

      rise = _____

      run = _____

      slope =

   ii) *A* and *C*

      rise = _____

      run = _____

      slope =

   iii) *B* and *C*

      rise = _____

      run = _____

      slope =

   iv) *A* and *D*

      rise = _____

      run = _____

      slope =

b) What do you notice about the slopes in part a)? _____

c) Does the slope of the line depend on the points used to find the slope? _____

d) What is the *y*-intercept of the line *AD*? _____

e) Use the slope and the *y*-intercept to write the equation of the line. _____

f) Use your answers to Question 6 to explain why the slope of the line does not depend on the choice of the points used to find the slope.

G8-38 Lines and Transformations

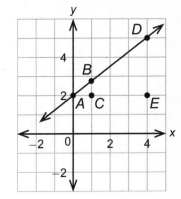

1. a) Find the length of the line segments.

    $DE =$ _____ units

    $AE =$ _____ units

    $AC =$ _____ unit

    b) Use the coordinates of points A and D to find the slope of the line AD.

    slope of $AD =$

    c) Write a symbol to make the statement true: $\triangle ABC$ _____ $\triangle ADE$.

    d) What do you know about the ratios $\dfrac{AE}{AC}$ and $\dfrac{DE}{BC}$? _____

    e) Use your answer to part d) to find the exact length of BC. _____ units

    f) What do you notice about the slope of AD and the length of BC? _____

    Use the length of AC to explain why this happens. _____

    _____

    _____

    g) What is the y-intercept of line AB? _____

    h) Write the equation for line AB in slope-intercept form. _____

    i) Draw line ℓ parallel to AD through the origin.

    j) To get from line ℓ to line AB, you can translate line ℓ _____ units up.

    Write the formula for this translation. $(x, y) \rightarrow ($ _____ , _____ $)$

    k) Circle the y-intercept of AB in your answers in part j).

    l) What is the y-intercept of line ℓ? _____ What is its slope? _____

    Write the equation for line ℓ in slope-intercept form. _____

    m) Is the point $\left(1, \dfrac{3}{4}\right)$ on line ℓ? _____ Explain.

    _____

    n) Draw a triangle with vertices $O\,(0, 0)$, $P\,(1, 0)$, and $Q\left(1, \dfrac{3}{4}\right)$. What can you tell

    about $\triangle OPQ$ and $\triangle ADE$? Explain. _____

    _____

    o) What sequence of transformations will take $\triangle OPQ$ to $\triangle ADE$?

    _____

    _____

2. a) Draw the line $y = 3x + 1$ on the grid.

b) Write the coordinates of two points on the line.

A (0,   ), B (1,   )

c) Where does the y-intercept of AB appear in your answer

to part b)? _____

How can you get the slope of AB from the coordinates of B and the y-intercept?

_____

_____

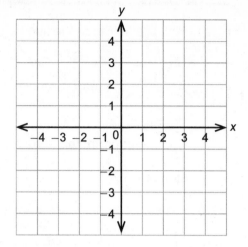

d) Reflect line AB in the y-axis.

Write the formula for the reflection. $(x, y) \rightarrow ($, $)$

e) What are the coordinates of the images of A and B under the reflection in the y-axis?

A' (,   ), B' (,   )

f) What is the slope of line $A'B'$? _____ What is the y-intercept? _____

What is the equation of line $A'B'$ in slope-intercept form? _____

g) Reflect line AB in the x-axis. Write the formula for the reflection.

$(x, y) \rightarrow ($, $)$

h) What are the coordinates of the images of A and B under the reflection in the x-axis?

A^* (,   ), B^* (,   )

i) What is the slope of line A^*B^*? _____ What is the y-intercept? _____

What is the equation of line A^*B^* in slope-intercept form? _____

j) What do you notice about lines $A'B'$ and A^*B^*? Do the slopes of the lines agree with your answer?

_____

_____

Bonus ▶ For the equation $y = 3x + 1$, substitute the formulas for the images of x and y after the given reflection. Then rewrite each equation for an image line in slope-intercept form.

    i) Reflection in the y-axis: **ii)** Reflection in the x-axis:

    _____ $= 3($ $) + 1$ _____ $= 3($ $) + 1$

    _____   _____

Did you get the same equations as in parts f) and i)? If not, find your mistake.

NS8-1 Square Roots

$6 \times 6 = 36$, so $6^2 = 36$. We say the **square** of 6 is 36.

Examples: $\left(\dfrac{2}{7}\right)^2 = \dfrac{2}{7} \times \dfrac{2}{7} = \dfrac{4}{49}$ $0.5^2 = 0.5 \times 0.5 = 0.25$

1. Evaluate the power.

a) $7^2 = \underline{49}$

b) $9^2 = \underline{}$

c) $10^2 = \underline{}$

d) $8^2 = \underline{}$

e) $\left(\dfrac{1}{4}\right)^2 = \underline{}$

f) $\left(\dfrac{3}{10}\right)^2 = \underline{}$

g) $0.2^2 = \underline{}$

h) $1.1^2 = \underline{}$

The **square root** of 25 is 5 because $5^2 = 25$. We write $\sqrt{25} = 5$.

Examples: $\sqrt{\dfrac{9}{16}} = \dfrac{3}{4}$ because $\left(\dfrac{3}{4}\right)^2 = \dfrac{9}{16}$ $\sqrt{0.01} = 0.1$ because $(0.1)^2 = 0.01$

2. Find the square root.

a) $\sqrt{49} = \underline{7}$

b) $\sqrt{16} = \underline{}$

c) $\sqrt{9} = \underline{}$

d) $\sqrt{36} = \underline{}$

e) $\sqrt{1} = \underline{}$

f) $\sqrt{100} = \underline{}$

g) $\sqrt{81} = \underline{}$

h) $\sqrt{64} = \underline{}$

i) $\sqrt{\dfrac{4}{9}} = \underline{}$

j) $\sqrt{\dfrac{49}{100}} = \underline{}$

k) $\sqrt{0.09} = \underline{}$

l) $\sqrt{1.44} = \underline{}$

3. Evaluate the square roots and then multiply, divide, add, or subtract.

a) $\sqrt{1} + \sqrt{64}$

b) $\sqrt{81} - \sqrt{25}$

c) $\sqrt{36} \div \sqrt{4}$

d) $\sqrt{25} + \sqrt{16} \times \sqrt{9}$

$= 1 + 8$

$= 9$

4. Evaluate both expressions. Then write $=$ or $\neq$ in the box.

a) $\sqrt{4 \times 9}$ $\boxed{=}$ $\sqrt{4} \times \sqrt{9}$

$= \sqrt{36}$ $= 2 \times 3$

$= 6$ $= 6$

b) $\sqrt{9 + 16}$ $\boxed{}$ $\sqrt{9} + \sqrt{16}$

c) $\sqrt{169 - 25}$ $\boxed{}$ $\sqrt{169} - \sqrt{25}$

d) $\sqrt{100 \div 4}$ $\boxed{}$ $\sqrt{100} \div \sqrt{4}$

5. a) Evaluate the powers.

    i) $5^2 = $ _____   ii) $11^2 = $ _____   iii) $12^2 = $ _____   iv) $3^2 = $ _____

      $(-5)^2 = $ _____ $(-11)^2 = $ _____ $(-12)^2 = $ _____ $(-3)^2 = $ _____

b) Write "positive" or "negative."

    i) The square of a positive number is a _____ number.

    ii) The square of a negative number is a _____ number.

Every positive number has a positive square root and a negative square root.

Example: $(4)^2 = 16$ and $(-4)^2 = 16$, so 4 and -4 are square roots of 16.

---

6. Write two square roots of the number.

  a) 81   b) 49   c) 25   d) 0.16

    _9_ and _−9_   ____ and ____   ____ and ____   ____ and ____

7. Write two solutions for the equation.

  a) $x^2 = 1$ b) $x^2 = 9$ c) $x^2 = 121$ d) $x^2 = 0.04$

    $x = $ _1_ and _−1_ $x = $ ____ and ____ $x = $ ____ and ____ $x = $ ____ and ____

The equation $x^2 = 81$ has two solutions: $x = 9$ and $x = -9$. We write $x = \pm 9$ to indicate that the solution can be positive or negative.

    $x^2 = 81$ Check: $x^2 = 81$

    $x = 9$ and $x = -9$ $(9)^2 = 81$ ✓

    $x = \pm 9$ $(-9)^2 = 81$ ✓

---

8. Solve the equation.

  a) $x^2 = 144$ b) $x^2 = 9$ c) $x^2 = \dfrac{36}{49}$ d) $x^2 = 0.09$

    $x = 12$ and $x = -12$

    $x = \pm 12$

  e) $x^2 + 5 = 41$ f) $4x^2 - 6 = 10$ g) $x^2 + \dfrac{1}{2} = \dfrac{3}{4}$ **Bonus ▶** $\dfrac{2}{3}x^2 - 15 = 1\dfrac{2}{3}$

9. Jayden's garden is a square. The area is 49 ft². What is the perimeter?

10. A square painting has an area of 36 in². Kathy says the length of one side could be 6 inches or −6 inches. What is Kathy's mistake?

The **principal square root** of a number is the positive square root of the number. We write $\sqrt{36} = 6$.

To indicate the negative square root, we write $-\sqrt{36} = -6$.

To indicate both the positive and negative square roots, we write $\pm\sqrt{36} = \pm6$.

11. Evaluate.

a) $-\sqrt{100} = \underline{\ -10\ }$ b) $\pm\sqrt{121} = \underline{\hspace{2cm}}$ c) $\sqrt{0.0144} = \underline{\hspace{2cm}}$ d) $\pm\sqrt{1} = \underline{\hspace{2cm}}$

e) $\pm\sqrt{30-5}$ f) $-\sqrt{81} - \sqrt{1}$ g) $\pm\sqrt{29+7}$ h) $\sqrt{36} + \sqrt{1} - \sqrt{25}$

$= \pm\sqrt{25}$

$= \pm5$

Since the solution to the equation $x^2 = 49$ can be positive or negative, we write $x = \pm\sqrt{49} = \pm7$.

12. Solve the equation.

a) $x^2 = 4$ b) $x^2 = 25$ c) $x^2 = \dfrac{1}{100}$ d) $x^2 = 1.44$

$x = \pm\sqrt{4}$

$x = \pm2$

13. a) Evaluate using the standard order of operations.

i) $\left(\sqrt{16}\right)^2$ ii) $\left(\sqrt{100}\right)^2$ iii) $\left(\sqrt{64}\right)^2$ iv) $\left(\sqrt{81}\right)^2$

$= (4)^2$

$= 16$

b) What do you notice about your answers to part a)?

14. a) To solve for x, square both sides of the equation. Group any like terms first.

i) $\sqrt{x} = 8$ ii) $\sqrt{x} = \dfrac{2}{5}$ iii) $5 - 2 = \sqrt{x}$ **Bonus ▶** $8 = \sqrt{x} + 7$

$\left(\sqrt{x}\right)^2 = 8^2$

$x = 64$

b) Check your answers to part a).

i) $\sqrt{x} = 8$ ii) iii) **Bonus ▶**

$\sqrt{64} = 8$ ✓

NS8-2 Cube Roots

$2 \times 2 \times 2 = 8$, so $2^3 = 8$. We say the **cube** of 2 is 8.

Examples: $4^3 = 4 \times 4 \times 4 = 64$ $\qquad\qquad$ $(-11)^3 = (-11)(-11)(-11) = -1{,}331$

1. Evaluate the power.

a) $0^3 = \underline{0}$ $\qquad$ b) $3^3 = \underline{}$ $\qquad$ c) $5^3 = \underline{}$ $\qquad$ d) $6^3 = \underline{}$

e) $7^3 = \underline{}$ $\qquad$ f) $8^3 = \underline{}$ $\qquad$ g) $9^3 = \underline{}$ $\qquad$ h) $10^3 = \underline{}$

2. a) Evaluate the powers.

i) $4^3 = \underline{64}$ $\quad$ ii) $1^3 = \underline{}$ $\quad$ iii) $2^3 = \underline{}$ $\quad$ iv) $3^3 = \underline{}$

$(-4)^3 = \underline{-64}$ $\quad$ $(-1)^3 = \underline{}$ $\quad$ $(-2)^3 = \underline{}$ $\quad$ $(-3)^3 = \underline{}$

b) Write "positive" or "negative."

i) The cube of a positive number is a _____ number.

ii) The cube of a negative number is a _____ number.

The **cube root** of 8 is 2 because $2^3 = 8$. We write $\sqrt[3]{8} = 2$.

Examples: $\sqrt[3]{125} = 5$ because $5^3 = 125$ $\qquad$ $\sqrt[3]{-64} = -4$ because $(-4)^3 = -64$

3. Find the cube root.

a) $\sqrt[3]{0} = \underline{0}$ $\quad$ b) $\sqrt[3]{512} = \underline{}$ $\quad$ c) $\sqrt[3]{-216} = \underline{}$ $\quad$ d) $\sqrt[3]{-27} = \underline{}$

e) $\sqrt[3]{1} = \underline{}$ $\quad$ f) $\sqrt[3]{-1{,}000} = \underline{}$ $\quad$ g) $\sqrt[3]{-343} = \underline{}$ $\quad$ h) $\sqrt[3]{729} = \underline{}$

4. Write "positive" or "negative."

a) The cube root of a positive number is a _____ number.

b) The cube root of a negative number is a _____ number.

5. Evaluate the expression. Remember to follow the standard order of operations.

a) $\sqrt[3]{3-30}$ $\qquad\qquad$ b) $\sqrt[3]{56+8}$ $\qquad\qquad$ c) $\sqrt[3]{-64} \div \sqrt[3]{-8}$ $\qquad\qquad$ d) $\sqrt[3]{1} + \sqrt[3]{125} \times \sqrt[3]{-729}$

$= \sqrt[3]{-27}$

$= -3$

6. Find the cube root. Check your answer.

a) $\sqrt[3]{\dfrac{1}{1{,}000}} = \dfrac{1}{10}$

b) $\sqrt[3]{-\dfrac{1}{8}} =$

c) $\sqrt[3]{\dfrac{64}{343}} =$

$\dfrac{1}{10} \times \dfrac{1}{10} \times \dfrac{1}{10} = \dfrac{1}{1{,}000}$ ✓

7. a) Evaluate the powers.

i) $1^3 =$ _____

ii) $3^3 =$ _____

iii) $5^3 =$ _____

   $0.1^3 =$ _____

   $0.3^3 =$ _____

   $50^3 =$ _____

   $0.01^3 =$ _____

   $0.03^3 =$ _____

   $500^3 =$ _____

b) You know that $8^3 = 512$. Explain how you can quickly evaluate 0.8^3, 0.08^3, 80^3, and 800^3.
Hint: How many times do you move the decimal place and in which direction?

8. Evaluate the power.

a) $0.5^3 =$ _____

b) $0.02^3 =$ _____

c) $(-70)^3 =$ _____

d) $(-1.2)^3 =$ _____

e) $100^3 =$ _____

f) $0.11^3 =$ _____

9. Find the cube root.

a) $\sqrt[3]{0.729} =$ _____

b) $\sqrt[3]{-0.343} =$ _____

c) $\sqrt[3]{64{,}000} =$ _____

d) $\sqrt[3]{-1.331} =$ _____

e) $\sqrt[3]{-125{,}000} =$ _____

f) $\sqrt[3]{0.000027} =$ _____

10. Evaluate both expressions. Then write $=$ or $\neq$ in the box.

a) $\sqrt[3]{1 \times 8}$ $\boxed{=}$ $\sqrt[3]{1} \times \sqrt[3]{8}$

$= \sqrt[3]{8}$ $= 1 \times 2$

$= 2$ $= 2$

b) $\sqrt[3]{(-8) \times 27}$ $\square$ $\sqrt[3]{-8} \times \sqrt[3]{27}$

c) $\sqrt[3]{64} \div \sqrt[3]{8}$ $\square$ $\sqrt[3]{64 \div 8}$

Bonus ▶ $\sqrt[3]{27 \times (-1{,}000) \div (-125)}$ $\square$ $\sqrt[3]{27} \times \sqrt[3]{-1{,}000} \div \sqrt[3]{-125}$

11. Write the numbers in order from least to greatest.

a) $\sqrt[3]{1{,}000}$, 2^3, 200, 8^3, $\sqrt[3]{8}$

b) $\sqrt[3]{343}$, $\sqrt[3]{-512}$, $\sqrt[3]{125}$, $\sqrt[3]{-27}$, $\sqrt[3]{64}$

Bonus ▶ 0.5, $\sqrt[3]{\dfrac{1}{64}}$, 1.2^3, 0.3^3, $\sqrt[3]{0.512}$

12. a) Evaluate using the standard order of operations.

i) $\left(\sqrt[3]{8}\right)^3$ ii) $\left(\sqrt[3]{-1}\right)^3$ iii) $\left(\sqrt[3]{-27}\right)^3$ iv) $\left(\sqrt[3]{1{,}000}\right)^3$

$= (2)^3$

$= 8$

b) What do you notice about your answers to part a)?

13. To solve for x, cube both sides of the equation. Group any like terms first.

a) $\sqrt[3]{x} = 5$ **b)** $\sqrt[3]{x} = -1.2$ **c)** $\sqrt[3]{x} = 4 - 6$ **Bonus ▶** $\sqrt[3]{x} + \dfrac{1}{2} = \dfrac{3}{4}$

$\left(\sqrt[3]{x}\right)^3 = 5^3$

$x = 125$

Sara solves the equation $x^3 = 216$.		Tom solves the equation $x^3 - 7 = -71$.	
$x^3 = 216$	Check:	$x^3 - 7 = -71$	Check:
$\sqrt[3]{x^3} = \sqrt[3]{216}$	$x^3 = 216$	$x^3 = -71 + 7$	$x^3 - 7 = -71$
$x = \sqrt[3]{216}$	$(6)^3 = 216 \checkmark$	$x^3 = -64$	$(-4)^3 - 7$
$x = 6$		$x = \sqrt[3]{-64}$	$= -64 - 7$
		$x = -4$	$= -71 \checkmark$

14. Solve the equation.

a) $x^3 = 8$ **b)** $x^3 = -343$ **c)** $x^3 = 1{,}000$ **d)** $x^3 = -\dfrac{64}{729}$

e) $x^3 - 6 = -70$ **f)** $2x^3 - 50 = 200$ **g)** $x^3 + \dfrac{1}{4} = \dfrac{3}{8}$ **h)** $\dfrac{1}{3}x^3 + 12 = -60$

15. A cardboard box is cube-shaped and has a volume of 1.728 ft^3. What is the length of one side of the box?

16. Peter says that the solution to $x^3 = 216$ is $x = \pm 6$. What is Peter's mistake?

NS8-3 Rational Numbers

We use braces { } to show a set of numbers.

{0, 1, 2, 3, ...} is the set of whole numbers. Whole numbers do not have fractional or decimal parts. They cannot be negative numbers. Examples: 9, 74, 244

{... , −3, −2, −1, 0, 1, 2, 3, ...} is the set of integers. Integers do not have fractional or decimal parts. They can be negative numbers. Examples: −6, 52, −768

1. Classify the number. Write "whole number," "integer," "both," or "neither."

   a) 4 _____

   b) 12.5 _____

   c) −11 _____

   d) $-6\frac{3}{5}$ _____

   e) 275 _____

   f) −61 _____

2. Is the statement true or false? If the statement is false, provide a counterexample.

   a) All whole numbers are integers.

   b) All integers are whole numbers.

3. Write the integer as a fraction.

   a) $7 = \frac{7}{1}$

   b) $-65 =$

   c) $670 =$

   d) $-5{,}012 =$

4. Write the mixed number as a fraction.

   a) $8\frac{4}{9} = \frac{76}{9}$

   b) $6\frac{2}{3} =$

   c) $5\frac{6}{7} =$

   d) $-4\frac{1}{6} =$

5. Write the percent as a fraction.

   a) $41\% = \frac{41}{100}$

   b) $65\% =$

   c) $-7\% =$

   d) $210\% =$

Any number that can be written as a fraction is a **rational number**.

6. Explain why integers, mixed numbers, and percents belong to the set of rational numbers.

7. Show that the decimal number is rational by writing it as a decimal fraction.

   a) $-1.6 = -\frac{16}{10}$

   b) $0.05 =$

   c) $0.305 =$

   d) $-47.49 =$

8. Sort the numbers by writing them in the correct part of the diagram.

$1\frac{3}{4}$ -4 38

-99 526 3.25

0 -7.5 -200

Bonus ▶

3% 100% $-\dfrac{10}{2}$

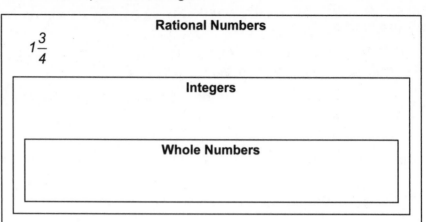

9. a) List the whole numbers less than 5. _____

b) List the integers between -3 and 4. _____

c) List five rational numbers between 1 and 2. _____

Bonus ▶ Marta says that she can list every rational number between 1 and 2. Do you think that she can? Explain.

10. Identify the set (whole numbers, integers, or rational numbers) that best describes the situation. Give two examples.

a) Scores in a golf game   *Integers such as -2 (under par) and $+1$ (over par)*

b) Number of concert tickets sold   c) Prices on tags in a clothing store

d) Temperatures to the nearest degree   e) Number of pets that a family has

A number can belong to more than one set of numbers.

Examples: 2 belongs to the sets of whole numbers, integers, and rational numbers.

$\sqrt[3]{-27} = -3$, so $\sqrt[3]{-27}$ belongs to the sets of integers and rational numbers.

11. List all sets that the number belongs to.

a) 3.08   b) 8   c) -9 d) $2\frac{1}{2}$

e) 0   f) $\sqrt{1.44}$ g) $\sqrt{25}$ h) $\sqrt[3]{-64}$

12. True (T) or false (F)?

a) All integers are rational numbers. ____   b) All rational numbers are integers. ____

c) All rational numbers are whole numbers. ____   d) All whole numbers are rational numbers. ____

NS8-4 Writing Fractions as Repeating Decimals

1. Find an equivalent decimal fraction. Then write the fraction as a decimal.

    a) $\dfrac{9}{25} = \dfrac{36}{100} = 0.36$

    b) $\dfrac{3}{4} =$

    c) $\dfrac{17}{40} =$

2. Use long division to write the fraction as a decimal. Keep dividing until the remainder is 0.

    a) $\dfrac{9}{25} = \underline{\quad 0.36 \quad}$

    b) $\dfrac{17}{20} = \underline{\qquad\qquad}$

    c) $\dfrac{5}{8} = \underline{\qquad\qquad}$

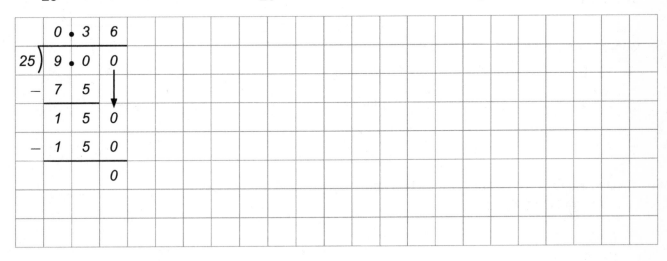

3. a) Calculate $2 \div 3$ by writing 2 as 2.0, 2.00, and 2.000.

    $2.0 \div 3$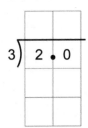

    $2.00 \div 3$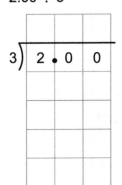

    $2.000 \div 3$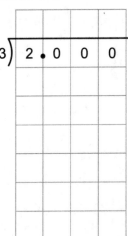

    b) If you continued the division to calculate $2.0000 \div 3$, what would the next digit in the quotient be? How do you know?

    c) Would you ever get a remainder of 0 if you continued the division? How do you know?

A **repeating decimal** is a decimal with a digit or group of digits that repeats forever. You can use a bar to show the digit or group of digits that repeats. Example: $0.45454\ldots = 0.\overline{45}$

A **terminating decimal** is a decimal that does not go on forever. Examples: 0.36, 6.685, 4.7

4. Write the repeating decimal to six decimal places.

a) $0.\overline{7} =$ ___0.777777...___

b) $-0.\overline{84} =$ _____

c) $1.\overline{822} =$ _____

d) $5.3\overline{60} =$ _____

e) $4.4\overline{8} =$ _____

f) $-8.0\overline{731} =$ _____

5. Use bar notation to write the repeating decimal.

a) $0.222222\ldots =$ ___$0.\overline{2}$___

b) $-0.949494\ldots =$ _____

c) $-6.0868686\ldots =$ _____

d) $4.754754\ldots =$ _____

e) $8.466666\ldots =$ _____

f) $-2.109090\ldots =$ _____

g) $0.101010\ldots =$ _____

h) $7.777777\ldots =$ _____

i) $-0.008888\ldots =$ _____

6. a) Use a calculator to write the fraction as a decimal. Use bar notation for repeating decimals.

i) $\dfrac{5}{9} =$ ___$0.\overline{5}$___

ii) $\dfrac{7}{25} =$ _____

iii) $\dfrac{4}{15} =$ _____

iv) $\dfrac{6}{11} =$ _____

v) $-\dfrac{5}{16} =$ _____

vi) $-\dfrac{17}{20} =$ _____

b) Which fractions in part a) can be written as terminating decimals?

c) Write the denominators of the fractions in part b) as products of only 2s and/or 5s. Can you do the same for the fractions in part a) that are written as repeating decimals?

To decide if a fraction can be written as a terminating decimal or a repeating decimal:

Step 1: Write the fraction in lowest terms.

Step 2: Look at the denominator. If it can be written as a product of only 2s and/or 5s, the decimal terminates. If it cannot be written as a product of only 2s and/or 5s, the decimal repeats.

7. Predict whether the decimal will terminate. Check with a calculator. Hint: Write the fraction in lowest terms first.

a) $\dfrac{10}{16}$

b) $\dfrac{21}{36}$

c) $\dfrac{63}{99}$

d) $-\dfrac{45}{250}$

e) $-\dfrac{35}{75}$

f) $\dfrac{9}{36}$

8. Can every rational number be written as a decimal that repeats eventually? Hint: $5.1 = 5.10 = 5.100\ldots$

NS8-5 Writing Repeating Decimals as Fractions

1. Use a calculator to write the fraction as a decimal. Write the decimal using bar notation.

    a) $\dfrac{1}{9} =$ ___0.$\overline{1}$___

    b) $-\dfrac{5}{9} =$ _____

    c) $\dfrac{31}{99} =$ _____

    d) $\dfrac{437}{999} =$ _____

    e) $5\dfrac{2}{9} =$ _____

    f) $-4\dfrac{68}{999} =$ _____

2. Find an equivalent fraction with a denominator of 9, 99, or 999. Then write the fraction as a decimal.

    a) $\dfrac{13}{33} = \dfrac{39}{99} = 0.\overline{39}$

    b) $-\dfrac{4}{11} =$

    c) $\dfrac{25}{333} =$

    d) $\dfrac{14}{18} =$

    e) $3\dfrac{48}{66} =$

    f) $-2\dfrac{15}{27} =$

3. Describe the pattern when you write a fraction with a denominator of 9, 99, or 999 as a decimal.

4. Use the pattern from Question 3 to write the decimal as a fraction or mixed number.

    a) $0.\overline{5} =$

    b) $0.\overline{74} =$

    c) $7.\overline{26} =$

    d) $0.\overline{321} =$

    e) $6.4444... =$

    f) $-2.6363... =$

5. Write the decimal as a decimal fraction.

    a) $0.5 =$

    b) $0.96 =$

    c) $3.001 =$

6. Fill in the blanks with "10, 100, etc." or "9, 99, etc."

    a) Terminating decimals can be written as fractions with denominators of _____.

    b) Repeating decimals can be written as fractions with denominators of _____.

7. Write the decimal as a fraction or mixed number. Reduce to lowest terms.

    a) $0.4 = \dfrac{4}{10} = \dfrac{2}{5}$

    b) $2.\overline{4} =$

    c) $4.35 =$

    d) $7.\overline{02} =$

    e) $-0.\overline{456} =$

    f) $-0.316 =$

8. Are all terminating decimals and repeating decimals rational numbers? Explain.

9. Multiply by moving the decimal point the correct number of places. Hint: Write the first few digits of the repeating decimal.

a) $0.\overline{8} \times 10$ 　　　　 b) $-1.\overline{7} \times 10$ 　　　　 c) $0.\overline{26} \times 100$ 　　　　 d) $-6.\overline{48} \times 100$

$= 0.88888... \times 10$

$= 8.8888...$ or $8.\overline{8}$

10. Write the power of 10 that makes the statement true.

a) $0.5555... \times \underline{\quad 10 \quad} = 5.555...$ 　　　　 b) $0.8787... \times \underline{\qquad} = 87.87...$

c) $1.6666... \times \underline{\qquad} = 16.666...$ 　　　　 d) $4.135135... \times \underline{\qquad} = 4{,}135.135...$

To write $0.\overline{6}$ as a fraction: 　　　　　　　　　　　　　 Let $x = 0.66666...$

Step 1: Multiply x by 10 because 1 digit repeats.
(Multiply x by 100 if 2 digits repeat.)

$$10x = 6.66666...$$
$$- x = 0.66666...$$

Step 2: Subtract x from $10x$ to eliminate the repeating part.

$$9x = 6.00000...$$

Step 3: Solve for x and reduce the fraction to lowest terms.

$$x = \frac{6}{9} = \frac{2}{3} \qquad \text{So } 0.\overline{6} = \frac{2}{3}.$$

11. Write the decimal as a fraction.

a) $0.\overline{4}$: Let $x =$

$10x =$

$- x =$

$\overline{\qquad\qquad\qquad\qquad}$

$9x =$

$x =$

b) $0.\overline{65}$: Let $x =$

$100x =$

$- x =$

$\overline{\qquad\qquad\qquad\qquad}$

$99x =$

$x =$

c) $0.\overline{3}$ 　　　　 d) $0.\overline{96}$ 　　　　 e) $0.\overline{715}$ 　　　　 f) $0.\overline{384}$

12. Write the decimal as a fraction. Write the answer as a mixed number.

a) $3.\overline{2}$: Let $x =$

$10x =$

$- x =$

$\overline{\qquad\qquad\qquad\qquad}$

$9x =$

$x =$

b) $5.\overline{43}$: Let $x =$

$100x =$

$- x =$

$\overline{\qquad\qquad\qquad\qquad}$

$99x =$

$x =$

c) $-12.\overline{4}$ 　　　　 d) $-8.\overline{29}$

NS8-6 Operations with Repeating Decimals

1. a) Add by lining up the decimal places.

   i) 0.8 + 0.5   ii) 0.88 + 0.55   iii) 0.888 + 0.555

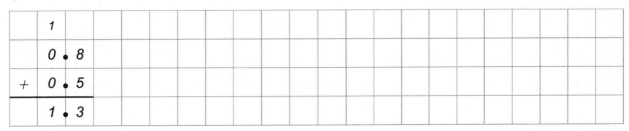

	1																	
	0 . 8																	
+	0 . 5																	
	1 . 3																	

   b) Use the pattern in part a) to predict $0.\overline{8} + 0.\overline{5}$. _____

2. a) Write $0.\overline{8}$ and $0.\overline{5}$ as fractions. $0.\overline{8} = \underline{\quad}$ $0.\overline{5} = \underline{\quad}$

   b) Add the fractions from part a). $\underline{\quad} + \underline{\quad} = \underline{\quad}$

   c) Write your answer to part b) as a mixed number, then as a decimal. _____ = _____

   d) Was your prediction from Question 1.b) correct? _____

   e) What problems can you see in trying to add $0.\overline{8} + 0.\overline{5}$ by lining up the decimal places? What advantage does writing the decimals as fractions give you?

To add repeating decimals:	Example: $0.\overline{4} + 0.\overline{79}$
Step 1: Write the decimals as fractions.	$0.\overline{4} = \dfrac{4}{9}$ $0.\overline{79} = \dfrac{79}{99}$
Step 2: Add the fractions.	$\dfrac{4}{9} + \dfrac{79}{99} = \dfrac{44}{99} + \dfrac{79}{99}$
	$= \dfrac{123}{99}$
	$= 1\dfrac{24}{99}$
Step 3: Write the answer as a decimal.	$= 1.\overline{24}$

3. Evaluate.

   a) $0.\overline{6} + 0.\overline{7}$ b) $0.\overline{85} + 0.\overline{6}$ c) $0.\overline{745} + 0.\overline{679}$

   d) $0.\overline{63} - 0.\overline{47}$ e) $0.\overline{512} - 0.\overline{4}$ f) $0.\overline{31} - 0.\overline{6}$

   Bonus ▶ $0.\overline{1} - 0.\overline{2} + 0.\overline{03} - 0.\overline{04}$

---

4. a) Multiply.

   i)   0.8
       $\times$ 4

   ii)   0.88
       $\times$ 4

   iii)   0.888
       $\times$ 4

b) Use the pattern in part a) to predict $0.\overline{8} \times 4$. What problems can you see in trying to multiply $0.\overline{8} \times 4$ as if the decimal was a whole number?

5. a) Write $0.\overline{8}$ as a fraction. $0.\overline{8} = $ ——

   b) Multiply the fraction from part a) by 4.   —— $\times 4 = $ ——

   c) Write your answer to part b) as a mixed number, then as a decimal.   _____ = _____

   d) Was your prediction in Question 4.b) correct? _____

6. Write the decimal as a fraction. Multiply or divide. Write the answer as a mixed number and then as a decimal.

   a) $0.\overline{4} \times 7$

   b) $0.\overline{43} \times 3$

   c) $0.\overline{6} \times 0.\overline{3}$

   d) $0.\overline{7} \div 0.\overline{2}$

   e) $0.\overline{6} \div 0.\overline{5}$

   f) $0.\overline{14} \div 0.\overline{18}$

To write a fraction as a percent:	Example: $\dfrac{5}{9} = $ _____%
Step 1: Write the fraction as a decimal.	$\dfrac{5}{9} = 0.55555...$
Step 2: Multiply by 100.	$0.55555... \times 100 = 55.55555...$
Step 3: Round to the nearest percent.	$\dfrac{5}{9} = 55.\overline{5}\% \approx 56\%$

7. Write the fraction as a percent.

   a) $\dfrac{7}{9} = $

   b) $\dfrac{3}{11} = $

   c) $\dfrac{12}{18} = $

8. Two bookstores are having a sale. Everything at Rick's Reads is $\dfrac{1}{3}$ off. At Bev's Books, there is a 30% discount. Which store offers a greater discount?

   Bonus ▶ What would be the difference in the sale price of a $20 book at these stores? Round to the nearest cent.

NS8-7 Rational Numbers on the Number Line

1. Name the fractions marked on the number line.

a)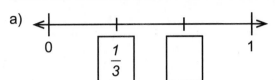

b)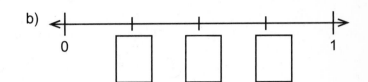

c)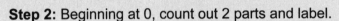

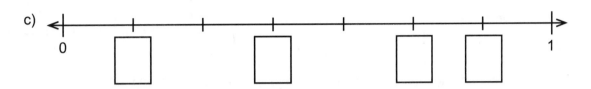

To show a fraction on a number line:

Step 1: Use a ruler to divide the interval from 0 to 1 into 5 equal parts.

Step 2: Beginning at 0, count out 2 parts and label.

Example: $\dfrac{2}{5}$

2. Show the fraction on the number line

a) $\dfrac{1}{3}$ 0 ——————————————————— 1

b) $\dfrac{3}{4}$ 0 ——————————————————— 1

c) $\dfrac{5}{6}$ 0 ——————————————————— 1

d) $5\dfrac{3}{8}$ 5 ——————————————————— 6

e) $2\dfrac{4}{5}$ 2 ——————————————————— 3

3. Show both numbers on the number line. Which number is greater?

a) $7\dfrac{3}{5}$ and $\sqrt{49}$

7 ———————————— 8

_____ < _____

b) $-3\dfrac{1}{4}$ and $\sqrt[3]{-27}$

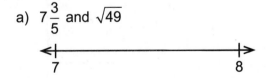

−4 ———————————— −3

_____ < _____

4. Mark the position of the decimal on each number line.

a) 0.463

b) 0.815

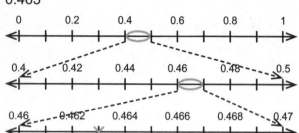
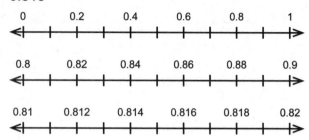

5. a) Explain why the terminating decimals in Question 4 have an exact position on the bottom number line.

b) Explain why a repeating decimal such as $0.\overline{5} = 0.555\ldots$ would not have an exact position on the bottom number line.

To show a repeating decimal on a number line:

Step 1: Write the repeating decimal as a fraction.

Step 2: Use a ruler to divide the interval from 5 to 6 into 9 equal parts.

Step 3: Beginning at 5, count out 4 parts and label.

Example: $5.\overline{4}$

$$5.\overline{4} = 5\frac{4}{9}$$

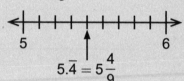

$$5.\overline{4} = 5\frac{4}{9}$$

---

6. Write the decimal as a fraction in lowest terms. Show the fraction on the number line.

a) $0.\overline{6} =$

0   1

b) $0.\overline{18} =$

0   1

c) $2.\overline{45} =$

2   3

7. What two numbers is the given number between if you count by ones, tenths, and hundredths?

		Ones	Tenths	Hundredths
a)	0.487	0 and 1	0.4 and 0.5	0.48 and 0.49
b)	5.628			
c)	$0.\overline{3} =$			
d)	$12.67\overline{} =$			

8. Does every rational number have a position on the number line? Explain.

NS8-8 Irrational Numbers

1. a) Write the terminating decimal as a fraction.

    i) $0.24 = \dfrac{24}{100}$ ii) $0.7 =$ iii) $0.348 =$ iv) $5.09 =$

    b) Write the repeating decimal as a fraction.

    i) $0.5555... = \dfrac{5}{9}$ ii) $0.2828... =$ iii) $0.\overline{01} =$ iv) $5.\overline{123} =$

    c) Explain why 1.41421356… is not a terminating decimal and not a repeating decimal.

    d) Can you write 1.41421356… as a fraction? Explain.

> Rational numbers are numbers that can be written as fractions. Terminating decimals and repeating decimals are rational numbers.
>
> **Irrational numbers** are numbers that cannot be written as fractions. Irrational numbers have decimal digits that continue forever and that never repeat.

2. a) Circle the numbers that are rational.

0.21	0.656565…	3.14159…	$0.\overline{3}$
0.818818881…	0.902	1.7	0.123456789…

    b) Choose four numbers that you circled in part a) and complete the sentence.

    _____ is rational because _____.

    _____ is rational because _____.

    _____ is rational because _____.

    _____ is rational because _____.

3. a) Show each number on the number line. Use a dot and letter label for the number.

    A. 1.1   **B.** $1.\overline{5}$ **C.** 1.414213…   **D.** $1\dfrac{7}{9}$

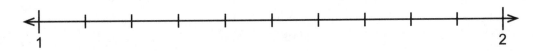

    b) Name a rational number between A and C. _____

    c) Name a rational number between B and D. _____

4. Evaluate the square roots and cube roots.

a) $\sqrt{64} =$ _____

b) $\sqrt{25} =$ _____

c) $\sqrt[3]{27} =$ _____

d) $\sqrt[3]{-512} =$ _____

e) $\sqrt{0.09} =$ _____

f) $\sqrt[3]{-0.008} =$ _____

g) $\sqrt{\dfrac{1}{4}} = \underline{}$

h) $\sqrt[3]{\dfrac{8}{27}} = \underline{}$

> **Perfect squares** and **perfect cubes** are numbers that have integers as their roots.
>
> Examples: The square roots of 25 are 5 and −5, so 25 is a perfect square.
> The cube root of −8 is −2, so −8 is a perfect cube.

5. a) Circle the perfect squares in the list.

   49   99   78   81   3.6

b) Circle the perfect cubes in the list.

   $\dfrac{1}{64}$ 216   495   −97   −729

6. a) Evaluate $\sqrt{1}$ and $\sqrt{4}$. $\sqrt{1} =$ _____ $\sqrt{4} =$ _____

b) Is there an integer between 1 and 2? _____

c) Can $\sqrt{2}$ or $\sqrt{3}$ be integers? Explain.

d) Use a calculator to evaluate $\sqrt{2}$ and $\sqrt{3}$. Write the first six decimal places.

   $\sqrt{2} =$ _____ ... $\sqrt{3} =$ _____ ...

e) Are $\sqrt{2}$ and $\sqrt{3}$ rational numbers? Explain.

> The square root of a non-perfect square is an irrational number. Example: $\sqrt{24}$ is irrational.
>
> The cube root of a non-perfect cube is an irrational number. Example: $\sqrt[3]{10}$ is irrational.

7. Is the number rational or irrational? Explain.

a) $\sqrt{49}$ is ___*rational*___ because ___$\sqrt{49} = 7$___ .

b) $\sqrt{12}$ is ___*irrational*___ because ___*12 is not a perfect square*___ .

c) $\sqrt[3]{-1,000}$ is _____ because _____ .

d) $\sqrt{200}$

e) $\sqrt{144}$

f) $\sqrt[3]{25}$

g) $\sqrt{\dfrac{1}{49}}$

8. Classify the number. If possible, evaluate the number first. You may check more than one category.

	Number	Whole Number	Integer	Rational Number	Irrational Number
a)	$\sqrt[3]{-8} = -2$		✓	✓	
b)	$\sqrt{121}$				
c)	$\sqrt[3]{6}$				
d)	$0.\overline{48}$				
e)	$0.010010001\ldots$				
f)	9.4				
g)	$-\sqrt{81}$				
h)	$\sqrt{8}$				

9. Circle the interval on each number line where the irrational number should be placed.

a) $\pi = 3.14159\ldots$

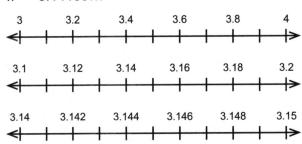

b) $\sqrt{3} = 1.73205\ldots$

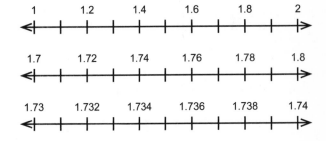

10. If you continued to draw number lines with smaller and smaller intervals, would the irrational numbers in Question 9 ever have an exact position? Explain.

11. Use a calculator to find the irrational number to 5 digits. What two numbers is the irrational number between if you count by ones, tenths, and hundredths?

		Decimal Equivalent (to 5 digits)	Ones	Tenths	Hundredths
a)	$\sqrt{12}$	3.46410...	3 and 4	3.4 and 3.5	3.46 and 3.47
b)	$\sqrt{138}$				
c)	$\sqrt[3]{417}$				
d)	$\sqrt[3]{734}$				
Bonus ▶	$\sqrt[3]{-185}$				

1. What is the corresponding perfect square for each whole number? Complete the table.

Whole Number	1	2	3	4	5	6	7	8	9	10
Perfect Square	1	4								

2. Which perfect squares is the number between? Which whole numbers is the square root between?

a) 13 is between ___9___ and ___16___

or 13 is between ___3^2___ and ___4^2___

so $\sqrt{13}$ is between ___3___ and ___4___

b) 33 is between _____ and _____

or 33 is between _____ and _____

so $\sqrt{33}$ is between _____ and _____

c) $\sqrt{7}$

d) $\sqrt{91}$

e) $\sqrt{70}$

Bonus ▶ $\sqrt{130}$

3. What is the corresponding perfect cube for each whole number? Complete the table.

Whole Number	1	2	3	4	5	6	7	8	9	10
Perfect Cube	1	8								

4. Which perfect cubes is the number between? Which integers is the cube root between?

a) 184 is between ___125___ and ___216___

or 184 is between ___5^3___ and ___6^3___

so $\sqrt[3]{184}$ is between ___5___ and ___6___

b) 789 is between _____ and _____

or 789 is between _____ and _____

so $\sqrt[3]{789}$ is between _____ and _____

c) $\sqrt[3]{101}$

d) $\sqrt[3]{-42}$

e) $\sqrt[3]{-480}$

f) $\sqrt[3]{25}$

$\sqrt{75}$ is between 8 and 9, so $\sqrt{75}$ must be greater than 8 ($\sqrt{75} > 8$) and less than 9 ($\sqrt{75} < 9$).

5. Find the integers that the root is between. Then write < or > in the box.

a) $\sqrt{7}$ $\boxed{<}$ 3

$\sqrt{7}$ is between

___2___ and ___3___

b) 8 $\boxed{}$ $\sqrt{55}$

$\sqrt{55}$ is between

_____ and _____

c) 1 $\boxed{}$ $\sqrt[3]{5}$

$\sqrt[3]{5}$ is between

_____ and _____

d) $\sqrt[3]{-444}$ $\boxed{}$ −8

$\sqrt[3]{-444}$ is between

_____ and _____

6. Order the set of numbers from least to greatest.

a) $\left\{\sqrt[3]{585},\ 8,\ \sqrt{61}\right\}$

b) $\left\{\sqrt{38},\ \sqrt{26},\ 5,\ \sqrt[3]{216}\right\}$

To compare expressions that include irrational numbers, find the integers that the irrational numbers are between. Then evaluate the expressions using the intervals.

Example: $\sqrt{10}+5$ ☐ $\sqrt{5}+10$ $3+5$ $4+5$

$\sqrt{10}$ is between 3 and 4, so $\sqrt{10}+5$ is between 8 and 9

$\sqrt{5}$ is between 2 and 3, so $\sqrt{5}+10$ is between 12 and 13

So $\sqrt{10}+5$ $\boxed{<}$ $\sqrt{5}+10$. $2+10$ $3+10$

7. Evaluate both expressions using intervals. Write $<$ or $>$ in the box to compare.

a) $\sqrt{3}+6$ ☐ $3+\sqrt{6}$ b) $6+\sqrt{7}$ ☐ $\sqrt{6}+7$ c) $10-\sqrt[3]{18}$ ☐ $18-\sqrt[3]{10}$

d) $5\times\sqrt{18}$ ☐ 18 e) $5+\sqrt[3]{60}$ ☐ $\sqrt[3]{817}-2$ f) $\dfrac{\sqrt[3]{480}}{4}$ ☐ $\dfrac{\sqrt{30}}{2}$

8. What two numbers is the expression between if you count by ones, tenths, and hundredths?

		Ones	Tenths	Hundredths
a)	$\pi = 3.14159...$	3 and 4	3.1 and 3.2	3.14 and 3.15
b)	$\pi + 5$			
c)	2π			
d)	$3\pi - 6$			

9. Yu has a triangular garden with side lengths as shown.

a) Write an expression for the perimeter of Yu's garden.

b) Yu has 17 m of fencing. Will this be enough to go around her garden?

c) The perimeter of Jay's garden is $8+\sqrt{70}$ m. Is Jay's garden bigger than Yu's garden?

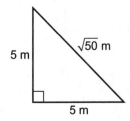
5 m $\sqrt{50}$ m   5 m

10. The golden ratio is an important number. The golden ratio is equal to $\dfrac{1+\sqrt{5}}{2}$.

a) What two numbers is $\sqrt{5}$ between if you count by ones, tenths, and hundredths?

Use the intervals for $\sqrt{5}$ to estimate the value of the golden ratio.

	Ones	Tenths	Hundredths
$\sqrt{5} = 2.23606...$			
$\dfrac{1+\sqrt{5}}{2}$			

b) Explain why the golden ratio is an irrational number.

The closest perfect square to 19 is 16, so the closest whole number to $\sqrt{19}$ is 4.

On a number line, $\sqrt{19}$ is to the right of 4.

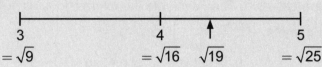

$$\begin{array}{cccc} 3 & 4 & & 5 \\ =\sqrt{9} & =\sqrt{16} & \sqrt{19} & =\sqrt{25} \end{array}$$

11. a) The closest whole number to $\sqrt{34}$ is __6__. On the number line, $\sqrt{34}$ is to the __*left of 6*__.

b) The closest whole number to $\sqrt{71}$ is _____. On the number line, $\sqrt{71}$ is to the _____.

c) The closest whole number to $\sqrt[3]{26}$ is _____. On the number line, $\sqrt[3]{26}$ is to the _____.

d) The closest whole number to $\sqrt[3]{349}$ is _____. On the number line, $\sqrt[3]{349}$ is to the _____.

12. Show $\sqrt{58}$, $\sqrt{40}$, $\sqrt{90}$, $\sqrt{43}$, $\sqrt{30}$, and $\sqrt{51}$ on the number line.

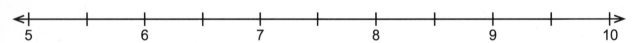

13. a) Show $\sqrt{16}$, $\sqrt{23}$, $\sqrt{25}$, and $\sqrt{19}$ on the number line.

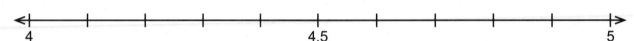

b) Is $\sqrt{19}$ closer to 4, 4.5, or 5? _____   c) Is $\sqrt{23}$ closer to 4, 4.5, or 5? _____

To simplify an expression, you can treat irrational numbers like variables.

Just as $3x + 5x = 8x$, $3\pi + 5\pi = 8\pi$ and $3\sqrt{2} + 5\sqrt{2} = 8\sqrt{2}$.

14. Simplify the expression.

a) $5\sqrt{7} + 8\sqrt{7}$

$= 13\sqrt{7}$

b) $9\sqrt{6} - 2\sqrt{6}$

c) $4\pi + 7\pi - 6\pi$

d) $\sqrt[3]{4} + \sqrt[3]{4} + \sqrt[3]{4}$

e) $8\left(\sqrt{3} + 4\right)$

f) $9(2\pi + 1)$

g) $3\left(\sqrt{5} - 4\right) - 4\sqrt{5}$

h) $11\sqrt[3]{9} - \left(2\sqrt[3]{9} + 5\sqrt[3]{9}\right)$

18 is between $16 = 4^2$ and $25 = 5^2$. You can use a mixed number to approximate $\sqrt{18}$.

Start by drawing a number line.

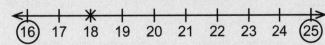

18 is $\frac{2}{9}$ of the way from 16 to 25. So $\sqrt{18}$ is approximately $\frac{2}{9}$ of the way from 4 to 5.

So $\sqrt{18} \approx 4\frac{2}{9}$.

1. Use the number line to approximate the square root. Write your answer as a mixed number.

   a) 11 is —— of the way from 9 to 16.

   So $\sqrt{11}$ is approximately —— of the way from 3 to 4.

   So $\sqrt{11} \approx$ _____.

   b) $\sqrt{15}$ c) $\sqrt{10}$ d) $\sqrt{14}$ e) $\sqrt{12}$

2. Complete the number line to approximate the square root. Write your answer as a mixed number.

4   9

   a) $\sqrt{5} \approx$ b) $\sqrt{6} \approx$ c) $\sqrt{7} \approx$ d) $\sqrt{8} \approx$

3. Complete the number line to approximate the square root. Write your answer as a mixed number.

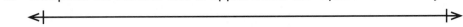

   a) $\sqrt{26} \approx$ b) $\sqrt{29} \approx$ c) $\sqrt{32} \approx$ d) $\sqrt{35} \approx$

4. Approximate the roots with a mixed number. Then order the set of numbers from least to greatest.

   a) $\left\{ \sqrt{23}, \sqrt{19}, 4\frac{5}{9}, \frac{40}{9} \right\}$

   b) $\left\{ \sqrt{31}, 5\frac{35}{99}, 5\frac{2}{3}, \sqrt{28} \right\}$

   Bonus ▶ $\left\{ \sqrt{20} - 1, 4\frac{1}{2}, \sqrt{13} + 2, \sqrt{30} - 3 \right\}$

5. a) Use the number line to approximate the square root. Write your answer as a mixed number.

i) $\sqrt{21} \approx 4\frac{5}{9}$ ii) $\sqrt{17} \approx$ ____   iii) $\sqrt{23} \approx$ ____   iv) $\sqrt{19} \approx$ ____

b) Write the mixed numbers in part a) as repeating decimals.

i) $\sqrt{21} \approx \underline{4.\overline{5}}$ ii) $\sqrt{17} \approx$ ____   iii) $\sqrt{23} \approx$ ____   iv) $\sqrt{19} \approx$ ____

c) Round your answers from part b) to the nearest tenth.

i) $\sqrt{21} \approx \underline{4.6}$ ii) $\sqrt{17} \approx$ ____   iii) $\sqrt{23} \approx$ ____   iv) $\sqrt{19} \approx$ ____

6. Evaluate the powers. Use the closest answer to 28 to approximate $\sqrt{28}$.

$5.1^2 =$ _____ $5.2^2 =$ _____ $5.3^2 =$ _____   So $\sqrt{28} \approx$ _____

7. Evaluate the powers. Use the closest answer to 53 to approximate $\sqrt[3]{53}$.

$3.9^3 =$ _____ $3.8^3 =$ _____ $3.7^3 =$ _____   So $\sqrt[3]{53} \approx$ _____

You can use a table to approximate $\sqrt{45}$ to one decimal place.

$\sqrt{45}$ is between 6 and 7, but closer to 7.

Try 6.7^2. Is this estimate too high or too low?

Try a second value. If your first estimate was too low, try a higher value. If it was too high, try a lower value.

Use the closest number to approximate $\sqrt{45}$.

x	x^2	Estimate is ...
6.7	44.89	too low
6.8	46.24	too high

6.7^2 is closest to 45, so $\sqrt{45} \approx 6.7$.

---

8. Use a table to approximate the irrational number to one decimal place.

a) $\sqrt{68}$ is between __8__ and __9__ ,

but closer to __8__ .

x	x^2	Estimate is ...
8.2	67.24	*too low*
8.3	68.89	*too high*

So $\sqrt{68} \approx \underline{8.2}$.

b) $\sqrt[3]{101}$ is between __4__ and __5__ ,

but closer to __5__ .

x	x^3	Estimate is ...
4.7		

So $\sqrt[3]{101} \approx$ ____ .

c) $\sqrt{85}$ **d)** $\sqrt{13}$ **e)** $\sqrt[3]{240}$ **f)** $\sqrt[3]{700}$

Bonus ▶ Use a table to approximate $\sqrt{68}$ to two decimal places. Hint: Try 8.23^2.

---

9. a) Write the number as a decimal to the nearest tenth.

i) $5\dfrac{1}{5} =$ _____   ii) $\sqrt{30} \approx$ _____   iii) $5\dfrac{2}{3} \approx$ _____   iv) $\sqrt[3]{130} \approx$ _____

b) Show the numbers from part a) on the number line.

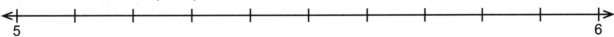
5   6

c) Order the numbers from part a) from least to greatest. _____ , _____ , _____ , _____

10. a) Order the numbers in the set from least to greatest: $\left\{ \sqrt{51},\ 8,\ \dfrac{23}{3},\ 7.\overline{30} \right\}$

b) Show the numbers from part a) on the number line.

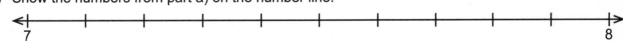
7   8

11. The side length (s) of a square with area A is given by the formula $s = \sqrt{A}$.

a) Find the side length of a square with area 130 cm² to one decimal place.

b) Find the perimeter of a square with area 55 in² to one decimal place.

c) About how much fencing do you need to fence a garden with an area of 5 m²?

12. The side length (s) of a cube with volume V is given by the formula $s = \sqrt[3]{V}$.

a) Find the side length of a cube with volume 485 in³ to one decimal place.

b) Find the side length of a cube with volume 0.2 m³ to one decimal place.

c) A foot stool in the shape of a cube has a volume of 4,000 in³. Will the foot stool fit under a coffee table that is 1.5 feet tall?

13. Solve the equation. Estimate the answer to one decimal place.

a) $x^2 = 67$ **b)** $x^3 = 492$

$x = \pm\sqrt{67}$

$x \approx \pm 8.2$

c) $5x^2 - 18 = 87$ **Bonus ▶** $0.3x^3 + 4 = 0.2x^3 - 1.4$

REMINDER: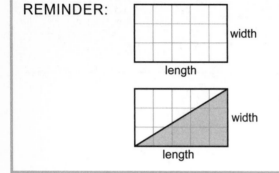

Area of a rectangle $=$ length $\times$ width

$ = 5 \times 3$

$ = 15$ square units

Area of a right triangle $=$ area of rectangle $\div 2$

$ = 5 \times 3 \div 2$

$ = 7.5$ square units

1. Find the area of the right triangles.

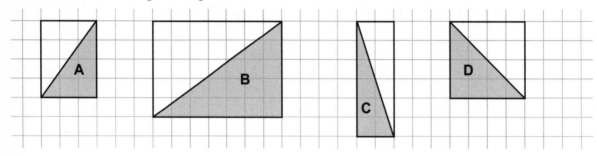

Area of A = _____ × _____ ÷ 2

$ =$ _____ square units

Area of B = _____ × _____ ÷ 2

$ =$ _____ square units

Area of C = _____ × _____ ÷ 2

$ =$ _____ square units

Area of D = _____ × _____ ÷ 2

$ =$ _____ square units

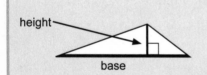 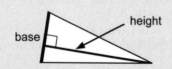 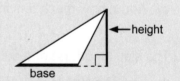

The height of a triangle is the length of a perpendicular line segment from the vertex to the base.

2. Use a ruler to draw the height of the triangle.

a)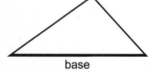

b)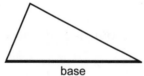

c)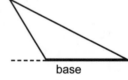

d)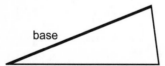

e)

f)

The area of an acute triangle is one half the area of a rectangle with the same base and height.

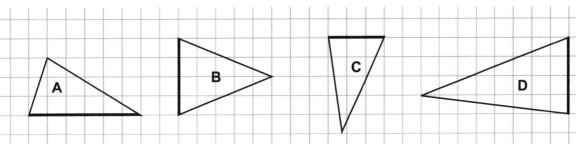

Area of triangle = base × height ÷ 2
= 8 × 3 ÷ 2
= 12 square units

3. Count squares to find the base and height. Then use the formula to find the area of the acute triangle.

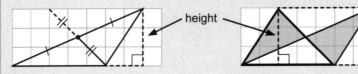

Area of A = _____ × _____ ÷ 2

    = _____ square units

Area of B = _____ × _____ ÷ 2

    = _____ square units

Area of C = _____ × _____ ÷ 2

    = _____ square units

Area of D = _____ × _____ ÷ 2

    = _____ square units

The area of an obtuse triangle is one half the area of a rectangle with the same base and height.

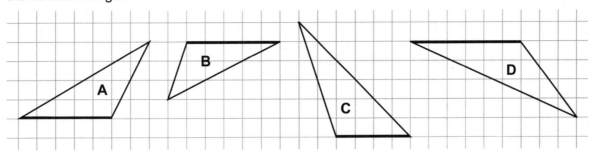

height

Area of triangle = base × height ÷ 2
= 5 × 3 ÷ 2
= 7.5 square units

4. Count squares to find the base and height. Then use the formula to find the area of the obtuse triangle.

Area of A = _____ × _____ ÷ 2

    = _____ square units

Area of B = _____ × _____ ÷ 2

    = _____ square units

Area of C = _____ × _____ ÷ 2

    = _____ square units

Area of D = _____ × _____ ÷ 2

    = _____ square units

5. The triangles are congruent. Measure the base and height of each triangle to the nearest tenth of a centimeter. Then find the area.

A.

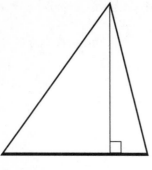

base = _____ cm

height = _____ cm

Area = _____ × _____ ÷ 2

= _____ cm²

B.

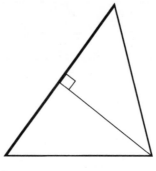

base = _____ cm

height = _____ cm

Area = _____ × _____ ÷ 2

= _____ cm²

6. a) What do you notice about your answers to Question 5?

b) Does the area change if you choose a different side of the triangle to be the base?

c) Draw an obtuse triangle and find the area using different sides as the base. The area should be the same. If not, find your mistake.

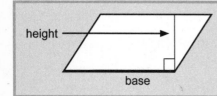

The height of a parallelogram is the length of a perpendicular line segment from the base to the opposite side.

7. Sketch a line to show the height of the parallelogram for the given base.

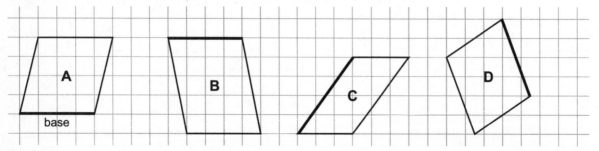

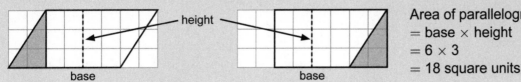

The area of a parallelogram is the same as the area of a rectangle with the same base and height.

height

base   base

Area of parallelogram
= base × height
= 6 × 3
= 18 square units

8. Mark and measure the height and base to the nearest tenth of a centimeter. Then find the area.

a)

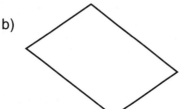

Area = _____ cm × _____ cm

= _____ cm²

b)

Area = _____ cm × _____ cm

= _____ cm²

9. Find the area of parallelogram *ABCD* in two different ways. First use *AB* as the base. Then use *BC* as the base. How do the answers compare? Why?

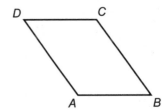

10. Find the area of the trapezoid. Hint: Add the areas of the parallelogram and triangle.

a)

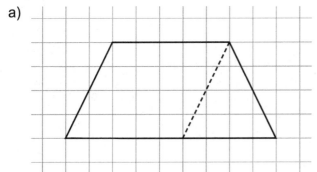

Area of
parallelogram = _____ × _____ = _____

Area of
triangle = _____ × _____ ÷ 2 = _____

Area of
trapezoid = _____ + _____ = _____ units²

b)

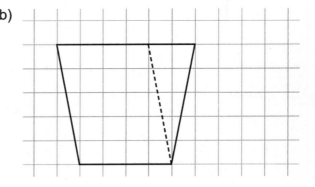

Area of
parallelogram = _____ × _____ = _____

Area of
triangle = _____ × _____ ÷ 2 = _____

Area of
trapezoid = _____ + _____ = _____ units²

All points on a circle are the same distance from a point called the **center**. This distance is called the **radius**. The plural of radius is **radii**.

To construct a circle using a compass when given the center and radius:

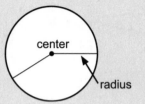

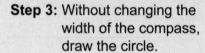
center
radius

Step 1: Set the compass width to the given radius.

Step 2: Set the compass point on the center point.

Step 3: Without changing the width of the compass, draw the circle.

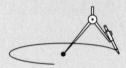

1. Construct a circle with center *O* and radius *AB*.

a) *A*

B

•*O*

b) *A*

B

•*O*

The **diameter** (*d*) of a circle is the distance across a circle through its center.

The radius (*r*) is half the diameter (*d*).

$r = d \div 2$

2. Find the radius or diameter. The diagrams are not drawn to scale.

a)

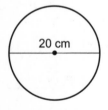
20 cm

radius = _____

diameter = _____

b)

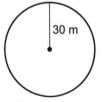
30 m

radius = _____

diameter = _____

c)

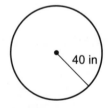
40 in

radius = _____

diameter = _____

REMINDER:

The distance around a polygon is called its **perimeter** (*P*).

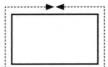

The distance around a circle is called its **circumference** (*C*).

3. Maya wants to estimate the circumference of a circle. The circle has a diameter of 3 cm. Inside the circle, she draws different polygons. Each polygon has all sides the same length.

A.

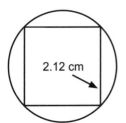

2.12 cm

B.

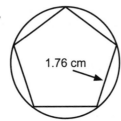

1.76 cm

C.

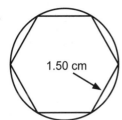

1.50 cm

D.

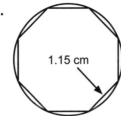

1.15 cm

E.

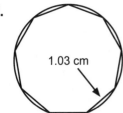

1.03 cm

F.

0.93 cm

a) Fill in the number of sides and calculate the perimeter of the polygon. Leave the last row blank.

Polygon	A	B	C	D	E	F
Length of One Polygon Side	2.12					
Number of Sides	4					
Perimeter (*P*)	8.48					
P ÷ *d*						

b) In each diagram above, the perimeter of the polygon is less than the circumference of the circle. What can we do with the number of sides to get an even better approximation of the circumference?

_____

c) The diameter (*d*) of the circle is 3 cm. Fill in the last row of the table by calculating *P* ÷ *d* for each polygon.

Geometry 8-40

115

The ratio of circumference to diameter is the same for all circles. This number has an infinite number of digits after its decimal point. We use the Greek letter π (pronounced "pie") to identify it.

Rounded to 2 decimal places, $\pi \approx 3.14$.

The circumference of a circle is π times larger than the diameter.

Circumference $= \pi \times$ diameter $= \pi \times d$. But the diameter is twice the radius, so:

Circumference $= \pi \times 2 \times$ radius $= 2 \times \pi \times r = 2\pi r$.

4. For the given measurement, find the approximate circumference (C) of the circle. Use 3.14 for π.

a) diameter = 5 cm   b) radius = 2 in   c) diameter = 10 m   d) radius = 3 ft

$\underline{\quad C = \pi \times d \quad}$ $\underline{\quad C = 2 \times \pi \times r \quad}$ $\underline{\qquad\qquad}$ $\underline{\qquad\qquad}$

$\underline{\quad C \approx 3.14 \times 5 \quad}$ $\underline{\qquad\qquad}$ $\underline{\qquad\qquad}$ $\underline{\qquad\qquad}$

$\underline{\quad = 15.7 \text{ cm} \quad}$ $\underline{\qquad\qquad}$ $\underline{\qquad\qquad}$ $\underline{\qquad\qquad}$

5. The High Roller Ferris Wheel in Las Vegas, Nevada, has a diameter of 520 ft.

a) Find the approximate circumference of the wheel.

b) It takes about 30 minutes (1,800 seconds) for one full turn. Approximately how fast does the wheel move in feet per second?

6. Earth's radius, from its center to its surface, is approximately 6,371 km. Earth's equator forms a circle. Find the approximate circumference of the equator.

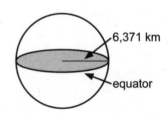

6,371 km

equator

    Geometry 8-40

G8-41 Area of Circles

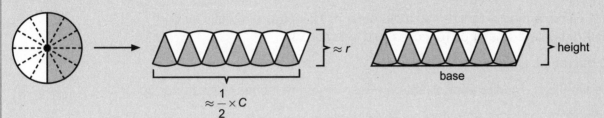

The area of a circle can be approximated by finding the area of a parallelogram.

$\approx \frac{1}{2} \times C$

height

base

Area of circle (A) = base × height = $\frac{1}{2} \times C \times r = \frac{1}{2} \times 2 \times \pi \times r \times r = \pi r^2$ $A = \pi r^2$

1. Find the approximate area of a circle with the given radius. Use 3.14 for π.

   a) $r = 5$ cm   b) $r = 10$ m   c) $r = 8$ ft   d) $r = 6$ km

   $\underline{A = \pi r^2}$ _____   _____   _____

   $\underline{A \approx 3.14 \times 5 \times 5}$ _____   _____   _____

   $\underline{= 78.5 \ cm^2}$ _____   _____   _____

2. Measure the radius in cm. Then find the approximate area. Use $\pi = 3.14$.

   a)   b)

   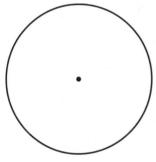   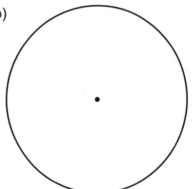

3. Find the area by first finding the radius. Use $\pi = 3.14$. The diagrams are not drawn to scale.

   a)   b)   c)   d)

   $r = \underline{\ 4 \ m\ }$ $r = $ _____ $r = $ _____ $r = $ _____

   $\underline{A = \pi r^2}$ _____   _____   _____

   $\underline{A \approx 3.14 \times 4 \times 4}$ _____   _____   _____

   $\underline{= 50.24 \ m^2}$ _____   _____   _____

4. A rotating water sprinkler can spray a distance of 15 m. Approximately what area of grass can the sprinkler cover?

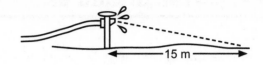

5. At a pizza place, a medium pizza has a diameter of 12 inches and sells for $14. A large pizza has a diameter of 16 inches and sells for $18.

   a) Find the radius and area of each pizza.

   b) For each pizza, find the approximate number of square inches of pizza per dollar.

   c) Which pizza size gives you more pizza per dollar?

6. The circle on the right has a diameter of 8 cm. The shaded area is a semicircle.

   a) Find the radius of the circle. $r =$ _____ $\div 2 =$ _____ cm

   b) Find the circumference of the circle.

      $C = \pi \times d \approx 3.14 \times$ _____ $=$ _____ cm

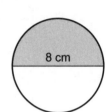

   c) Trace a line around the shaded semicircle. What is the line's length?
      Hint: Add half the circle's circumference and the diameter.

   _____

   d) Find the area of the circle. $A = \pi r^2 \approx 3.14 \times$ _____ $\times$ _____ $=$ _____ cm^2

   e) The area of a semicircle is half the area of a circle. Find the area of the semicircle.

      Area of semicircle $=$ _____ $\div 2 =$ _____ cm^2

7. a) Find the total area of the shape.   b) Trace a line around the outside of the shape. What is the line's length?

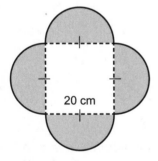

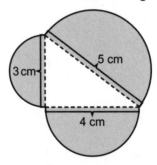

8. a) Each wheel on Rani's bike has a diameter of 56 cm. What is the circumference of each wheel?

   b) Rani pedals so that the wheels make 3 full rotations in 2 seconds. How far will she travel in 1 second? 2 seconds? 10 seconds? 1 minute? 1 hour?

G8-42 Introduction to the Pythagorean Theorem

1. Find the area of the right triangle.

   a)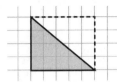

   Area = ___20___ ÷ 2 = ___10___

   b)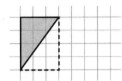

   Area = _____ ÷ 2 = _____

   c)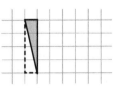

   Area = _____ ÷ 2 = _____

2. Find the area of each square by finding the area of 4 right triangles and what is left.

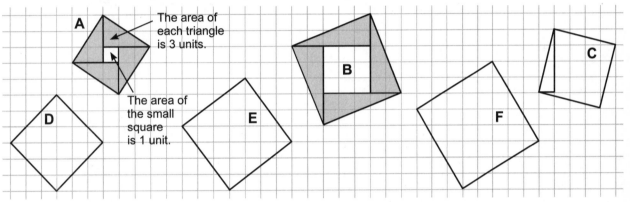

The area of each triangle is 3 units.

The area of the small square is 1 unit.

Area of A = 4 × ___3___ + ___1___ = ___13___

3. What is the side length of square E in Question 2? How do you know?

4. Find the side length of each square.

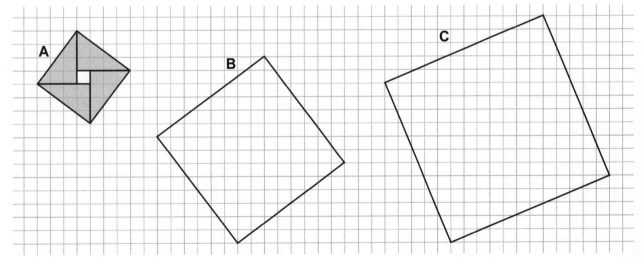

Side length of A

$=\sqrt{4 \times 6 + 1}$

$=\sqrt{25} = 5$

Side length of B

$=\sqrt{4 \times \rule{1cm}{0.4pt} + \rule{1cm}{0.4pt}}$

$=\sqrt{\rule{1.5cm}{0.4pt}} = \rule{1cm}{0.4pt}$

Side length of C

$=\sqrt{4 \times \rule{1cm}{0.4pt} + \rule{1cm}{0.4pt}}$

$=\sqrt{\rule{1.5cm}{0.4pt}} = \rule{1cm}{0.4pt}$

5. a) Find the area of the squares with side lengths *a*, *b*, and *c*. Write your answers in the table. Leave the last column empty.

i)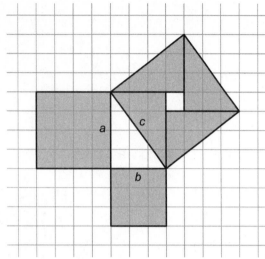

ii)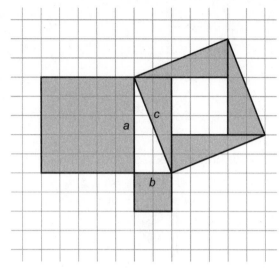

iii)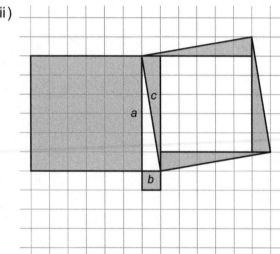

iv)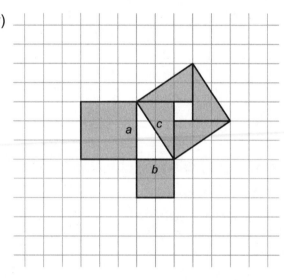

	a^2	b^2	c^2	$a^2 + b^2$
i)	$4 \times 4 = 16$	$3 \times 3 = 9$	$4 \times 6 + 1 = 25$	
ii)				
iii)				
iv)				

b) For each row in the table, calculate the value of $a^2 + b^2$. Fill in the last column.

c) Compare your answers to the last two columns: c^2 and $a^2 + b^2$. Make a conjecture: If *c* is the side opposite the right angle in a right triangle with sides *a*, *b*, *c*,

then _____.

Geometry 8-42

6. Check your conjecture from Question 5.c) by measuring the length of each side of the right triangle to the nearest tenth of a centimeter.

a)

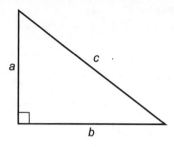

$a =$ _____ $b =$ _____ $c =$ _____

$a^2 =$ _____ $b^2 =$ _____ $c^2 =$ _____

$a^2 + b^2 =$ _____

b)

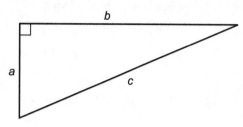

$a =$ _____ $b =$ _____ $c =$ _____

$a^2 =$ _____ $b^2 =$ _____ $c^2 =$ _____

$a^2 + b^2 =$ _____

7. Use $c^2 = a^2 + b^2$ to find the length of c.

a)

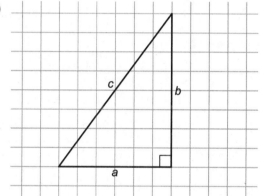

$c^2 = a^2 + b^2$

$= $ _____$^2 + $ _____^{2}

$= $ _____ $+ $ _____

$= $ _____

$c = \sqrt{\rule{1cm}{0pt}} = $ _____

b)

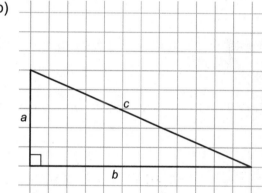

$c^2 = a^2 + b^2$

$= $ _____$^2 + $ _____^{2}

$= $ _____ $+ $ _____

$= $ _____

$c = \sqrt{\rule{1cm}{0pt}} = $ _____

8. The sides that are not opposite the right angle in a right triangle are given. Find the length of the side opposite the right angle.

a) 8, 15

b) 9, 12

In a right triangle, the side opposite the right angle is called the **hypotenuse**.

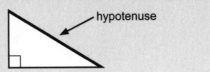

1. Mark the hypotenuse of the triangle with a thick line.

a)    b)   c) 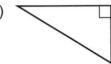   d)

Pythagorean Theorem

In a right triangle, the hypotenuse squared is the sum of the squares of the other two sides.

If the hypotenuse is labeled c, and the other sides are labeled a and b, then $c^2 = a^2 + b^2$.

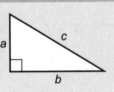

$$c^2 = a^2 + b^2$$

2. Use the Pythagorean Theorem to write an equation for the triangle.

a) 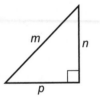   b) 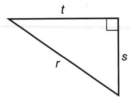   c)   d)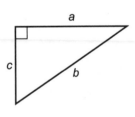

_____   _____   _____   _____

3. Use the Pythagorean Theorem to find the hypotenuse.

a) 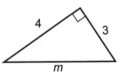   b) 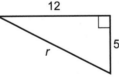   c) 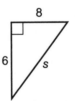   d)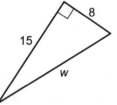

$\underline{m^2 = 4^2 + 3^2}$

$\underline{m^2 = 16 + 9}$

$\underline{m^2 = 25}$

$\underline{m = \sqrt{25} = 5}$

You can use the Pythagorean Theorem to find any side of a right triangle if two sides are given.

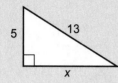

$$5^2 + x^2 = 13^2$$

$$25 + x^2 = 169$$

$$x^2 = 169 - 25 = 144$$

$$\text{so } x = \sqrt{144} = 12$$

4. Use the Pythagorean Theorem to write an equation for the triangle. Then find the missing side.

a)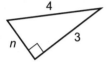

b)

c)

d)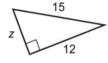

$$\underline{\quad n^2 + 3^2 = 4^2 \quad}$$

$$\underline{\quad n^2 + 9 = 16 \quad}$$

$$\underline{\quad n^2 = 16 - 9 = 7 \quad}$$

$$\underline{\quad n = \sqrt{7} \quad}$$

5. Find the missing side of the triangle using the Pythagorean Theorem.

a)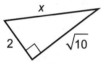

b)

c)

d)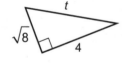

$$\underline{\quad 2^2 + \left(\sqrt{10}\right)^2 = x^2 \quad}$$

$$\underline{\quad 4 + 10 = x^2 \quad}$$

$$\underline{\quad 14 = x^2 \quad}$$

$$\underline{\quad x = \sqrt{14} \quad}$$

$$\underline{\quad x \approx 3.7 \quad}$$

6. Find the missing side of the triangle.

a)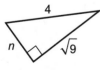

b)

c)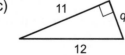

d)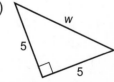

G8-44 Proving the Pythagorean Theorem

Figure 1

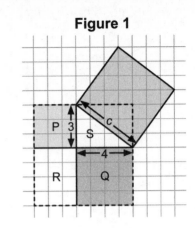

1. Look at Figure 1.

   a) What is the width of square P? _____

   b) What is the width of square Q? _____

   c) Do the rectangles R and S have the same area? _____

      How do you know? _____

   d) Fill in the blanks to write an expression for each area.

      Area of square P: _____²   Area of square Q: _____²

      Area of rectangle R: _____ × _____

      Area of rectangle S: _____ × _____

      Area of the square with the dashed outline: _____

Figure 2

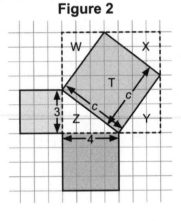

2. Look at Figure 2.

   a) Triangles Z and X make a rectangle. What is its area? _____ × _____

   b) Triangles W and Y make a rectangle. What is its area? _____ × _____

   c) Write an expression for the length and width of square T. _____

   d) Write an expression for the area of square T. _____²

   e) Use your answers in parts a), b), and d) to write an expression for the area of the square with the dashed outline.

      _____

3. a) In Figure 1, count the squares to find the width and length of the square with the

      dashed outline.   width = _____   length = _____

   b) In Figure 2, count the squares to find the width and length of the square with the

      dashed outline.   width = _____   length = _____

   c) What can you say about the areas of the dash-outlined squares in Figure 1 and

      Figure 2? _____

   d) Use your answers to Questions 2.e) and 1.d) to write an equation.

      _____

   e) In the equation above, cross out parts that are the same on both sides to find an

      equation for c^2. _____

4. Look at Figure 3.

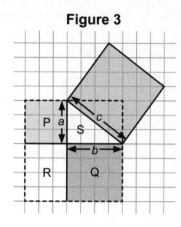

Figure 3

a) Write an expression for the width of square P. _____

b) Write an expression for the width of square Q. _____

c) Do rectangles R and S have the same area? _____

How do you know? _____

d) Fill in the blanks to write an expression for each area.

Area of square P: _____²   Area of square Q: _____²

Area of rectangle R: _____ × _____

Area of rectangle S: _____ × _____

Area of the square with the dashed outline: _____

5. Look at Figure 4.

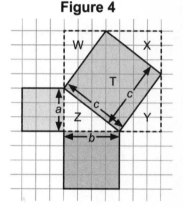

Figure 4

a) Triangles Z and X make a rectangle. Write an expression

for the area of the rectangle. _____ × _____

b) Triangles Y and W make a rectangle. Write an expression

for the area of the rectangle. _____ × _____

c) Write an expression for the length and width of square T. _____

d) Write an expression for the area of square T. _____²

e) Use your answers in parts a), b), and d) to write an expression
for the area of the square with the dashed outline.

_____

6. a) For Figure 3, write an expression for the width and length of the square with the

dashed outline.   width = _____   length = _____

b) For Figure 4, write an expression for the width and length of the square with the

dashed outline.   width = _____   length = _____

c) What can be said about the areas of the dash-outlined squares in Figure 3 and

Figure 4? _____

d) Use your answers to Questions 5.e) and 4.d) to write an equation.

_____

e) In the equation above, cross out parts that are the same on both sides to find

an equation for c^2. _____

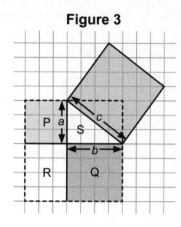

> REMINDER: An acute angle is less than 90°.
>
> An obtuse angle is greater than 90°.
>
> A right angle is exactly 90°.

1. Complete the chart. Use $<$, $>$, or $=$ to compare c^2 with $a^2 + b^2$.

a) i) 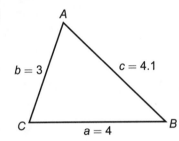 ii) 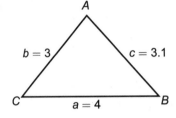 iii)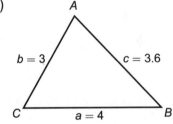

	a	b	c	a^2	b^2	c^2	$a^2 + b^2$	$c^2 \,\square\, a^2 + b^2$	Is $\angle C$ acute, obtuse, or a right angle?
i)	4	3	4.1	16	9	16.81	25	$c^2 < a^2 + b^2$	acute
ii)									
iii)									

b) i) 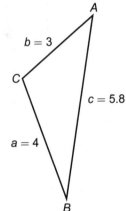 ii) 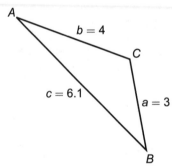 iii)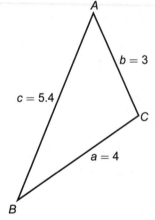

	a	b	c	a^2	b^2	c^2	$a^2 + b^2$	$c^2 \,\square\, a^2 + b^2$	Is $\angle C$ acute, obtuse, or a right angle?
i)									
ii)									
iii)									

c) i)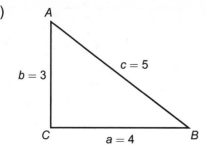

ii)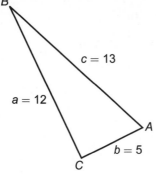

iii)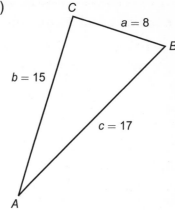

	a	b	c	a^2	b^2	c^2	$a^2 + b^2$	$c^2 \square a^2 + b^2$	Is ∠C acute, obtuse, or a right angle?
i)									
ii)									
iii)									

2. Summarize your findings from Question 1.

   a) When $c^2 < a^2 + b^2$, ∠C is an _____ angle.

   b) When $c^2 > a^2 + b^2$, ∠C is an _____ angle.

   c) When $c^2 = a^2 + b^2$, ∠C is a _____ angle.

To name the vertices and sides on a triangle:

Step 1: Label each vertex with a capital letter.

Step 2: Label sides with small letters. For each side, use the letter to match the opposite vertex. For example, side b is opposite ∠B.

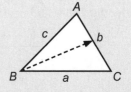

---

3. For the triangle, calculate a^2, b^2, c^2, and $a^2 + b^2$. Compare c^2 with $a^2 + b^2$. Predict whether ∠C will be acute, obtuse, or a right angle.

	Triangle Sides	a^2	b^2	c^2	$a^2 + b^2$	$c^2 \square a^2 + b^2$	∠C
a)	$a = 5, b = 9, c = 10$	25	81	100	106	$c^2 < a^2 + b^2$	acute
b)	$a = 6, b = 8, c = 10$						
c)	$a = 2.5, b = 6, c = 7$						
d)	$a = 2, b = 3.75, c = 4$						

Converse of the Pythagorean Theorem

In $\triangle ABC$, if $c^2 = a^2 + b^2$, then $\angle C$ is a right angle, and $\triangle ABC$ is a right triangle.

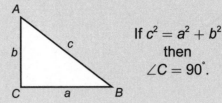

If $c^2 = a^2 + b^2$
then
$\angle C = 90°$.

4. John doesn't believe the Converse of the Pythagorean Theorem is true. He draws $\triangle ABC$ so that $c^2 = a^2 + b^2$ but he doesn't draw $\angle C$ as a right angle. Follow these steps to see if John's picture (shown with solid lines) makes sense.

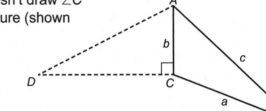

a) Line CD is drawn perpendicular to AC, such that $CD = BC$. Since $BC = a$, label $DC = a$.

b) Points D and A are joined to form $\triangle ADC$. Label the length of AD as y.

c) What is the measurement of $\angle ACD$? _____

d) What type of triangle is $\triangle ADC$? _____

e) $\triangle ADC$ is a right triangle. Use the Pythagorean Theorem to write an equation for y^2.

$y^2 = $ _____

f) Now we have $c^2 = a^2 + b^2$ and $y^2 = a^2 + b^2$. What can we say about c^2 and y^2?

_____

g) If $c^2 = y^2$, what can we say about c and y? _____

h) In $\triangle ADC$ and $\triangle ABC$, we drew $CD = CB$, side AC is shared by both triangles, and now we have $AD = AB$. What congruence rule allows us to say that $\triangle ADC \cong \triangle ABC$?

_____

i) In $\triangle ADC \cong \triangle ABC$, the corresponding sides and angles are equal.

What angle in $\triangle ABC$ is equal to $\angle ACD$? _____

j) But $\angle ACD = 90°$. So what is the measurement of $\angle ACB$? _____

k) Since $\angle ACB = 90°$, $\triangle ABC$ is a _____ triangle.

5. In $\triangle DEF$, $d = 7$, $e = 25$, $f = 24$.

a) Label each side with the correct letter: d, e, or f.

b) Is $\triangle DEF$ right-angled? Explain.

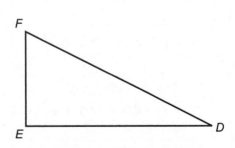

1. Tom lets out 80 m of string while flying his kite.
When he is 50 m way from Mary, the kite is directly above Mary.
How high is the kite above Mary?

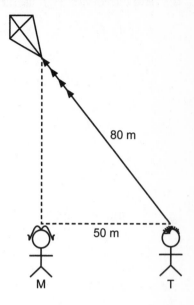

2. Ava wants to buy a new television. She has space for a TV screen
that is 43.6 inches wide and 24.5 inches tall. TVs are sold using one
measurement: the length of a diagonal line from one corner of the
screen to the opposite corner. What is the largest TV screen that
Ava can buy?

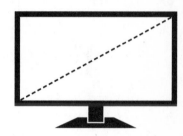

3. Sam must buy fencing to go around a field that is in the shape of a
right triangle, as shown on the right. Find the length of fencing needed,
rounded to the nearest meter.

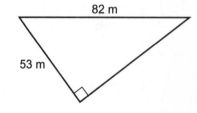

4. Mike is using a ladder that extends to reach a height of 32 feet up
a wall. For safety, he must place the base of the ladder 1 foot away
from the wall for every 4 feet in height.

a) Label 32 feet up the wall in the diagram. The diagram is not to scale.

b) How far should the base of the ladder be from the wall?
Label this distance on the diagram.

c) Find the length of the ladder to the nearest foot. Label the diagram.

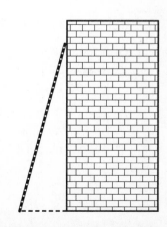

5. The isosceles triangle has equal sides each 8 cm long and a base 10 cm long.

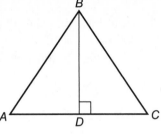

a) Find the length of *AD*.

b) Find the height of the triangle to the nearest tenth of a centimeter.

c) Find the approximate area of the triangle.

6. Find the height of the parallelogram shown on the right.

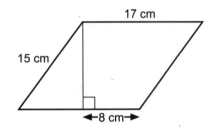

7. Marta usually walks to school by walking 2 km east, and then 1 km north. On Monday, Marta took a shortcut by walking through a park on a diagonal. To the nearest meter, how much shorter is her trip when she takes the shortcut?

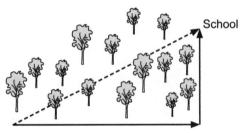

8. The bases on a baseball diamond are 90 feet apart.

a) If the catcher is at home plate and wants to throw the ball to second base, how far must the catcher throw the ball? Round your answer to the nearest tenth of a foot.

b) The pitcher pitches from a point 60.5 feet from home plate on a direct line from home plate to second base. Is the pitcher closer to home plate or second base? Explain.

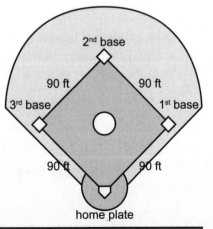

Answer all problems in your notebook.

1. A bridge needs to be built across a marsh. The distance across the marsh is too difficult to measure. Instead, three measurements around the marsh are taken. Find the length of the bridge to the nearest meter by following these steps:

   a) In $\triangle BCD$, find the length of BC.

   b) In $\triangle ACB$, find the length of AC.

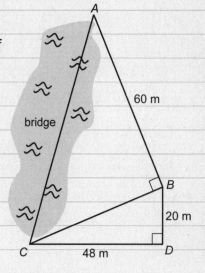

2. Find the length of the side labeled x to the nearest tenth of a meter by following these steps:

   a) In $\triangle ACD$, find the value of y.

   b) Find the length of BC.

   c) In $\triangle ABC$, find the value of x.

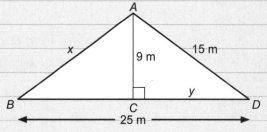

3. A 25 m tower has steel wires bracing the tower. The longer wires are each 65 m long. The shorter wires are fastened 28 m closer to the base. Find the length of a shorter wire to the nearest tenth of a meter by following these steps:

   a) In $\triangle ABD$, find the length of BD.

   b) Find the length of CD.

   c) In $\triangle ACD$, find the length of AC.

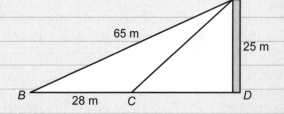

4. A playground tower has two slides. One slide is 5 m long and its base is 4 m from the bottom of the tower. The second slide has its base 3 m from the bottom.

   a) How high off the ground is the top of the first slide?

   b) How high off the ground is the top of the second slide? Explain.

   c) To the nearest tenth of a meter, how long is the second slide?

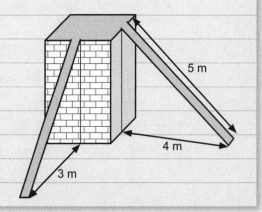

5. The same rectangular prism is shown twice, below.

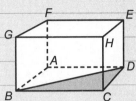 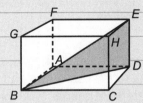

a) *BD* is a diagonal on the base of the prism. What type of triangle is △*BCD*?

b) *BE* is a diagonal from the base of the prism to the diagonally opposite corner. What type of triangle is △*BDE*?

c) What side is shared by △*BCD* and △*BDE*?

d) Draw a copy of the prism and sketch △*ABC* and △*ACF*.

e) What types of triangles are △*ABC* and △*ACF*?

f) What side is shared by △*ABC* and △*ACF*?

6. The rectangular prism shown on the right is 3 cm wide, 4 cm long, and 12 cm tall.

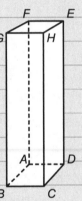

a) Draw the diagonal from *B* to *D*. What type of triangle is △*BCD*?

b) Use the Pythagorean Theorem and △*BCD* to find the length of *BD*.

c) Draw the diagonal from *B* to *E*. What type of triangle is △*BDE*?

d) What side do the two triangles share?

e) Use the Pythagorean Theorem and △*BDE* to find the length of *BE*.

7. A storage room is 12 feet wide, 16 feet long, and 8 feet tall. A spider spins a web that has one strand from a top corner of the room to the diagonally opposite bottom corner.

a) Draw a diagram of the room.

b) Find the length of the strand spun by the spider.

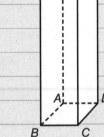

8. Ben's suitcase is 60 cm long, 20 cm wide, and 80 cm tall. Ben wants to fit the tallest Statue of Liberty souvenir possible in his suitcase.

a) Draw a diagonal from *A* to *C*. What shape is △*ABC*?

b) Draw a diagonal from *A* to *F*. What shape is △*ACF*?

c) What side is shared by the two triangles?

d) Use △*ABC* to find the length of *AC* to the nearest tenth of a centimeter.

e) Use △*ACF* to find the length of *AF* to the nearest tenth of a centimeter.

f) What is the tallest souvenir that Ben can fit in his suitcase?

G8-48 The Pythagorean Theorem in a Coordinate Grid

REMINDER:

1. To find the distance between two points on the same horizontal line, find the absolute value of the change in x.

   Length of $AB = $ |change in x| $= |1 - (-4)| = 5$

2. To find the distance between two points on the same vertical line, find the absolute value of the change in y.

   Length of $CD = $ |change in y| $= |4 - (-3)| = 7$

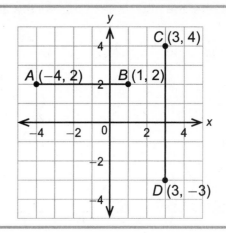

1. Find the coordinates of the points. Then find the distance between the points.

	Points	Distance
a)	A (_−5_ , _5_) B (_−5_ , _−1_)	$|5 - (-1)| = 6$
b)	G (___ , ___) H (___ , ___)	
c)	K (___ , ___) L (___ , ___)	

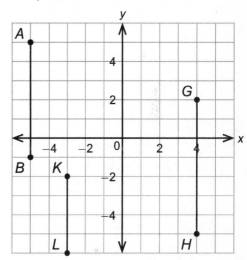

2. Find the coordinates of the points. Then find the distance between the points.

	Points	Distance
a)	C (___ , ___) D (___ , ___)	
b)	E (___ , ___) F (___ , ___)	
c)	I (___ , ___) J (___ , ___)	

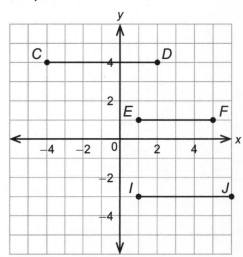

3. Find the distance between the points.

a) $A (-3, 4)$ $B (-3, 9)$ b) $C (-5, 3)$ $D (6, 3)$ c) $E (0, -3)$ $F (0, -9)$

4. a) Draw right triangles so that each given line segment is the hypotenuse of a triangle. Label the new vertex C. Label the appropriate sides a, b, and c.

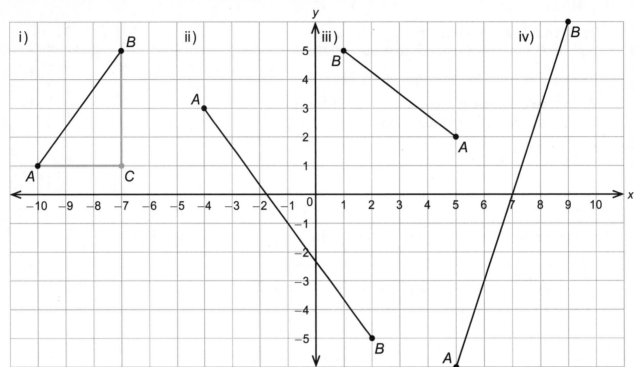

b) For each triangle in part a), find the coordinates of A, B, and C. Then find the lengths of a and b.

	Coordinates of A	Coordinates of B	Coordinates of C	Length of a	Length of b
i)	$(-10, 1)$	$(-7, 5)$	$(-7, 1)$	$\|5 - 1\| = 4$	$\|-7 - (-10)\| = 3$
ii)					
iii)					
iv)					

c) For each triangle above, use side lengths and the Pythagorean Theorem to find the length of c.

i) $a = \underline{\quad 4 \quad}$ $\qquad\qquad$ $b = \underline{\quad 3 \quad}$ $\qquad\qquad$ ii) $a = \underline{\qquad}$ $\qquad\qquad$ $b = \underline{\qquad}$

$\quad$ $c^2 = a^2 + b^2 = 4^2 + 3^2 = 25$

$\quad$ $c = \sqrt{25} = 5$

iii) $a = \underline{\qquad}$ $\qquad\qquad$ $b = \underline{\qquad}$ $\qquad\qquad$ iv) $a = \underline{\qquad}$ $\qquad\qquad$ $b = \underline{\qquad}$

To find the distance between two points:

Step 1: Find the |change in x|. $a = |2 - (-4)| = 6$

Step 2: Find the |change in y|. $b = |5 - (-3)| = 8$

Step 3: Find $c^2 = a^2 + b^2$. $c^2 = 6^2 + 8^2 = 100$

Step 4: Find the square root to find c. $c = \sqrt{100} = 10$

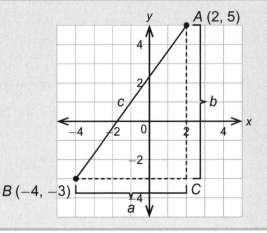

5. Draw the points A and B on a grid. Find the length of the line segment AB to the nearest tenth of a unit using the steps above.

a) $A(-4, 6)$ $B(-1, 2)$

b) $A(7, 1)$ $B(1, -7)$

c) $A(-4, -2)$ $B(1, 10)$

d) $A(3, -5)$ $B(-1, 1)$

e) $A(-2, 3)$ $B(-7, 9)$

f) $A(7, 0)$ $B(0, -3)$

To find the distance between two points, A and B, without a diagram, you can use the formula:

$$d_{AB} = \sqrt{|\text{change in } x|^2 + |\text{change in } y|^2}$$

Example: $A(3, 5)$ $B(8, -7)$ $d_{AB} = \sqrt{|8 - 3|^2 + |-7 - 5|^2}$

$$= \sqrt{5^2 + 12^2}$$

$$= \sqrt{169} = 13$$

6. Use the formula to find the distance between the two points to the nearest tenth of a unit.

a) $D(-3, -1)$ $E(4, 3)$

b) $C(7, -3)$ $D(2, 9)$

c) $A(-4, 7)$ $B(2, -1)$

d) $F(-4, -6)$ $G(4, 9)$

e) $H(2, 4)$ $J(3, -4)$

f) $K(-5, 2)$ $M(3, 5)$

7. A triangle has vertices with coordinates $A(0, 3)$, $B(-6, 3)$, and $C(-6, -5)$.

a) Use the distance formula to find the lengths of the sides AB, BC, and AC.

b) Find the perimeter of the triangle.

c) Use the Pythagorean Theorem to show that $\triangle ABC$ is a right triangle.

d) Find the area of the triangle.

> REMINDER: In the expression $3h + 2$, $3h$ is another way of writing $3 \times h$.

1. Replace the variable with the given number, then evaluate.

    a) $3h + 2$, $h = 4$

    $= 3(4) + 2$

    $= 12 + 2$

    $= 14$

    b) $2p + 8$, $p = -3$

    c) $-3x - 4$, $x = -2$

    d) $4q - 3$, $q = 0$

    e) $-5m + 2$, $m = 0.2$

    f) $\dfrac{-3}{4}d + \dfrac{3}{4}$, $d = \dfrac{3}{4}$

In a function table, the rule for the function shows how to calculate the output for each input. That calculation gives you an ordered pair.

Example: $y = 2x - 1$

$y = 2(3) - 1 = 5$ $(x, y) = (3, 5)$

x	y = 2x − 1
1	1
2	3
3	5
4	7

---

2. Use the rule for the function to complete the function table.

a) $y = 2x + 1$

x	y
1	
2	
3	
4	
5	

b) $y = -3x + 4$

x	y
1	
2	
3	
4	
5	

c) $y = x + 5$

x	y
1	
2	
3	
4	
5	

d) $y = 4x - 3$

x	y
−2	
−1	
0	
1	
2	

e) $y = -2x - 1$

x	y
−2	
−1	
0	
1	
2	

f) $y = -\dfrac{3}{4}x + 2$

x	y
−8	
−4	
0	
4	
8	

3. Find the ordered pair that appears in both tables.

a)

x	y
−2	1
−1	3
0	5
1	7
2	9

x	y
−1	1
0	4
1	7
2	10
3	13

b)

x	y
−3	6
−2	4
−1	2
0	0
1	−2

x	y
−4	−1
−3	0
−2	1
−1	2
0	3

c)

x	y
5	3
2	−1
−3	−5
0	−2
4	2

x	y
5	−7
0	−2
−3	1
4	−6
2	−4

_____(1, 7)_____　　　　　　　_____　　　　　　　_____

4. Complete each function table. Then find the ordered pair that appears in both tables.

a) $y = x - 3$　　$y = 2x - 2$

x	y
−2	
−1	
0	
1	
2	

x	y
−2	
−1	
0	
1	
2	

b) $y = -x + 4$　　$y = x + 8$

x	y
−5	
−4	
−3	
−2	
−1	

x	y
−5	
−4	
−3	
−2	
−1	

c) $y = \frac{1}{2}x - 3$　　$y = -\frac{1}{2}x - 1$

x	y
−2	
0	
2	
4	
6	

x	y
−2	
0	
2	
4	
6	

_____　　　　　　　_____　　　　　　　_____

d) $y = 2x - 1$, $y = 3x + 5$

Hint: Use $-10 \leq x \leq -5$.

e) $y = -3x - 3$, $y = -5x + 7$

Hint: Use $1 \leq x \leq 6$.

f) $y = \frac{1}{2}x + 2$, $y = \frac{3}{2}x - 4$

Hint: Use $2 \leq x \leq 8$.

5. Cathy thinks that the function tables for $y = x - 1$ and $y = 2x - 4$ will not have a common ordered pair.

a) Complete the function tables.

b) Do they appear to have an ordered pair in common? _____

c) Add one more row in each table where $x = 3$. Find the y-coordinates.

d) Was Cathy correct? Can you always tell by looking at functions tables whether two functions will have a common ordered pair? Explain.

$y = x - 1$　　$y = 2x - 4$

x	y
−2	
−1	
0	
1	
2	

x	y
−2	
−1	
0	
1	
2	

EE8-50 Graphing Systems of Linear Equations (Introduction)

If a point lies on a line, the point's coordinates satisfy the equation of the line.

Example: $y = 2x - 1$

(2, 3) lies on the line since $3 = 2(2) - 1$.
(3, 1) does not lie on the line since $1 \neq 2(3) - 1$.

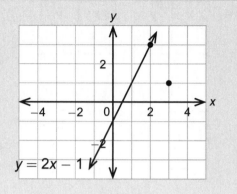

$y = 2x - 1$

1. Use the equation of the line to find whether each point lies on the line $y = -2x + 1$.

Point	Calculation	On the line?
(2, 3)	$3 \neq -2(2) + 1$	*no*
(−1, 3)	$3 = -2(-1) + 1$	*yes*
(0, 1)		
(1, −3)		
(1, −1)		
(−2, 2)		

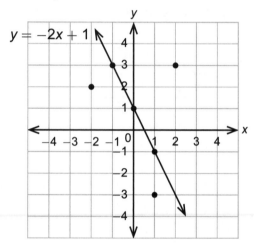

$y = -2x + 1$

2. Without graphing the equation, find whether the point lies on the line.

   a) $y = 3x - 4$

   point: (2, −3)

   b) $y = -2x + 5$

   point: (3, −1)

   c) $y = x + 5$

   point: (−1, 4)

   d) $y = -x - 2$

   point: (3, 5)

3. Show that the point lies on both lines.

   a) $y = 4x - 5$ $3 = 4(2) - 5$ *(2, 3) lies on the line $y = 4x - 5$.*

   $y = -2x + 7$ $3 = -2(2) + 7$ *(2, 3) lies on the line $y = -2x + 7$.*

   point: (2, 3)   *So (2, 3) lies on both lines.*

   b) $y = 3x - 2$

   $y = -5x + 6$

   point: (1, 1)

   c) $y = -2x + 1$

   $y = -6x - 3$

   point: (−1, 3)

The **intersection point** of two lines is the point common to both lines.

Example: $(-1, 1)$ is the intersection point of the lines $y = x + 2$ and $y = -2x - 1$.

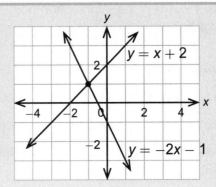

4. Write the coordinates of the intersection point.

a)

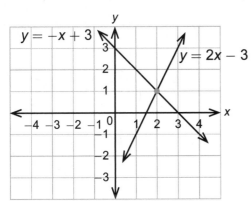

intersection point: (,   )

b)

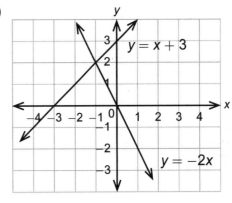

intersection point: (,   )

c)

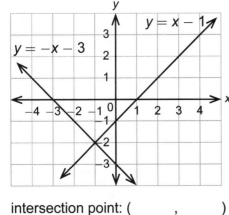

intersection point: (,   )

d)

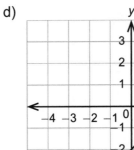

intersection point: (,   )

5. Show that the coordinates of each intersection point in Question 4 satisfy both equations.

	Point	First Line	Check	Second Line	Check
a)	$(2, 1)$	$y = -x + 3$	$1 = -(2) + 3$	$y = 2x - 3$	$1 = 2(2) - 3$
b)		$y = x + 3$		$y = -2x$	
c)		$y = -x - 3$		$y = x - 1$	
d)		$y = x - 2$		$y = -2x + 4$	

Expressions and Equations 8-50

6. Jennifer thinks that $(3, -1)$ is the intersection point for the lines $y = -x + 4$ and $y = 2x - 3$. Is she correct? Explain.

7. For each pair of lines:

a) Complete the function tables. Find the intersection point from the tables.

b) Use the coordinates to graph and label the lines. Label the intersection point on the grid.

c) Are the intersection points in a) and b) the same? Check that each intersection point satisfies both equations.

i) $y = -2x + 3$ $y = x - 3$

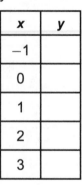

x	y
0	3
1	1
2	-1
3	-3
4	-5

x	y
1	
2	
3	
4	
5	

Checks:

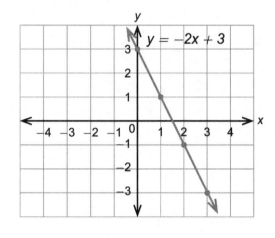

intersection point: (,   )

ii) $y = -x + 1$ $y = 2x - 2$

x	y
-2	
-1	
0	
1	
2	

x	y
-1	
0	
1	
2	
3	

Checks:

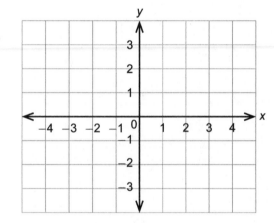

intersection point: (,   )

iii) $y = -3x + 2$ $y = x - 2$

x	y
-1	
0	
1	
2	
3	

x	y
-1	
0	
1	
2	
3	

Checks:

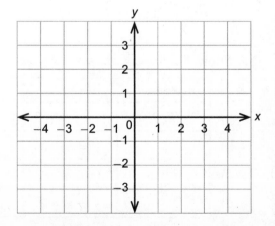

intersection point: (,   )

Expressions and Equations 8-50

EE8-51 Solving Systems of Linear Equations by Graphing

REMINDER: A line with the equation $y = 2x + 3$ has slope $= 2$ and y-intercept $= 3$.

1. Find the slope and the y-intercept for each equation.

Equation	$y = 3x + 4$	$y = -2x + 5$	$y = -x + 2$	$y = 5x$	$y = -3x - 2$
Slope	3				
y-intercept	4				

REMINDER: To graph the line $y = -2x + 1$:

Step 1: Draw a dot for the y-intercept.

Step 2: For a slope that will be $\dfrac{-2}{1}$, count 1 unit to the right from the y-intercept (for a run of 1) and 2 units down (for a rise of -2), and draw another dot.

Step 3: Join the dots with a line.

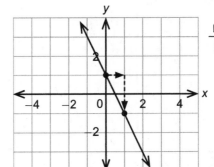

$$\frac{\text{rise}}{\text{run}} = \frac{-2}{1}$$

2. Find the slope (m) and y-intercept (y-int.). Then draw the graph of the line.

a) $y = 2x - 1$ $m =$ _____ y-int. $=$ _____

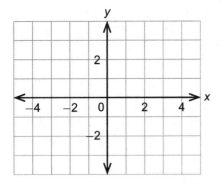

b) $y = -3x + 1$ $m =$ _____ y-int. $=$ _____

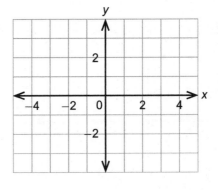

c) $y = -x + 2$ $m =$ _____ y-int. $=$ _____

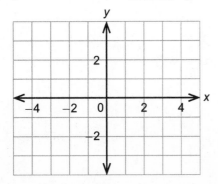

d) $y = 3x - 2$ $m =$ _____ y-int. $=$ _____

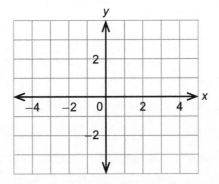

A **system of linear equations** is a set of two equations. The graph of the system is two lines.
To **solve a system of equations** means to find the point where the two lines intersect.

3. Graph each line by first finding its slope and *y*-intercept. Then solve the system of equations.

a) $y = 2x - 3$ $m =$ _____   *y*-int. = _____

   $y = -3x + 2$ $m =$ _____   *y*-int. = _____

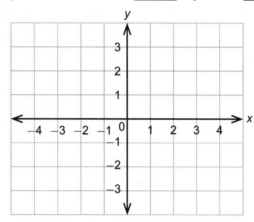

intersection point: (,   )

b) $y = x + 3$ $m =$ _____   *y*-int. = _____

   $y = -x + 1$ $m =$ _____   *y*-int. = _____

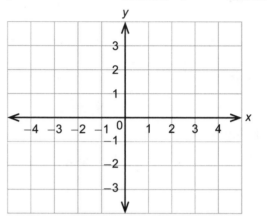

intersection point: (,   )

c) $y = 3x - 2$ $m =$ _____   *y*-int. = _____

   $y = -2x + 3$ $m =$ _____   *y*-int. = _____

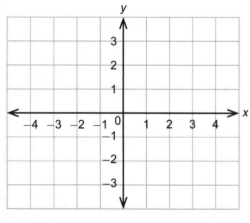

intersection point: (,   )

Bonus ▶ $y = 2x - 4$ $m =$ _____   *y*-int. = _____

   $y = -2$ $m =$ _____   *y*-int. = _____

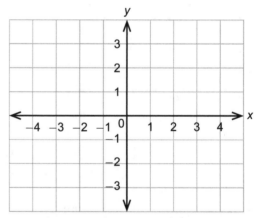

intersection point: (,   )

4. Roy graphed the lines $y = 2x - 3$ and $y = 2x + 1$, but he can't seem to find the intersection point.

a) Find the slope of each line. What do you notice?

b) What can we say about lines that have the same slope?

c) Explain whether Roy should be able to find the intersection point.

Expressions and Equations 8-51

COPYRIGHT © 2015 JUMP MATH: NOT TO BE COPIED. CC EDITION

Some word problems involve a cost per unit and a flat fee. Example: Sam wants to rent a bike, and the cost (y) will include a flat fee and a cost for each hour (x).

At Wheels Are Us, a rental costs $3 for each hour plus a flat fee of $7.

$y = 3x + 7$ ⟶ flat fee
⟶ charge per hour

At Best Bikes, a rental costs $2 for each hour, but the flat fee is $11.

$y = 2x + 11$ ⟶ flat fee
⟶ charge per hour

1. Write two formulas for the word problems involving a flat fee.

   a) At Tony's Tops, it costs $6 to print each shirt plus a set-up fee of $32. _____

   At Victory V-Necks, it costs $4 for each shirt plus a set-up fee of $38. _____

   b) Westside Wedding Videos charges $50 per hour plus a flat fee of $330. _____

   Downtown Photography charges $60 per hour plus a flat fee of $250. _____

   c) At Paper Plus, photocopying costs 5¢ per page plus a flat fee of 150¢. _____

   At Copy Quick, it costs 3¢ for each page plus a flat fee of 240¢. _____

Alice wants to rent a bike for a certain number of hours. She says the cost is the same at Wheels Are Us and Best Bikes. What is the number of hours Alice wants to rent for? How much will it cost?

Equation	Slope	y-intercept
$y = 3x + 7$	3	7
$y = 2x + 11$	2	11

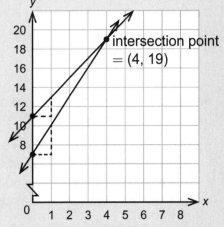

intersection point = (4, 19)

intersection point = (4, 19)

So Alice wants to rent a bike for 4 hours. The total cost is $19.

Checks: $19 = 3(4) + 7$ and $19 = 2(4) + 11$

2. Write the equations for the word problem. Then solve by graphing.

   a) Prime Plumbers charges $24 per hour plus a flat fee of $50. Acme Plumbing charges $20 per hour and a flat fee of $70. After how many hours would the two services charge the same total?

   b) Phone Plan A charges $40 for a basic plan and $15 for each extra unit of data. Plan B charges $55 for the basic plan and $10 for each extra unit of data. In what situation would both phone plans cost the same?

The intersection point may contain fractions or decimals.

Example: Peter's Parking Palace charges a flat fee of $12 to park a car and $6 per hour. At Vince's Valet Services, the flat fee is $19 and $4 per hour.

Maria calculates the total cost is the same at both businesses for the number of hours she needs to park her car.

For how many hours does Maria need to park her car? What is the total cost of parking?

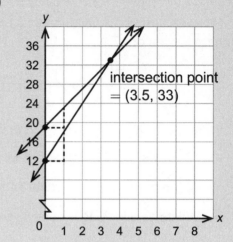

intersection point = (3.5, 33)

Equation	Slope	y-intercept
$y = 6x + 12$	6	12
$y = 4x + 19$	4	19

intersection point = (3.5, 33)

So Maria needs to park for 3.5 hours. The total cost is $33.

Checks: $33 = 6(3.5) + 12$ and $33 = 4(3.5) + 19$

3. Explain why it might be difficult to find the exact intersection point from the graph when the intersection point involves fractions or decimals.

4. Write the equations for the word problem. Then solve by graphing. The intersection point may have fractions or decimals.

a) Two trains left Union Station at different times. Train A is 12 km from the station and is traveling 60 km/h. Train B is 27 km from the station and is traveling 50 km/h. When will Train A catch up to Train B? How far will they be from the station?

b) Some species of bamboo can grow many inches in one day. Bamboo Shoot A is 28 inches tall and grows 3 inches per day. Bamboo Shoot B is 21 inches tall and grows 5 inches per day. When will the two shoots be the same height? What will the height be?

c) Ace Appliance Repair charges $92.50 for a service call and $20 for every 30 minutes on the job. The Fridge Fixer charges $80 for a service call plus $25 for every 30 minutes on the job. After how much time would a repair cost the same from both companies?

d) Jay earns $35,000 per year and gets a $2,000 raise each year. Helen earns $45,000 per year and gets a $1,500 raise each year. After how many years will Jay and Helen earn the same amount?

In a function table, an equation gives the rule for finding the values. The equation $y = 2x + 1$ tells us that, to find the y-coordinate, we need to multiply the x-coordinate by 2, then add 1.

We write that the **general point** on the line $y = 2x + 1$ has coordinates $(x, 2x + 1)$.

x	$y = 2x + 1$
1	3
2	5
3	7
4	9
x	$2x + 1$

1. Complete the table. Write the coordinates of the general point.

a)

x	$y = 2x - 1$
1	
2	
3	
4	
x	

general point: (,   )

b)

x	$y = 3x - 4$
1	
2	
3	
4	
x	

general point: (,   )

c)

x	$y = -2x + 5$
1	
2	
3	
4	
x	

general point: (,   )

2. Write the coordinates of the general point for the line.

a) $y = 4x + 3$

_(x, 4x + 3)_

b) $y = x - 5$

_____

c) $y = -x + 3$

_____

REMINDER: The coordinates of the intersection point satisfy the equations of both lines.

3. The equations for two lines that intersect and the x-coordinate of the intersection point (int. point) are given. Use the x-coordinate in the equation of either line to find the y-coordinate of the intersection point.

a) $y = 3x - 2$

$y = 2x + 5$

int. point $= (7, ?)$

$y = 3(7) - 2 = 19$
          or
$y = 2(7) + 5 = 19$

So int. point $= (7, 19)$

b) $y = -2x + 1$

$y = 2x - 3$

int. point $= (1, ?)$

c) $y = 2x + 4$

$y = -x - 2$

int. point $= (-2, ?)$

To find the intersection point of two lines algebraically:

Step 1: Write an equation using the *y*-coordinates of both general points.

Example: $-2x + 1 = 2x - 3$

Step 2: Solve the equation for *x*.

$x = 1$

Step 3: Use the answer for *x* in the equation of either line to solve for *y*.

$y = -1$

Step 4: Write the intersection point (x, y) using the answers from Step 2 and Step 3.

int. point $= (1, -1)$

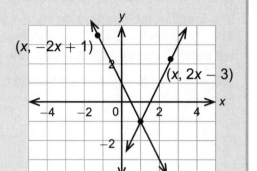

4. Perform Step 1 of finding the intersection point algebraically.

a) $y = 2x - 3$

$y = -2x + 1$

At the int. point:

$2x - 3 = -2x + 1$

b) $y = -3x - 4$

$y = 2x + 1$

c) $y = x - 4$

$y = -3x + 8$

d) $y = 4x - 8$

$y = -3x + 13$

e) $y = 2x - 1$

$y = -3x - 11$

f) $y = 6x - 17$

$y = -3x + 19$

5. For the equations in Question 4, perform Step 2 by solving for *x*.

a) $2x - 3 = -2x + 1$

$2x + 2x = 1 + 3$

$4x = 4$

$4x \div 4 = 4 \div 4$

$x = 1$

b)

c)

d)

e)

f)

6. For the lines in Questions 4 and 5, perform Steps 3 and 4 to find the intersection point.

a) $y = 2x - 3$

$y = -2x + 1$

$x = 1$

$y = 2(1) - 3 = -1$

    or

$y = -2(1) + 1 = -1$

So the int. point $= (1, -1)$

b) $y = -3x - 4$

$y = 2x + 1$

c) $y = x - 4$

$y = -3x + 8$

d) $y = 4x - 8$

$y = -3x + 13$

e) $y = 2x - 1$

$y = -3x - 11$

f) $y = 6x - 17$

$y = -3x + 19$

7. Find the intersection point of the lines. Check that the intersection point satisfies the equation of both lines.

a) $y = 2x + 3$

$y = -3x - 7$

At the int. point:

$2x + 3 = -3x - 7$

$2x + 3x = -7 - 3$

$5x = -10$

$5x \div 5 = -10 \div 5$

$x = -2$

At the int. point:

$y = 2(-2) + 3 = -1$

So int. point $= (-2, -1)$

Checks: $-1 = 2(-2) + 3$

$\qquad -1 = -3(-2) - 7$

b) $y = -x + 3$

$y = x + 7$

c) $y = -2x - 8$

$y = -x + 2$

d) $y = 6x + 32$

$y = -2x - 24$

e) $y = -x + 3$

$y = -2x + 1$

f) $y = -3x - 8$

$y = -4x + 6$

EE8-54 Solving Systems of Equations Algebraically II

To find the slope and *y*-intercept of a line, isolate for *y*.

Example: $x + 2y = 4$
$x + 2y - x = 4 - x$
$2y = -x + 4$
$y = -\dfrac{1}{2}x + 2$ ← *y*-intercept
                    slope

1. Isolate for *y*. Then find the slope and the *y*-intercept.

   a) $3x + y = 5$ b) $x - 3y = 1$ c) $2x + 3y = 4$

   $m =$ _____ $m =$ _____ $m =$ _____

   y-intercept = _____   *y*-intercept = _____   *y*-intercept = _____

2. For each line, isolate for *y* to find the slope and the *y*-intercept. Write your answers
   in the table. Then graph each line and find the intersection point of the lines.

a)

Equation	$y = mx + b$ Form	Slope	*y*-intercept
$x + 2y = -2$	$y = \dfrac{-1}{2}x - 1$	$\dfrac{-1}{2}$	-1
$x - y = 4$	$y = x - 4$		

intersection point: (,   )

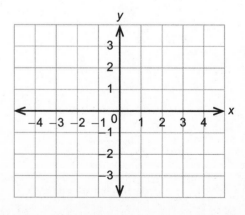

b)

Equation	$y = mx + b$ Form	Slope	*y*-intercept
$x + y = 4$			
$2x - y = -1$			

intersection point: (,   )

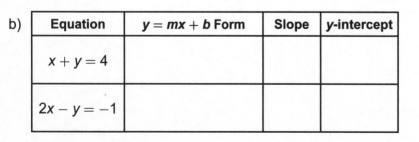

Expressions and Equations 8-54

To solve the system $\begin{array}{l} x - y = 5 \\ x + 2y = -1 \end{array}$ algebraically:

Step 1: Isolate for the variable y in each equation.

$y = x - 5$

$y = -\dfrac{1}{2}x - \dfrac{1}{2}$

Step 2: At the intersection point, the y-coordinates are equal. Write the equation.

$x - 5 = -\dfrac{1}{2}x - \dfrac{1}{2}$

...

Step 3: Solve for x.

$\dfrac{3}{2}x = \dfrac{9}{2}$

$3x = 9$

$x = 3$

Step 4: Use either of the original equations to solve for y at the intersection point.

At the intersection point:

$3 - y = 5$

$y = 3 - 5 = -2$

Step 5: Write the intersection point and check using both equations.

int. point $= (3, -2)$

Check: $3 - (-2) = 5$

$3 + 2(-2) = -1$

3. Solve the system algebraically. Check that your answer works in both equations.

a) $x - y = 3$

$x + y = 7$

b) $2x - y = 5$

$3x + y = 10$

c) $x + y = -2$

$x + 3y = -8$

d) $x + 2y = 6$

$x + 3y = 9$

In word problems, watch for these frequent words and the operations they usually refer to:

- **addition**—"sum," "plus," "more than," "total"
- **multiplication**—"product," "twice," "double"
- **subtraction**—"less than," "minus," "difference"
- **division**—"quotient," "ratio," "one-half," "one-third"

Words such as "is," "are," "was," and "were" usually show us where to put the **equal sign**.

The sum of two numbers x and y is 35.

$$x + y \qquad = 35$$

One number is 5 more than twice another number.

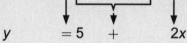

$$y \qquad = 5 \quad + \quad 2x$$

1. Translate each sentence into an equation using two variables, *x* and *y*. Start by explaining what each variable represents.

   a) A number is 3 less than twice another number.

   Let x be the first number. Let y be the second number. $\underline{\quad x = 2y - 3 \quad}$

   b) The difference between two numbers is 7.

   Let x be the larger number. Let y be the smaller number. $\underline{\hspace{3cm}}$

   c) The sum of twice a number and three times a different number is 35.

   $\underline{\hspace{3cm}}$

   d) Ivan has 23 coins made up of nickels and dimes.

   $\underline{\hspace{3cm}}$

   e) Nina has $37 in her wallet made up of $5 bills and $1 bills.

   $\underline{\hspace{3cm}}$

2. For the word problem, write two equations. Each equation should use two variables.

   a) The length of a rectangle is twice its width. The perimeter is 100 cm. What are the length and width?

   Let x be the length of the rectangle. Let y be its width.

   $\underline{\quad x = 2y \quad}$ $\underline{\quad 2x + 2y = 100 \quad}$

   b) Will has $150 in $5 bills and $10 bills. If he has 20 bills altogether, what bills does he have?

   $\underline{\hspace{3cm}}$ $\underline{\hspace{3cm}}$

   c) There are 140 people in the audience. Adult tickets cost $5. Child tickets cost $3. The total value of the tickets sold is $620. How many tickets were sold for adults and children?

   $\underline{\hspace{3cm}}$ $\underline{\hspace{3cm}}$

To solve a word problem with a system of linear equations:

Step 1: State what each variable represents and write the equations.

Step 2: Isolate for y in each equation.

Step 3: Write an equation for the y-value at the intersection point.

Step 4: Solve the equation.

Step 5: Find the y-coordinate of the intersection point.

Step 6: Write a concluding statement.

Step 7: Check that your answers work.

Example: The sum of two numbers is 12. Their difference is 6. What are the numbers?

Let x be the larger number.
Let y be the smaller number.

the sum of two numbers

$x + y = 12$

$x - y = 6$

the difference between the numbers

$y = 12 - x$
$y = x - 6$

At the intersection point:
$12 - x = x - 6$

$-2x = -18$
$x = 9$

$y = 12 - 9 = 3$

The larger number is 9. The smaller number is 3.

Check: $9 + 3 = 12$
$9 - 3 = 6$

3. The sum of two numbers is 15. The difference between the two numbers is 3. Find the numbers.

4. John has cash in the form of $5 bills and $1 bills. He has 20 bills altogether and they are worth $64. How many $5 bills does he have?

5. Clara has 5 more stamps than Anwar. If she had 6 more stamps, she would have twice as many stamps as Anwar. How many stamps does each person have?

6. Divide 36 into two parts so that the larger part is 3 times the smaller part. What size are the parts?

7. Angles *A* and *B* are complementary angles. Angle *A* is 18 degrees greater than Angle *B*. What are the measurements of the angles?

8. Bo is 5 years older than Blanca. In 3 years, the sum of their ages will be 25. How old is Bo today?

9. There are 13 animals in a barn. Some are chickens and the rest are cows. There are 40 legs altogether. How many chickens are in the barn?

10. The sum of the digits of a two-digit number is 7. The number formed by reversing the digits is 45 less than the original number. What was the original number? Remember, the value of a two-digit number can be found by multiplying each digit by its place value and adding the products.

EE8-56 Solving Systems of Linear Equations by Inspection

1. Circle whether the lines are parallel or not parallel.

a)

parallel   not parallel

b)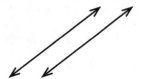

parallel   not parallel

c)

parallel   not parallel

2. Use the rise and run to find the slope of each line. Then circle whether the lines are parallel or not parallel.

a)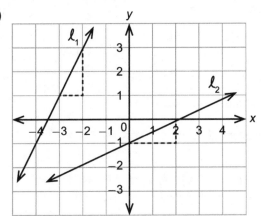

$$m_1 = \frac{2}{1} = 2 \qquad m_2 = \frac{1}{2}$$

parallel   (not parallel)

b)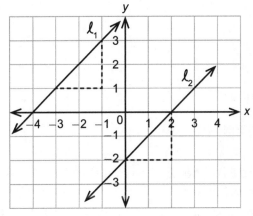

$$m_1 = \underline{\quad} \qquad m_2 = \underline{\quad}$$

parallel   not parallel

c)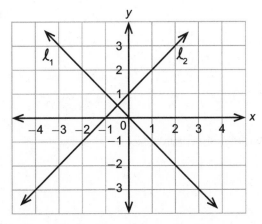

$$m_1 = \underline{\quad} \qquad m_2 = \underline{\quad}$$

parallel   not parallel

d)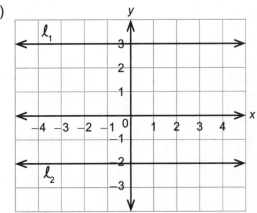

$$m_1 = \underline{\quad} \qquad m_2 = \underline{\quad}$$

parallel   not parallel

3. Write the slope for each line. Circle whether the lines are parallel and whether they intersect.

a) $y = 2x - 1$ $m =$ _____

   $y = 3x - 1$ $m =$ _____

   Parallel?   yes   no

   Intersect?   yes   no

b) $y = 3x - 1$ $m =$ _____

   $y = 3x + 5$ $m =$ _____

   Parallel?   yes   no

   Intersect?   yes   no

c) $y = -x + 3$ $m =$ _____

   $y = -x - 7$ $m =$ _____

   Parallel?   yes   no

   Intersect?   yes   no

d) $y = 6$ $m =$ _____

   $y = -3$ $m =$ _____

   Parallel?   yes   no

   Intersect?   yes   no

4. Use the slopes to predict whether or not there is a solution to the system of equations.

a) $y = 4x - 2$ $m =$ _____

   $y = -2x + 6$ $m =$ _____

   Solution?   yes   no

b) $y = x + 5$ $m =$ _____

   $y = x - 2$ $m =$ _____

   Solution?   yes   no

c) $y = 7$ $m =$ _____

   $y = -2$ $m =$ _____

   Solution?   yes   no

d) $y = 5x + 7$ $m =$ _____

   $y = -2x$ $m =$ _____

   Solution?   yes   no

5. For the parts in Question 4 that can be solved, find the solution algebraically.

Expressions and Equations 8-56

6. Write the equation of each line in the form $y = mx + b$. Then predict whether there is a solution to the system of equations.

a) $x + y = 7$ ⟶ $\underline{\quad y = -x + 7 \quad}$ $m = \underline{\quad -1 \quad}$ Parallel?   yes   no

    $x - y = 2$ ⟶ $\underline{\quad y = x - 2 \quad}$ $m = \underline{\quad 1 \quad}$ Solution?   yes   no

b) $x - y = 5$ ⟶ $\underline{\qquad\qquad}$ $m = \underline{\qquad}$ Parallel?   yes   no

    $x - y = 2$ ⟶ $\underline{\qquad\qquad}$ $m = \underline{\qquad}$ Solution?   yes   no

c) $2x - y = 8$ ⟶ $\underline{\qquad\qquad}$ $m = \underline{\qquad}$ Parallel?   yes   no

    $3x + y = 4$ ⟶ $\underline{\qquad\qquad}$ $m = \underline{\qquad}$ Solution?   yes   no

d) $3x + y = 1$ ⟶ $\underline{\qquad\qquad}$ $m = \underline{\qquad}$ Parallel?   yes   no

    $3x + y = 7$ ⟶ $\underline{\qquad\qquad}$ $m = \underline{\qquad}$ Solution?   yes   no

e) $-3x + y = 1$ ⟶ $\underline{\qquad\qquad}$ $m = \underline{\qquad}$ Parallel?   yes   no

    $3x + y = 7$ ⟶ $\underline{\qquad\qquad}$ $m = \underline{\qquad}$ Solution?   yes   no

---

A variable represents only one number at a time. So, for example, the variable x cannot represent two numbers at the same time.

The system of linear equations $\begin{array}{l} x = 6 \\ x = 7 \end{array}$ has no solution because x cannot simultaneously be 6 and 7.

In the same way, the system $\begin{array}{l} x + 2y = 6 \\ x + 2y = 7 \end{array}$ has no solution because $x + 2y$ cannot simultaneously be 6 and 7.

---

7. Without finding the slope, circle the systems that have no solution.

A. $3x - 2y = 4$ **B.** $2x + 3y = -2$ **C.** $3x - 2y = 4$

    $3x - 2y = 5$ $2x - 3y = 4$ $2x - 3y = -1$

D. $x - 4y = 1$ **E.** $4x + 3y = 9$ **F.** $2x - y = 4$

    $x - 5y = -2$ $4x + 3y = 0$ $2x + y = -6$

8. Emma thinks that the system $\begin{array}{l} 3x - 2y = 2 \\ -3x + 2y = 4 \end{array}$ has no solution. Is she correct? Explain.

G8-49 Volume of Prisms

Prisms are three-dimensional (3-D) shapes that have faces, edges, vertices, and bases.

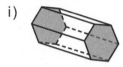 Faces are the flat surfaces.

Faces meet at edges.

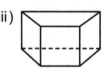 Dashed lines show hidden edges.

Edges meet at vertices.

Every prism has two parallel faces that are bases. The bases are always congruent polygons.

1. a) Shade the two bases of the prism. Identify the type of polygon that makes the base.

   i)

   ii)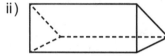

   iii)

   <u>   hexagon   </u>   _____   _____

   b) What shapes are the faces that are not bases? _____

When a prism stands on one base, the other base becomes the top face.

In a **right prism**, the top face is directly above the bottom face. The side edges are vertical.

In a **skew prism**, the top face is not directly above the bottom face. The side edges are not vertical.

---

2. a) Sort the 3-D shapes.

   A.   **B.**   **C.**   **D.**   **E.**   **F.**

   Right prisms _____   Skew prisms _____   Not prisms _____

   b) Choose one 3-D shape from the last group and explain why it is not a prism.

The height of a prism is the distance between its two bases.

---

3. Circle the measurement that gives the height of the prism. Hint: Shade the two bases.

   a)
   6 cm   4 cm   5 cm

   b)
   5 in   2 in   3 in   4 in   2.5 in

   c)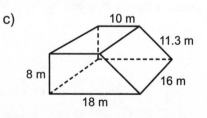
   10 m   11.3 m   8 m   16 m   18 m

Volume is the amount of space taken up by a 3-D shape. We measure volume in unit cubes or cubic units—for example, cubic inches (in^3) and cubic centimeters (cm^3).

4. a) Count the cubes to determine the volume of the prism.

i)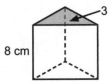

$V = $ ___8 in^3___

ii)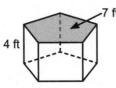

$V = $ _____

iii)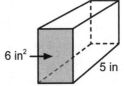

$V = $ _____

b) Complete the chart for each prism in part a).

	Area of Shaded Base (in^2)	Height (in)	Area of Shaded Base × Height (in^3)
i)	4 in^2	2 in	8 in^3
ii)			
iii)			

c) What do you notice about the volume of each prism in part a) and the product (area of shaded base) × (height) in part b)?

d) Write a formula for the volume of a prism.

5. Use the formula you developed in Question 4 to find the volume of the prism.

a)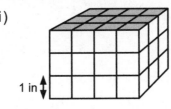

$V = $ ___(3 cm^2)(8 cm)___

$= $ ___24 cm^3___

b)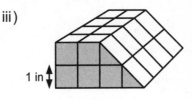

$V = $ _____

$= $ _____

c)

$V = $ _____

$= $ _____

6. The volume of a prism is 600 in^3 and the height is 15 inches. What is the area of the base of the prism?

7. The volume of a rectangular prism is 48 in^3 and the height is 3 inches. List 3 possible dimensions (length and width) for the base.

| Area of rectangle
= length × width | Area of triangle
= base × height ÷ 2 | Area of parallelogram
= base × height | Area of trapezoid
= (base₁ + base₂) × height ÷ 2 |

$$\text{Area of rectangle} = \text{length} \times \text{width}$$
$$\text{Area of triangle} = \text{base} \times \text{height} \div 2$$
$$\text{Area of parallelogram} = \text{base} \times \text{height}$$
$$\text{Area of trapezoid} = (base_1 + base_2) \times height \div 2$$

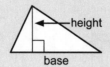 width, length

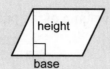 height, base

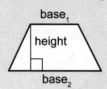 height, base

base₁, height, base₂

8. Calculate the area of the base (B). Hint: First shade the base and circle its measurements.

a)

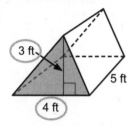

3 ft   5 ft   4 ft

$B = \underline{\quad (base \times height) \div 2 \quad}$

$= \underline{\quad (4\ ft)(3\ ft) \div 2 \quad}$

$= \underline{\quad 6\ ft^2 \quad}$

b)

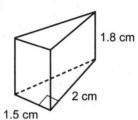

1.8 cm   2 cm   1.5 cm

$B = \underline{\hspace{5cm}}$

$= \underline{\hspace{5cm}}$

$= \underline{\hspace{5cm}}$

c)

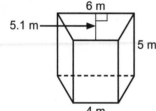

6 m   5.1 m   5 m   4 m

$B = \underline{\hspace{5cm}}$

$= \underline{\hspace{5cm}}$

$= \underline{\hspace{5cm}}$

d)

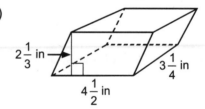

$2\frac{1}{3}$ in $3\frac{1}{4}$ in $4\frac{1}{2}$ in

$B = \underline{\hspace{5cm}}$

$= \underline{\hspace{5cm}}$

$= \underline{\hspace{5cm}}$

Volume of a prism = area of base × height   or $V = B \times h$ or $V = Bh$

9. Find the volume of the prisms in Question 8.

a) $V = \underline{\quad Bh \quad}$

$= \underline{\quad (6\ ft^2)(5\ ft) \quad}$

$= \underline{\quad 30\ ft^3 \quad}$

b) $V = \underline{\hspace{3cm}}$

$= \underline{\hspace{3cm}}$

$= \underline{\hspace{3cm}}$

c) $V = \underline{\hspace{3cm}}$

$= \underline{\hspace{3cm}}$

$= \underline{\hspace{3cm}}$

d) $V = \underline{\hspace{3cm}}$

$= \underline{\hspace{3cm}}$

$= \underline{\hspace{3cm}}$

A **composite solid** is a 3-D shape made up of two or more simpler shapes.

To find the volume of a composite solid:

Step 1: Divide the solid into shapes with volumes you know how to find.

Step 2: Find the volume of each simpler shape.

Step 3: Add the volumes.

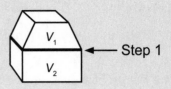

← Step 1

10. Find the volume of the composite solid.

a)

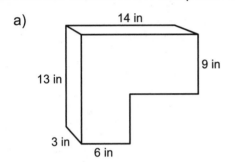

14 in

9 in

13 in

3 in

6 in

$V_1 = $ _____

$V_2 = $ _____

Total volume = _____

b)

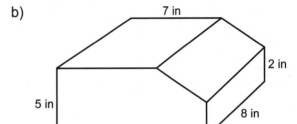

7 in

2 in

5 in

8 in

10 in

$V_1 = $ _____

$V_2 = $ _____

Total volume = _____

11. A rectangular prism has the following dimensions: height $\frac{3}{4}$ ft, length $\frac{5}{6}$ ft, and volume $\frac{5}{16}$ ft³.
What is the width?

12. Write two possible sets of dimensions (length, width, and height) for a rectangular prism
with the given volume.

a) $V = 12$ in³   b) $V = 8$ cm³   c) $V = \frac{1}{2}$ ft³   d) $V = 0.75$ m³

13. a) Ben wants to cover his yard with 4 inches of topsoil.
How many cubic feet of topsoil will he need? Hint: 1 in $= \frac{1}{12}$ ft.

b) 70 cubic feet of topsoil costs $149. How much will Ben pay
for the topsoil he needs?

Bonus ▶ How much more would it cost for Ben to cover his yard
with 4.5 inches of topsoil?

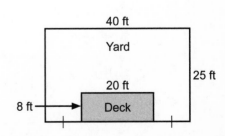

40 ft

Yard

25 ft

20 ft

8 ft

Deck

G8-50 Volume of Cylinders

Cylinders are 3-D shapes that have:

- two parallel bases that are congruent circles
- one curved surface

The height of a cylinder is the distance between the bases.

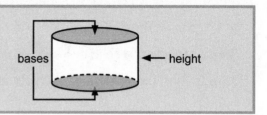

1. Shade the visible base of the cylinder.

a)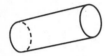

b)

c)

REMINDER: The diameter of a circle is twice the radius: $d = 2r$

The radius of a circle is half the diameter: $r = \frac{1}{2}d$

2. Which is given, the radius or the diameter? Find the measure that is not given.

a)

15 mm

$r =$ _____ mm

$d =$ _____ mm

b)

24 cm

$r =$ _____ cm

$d =$ _____ cm

Bonus ▶

1 ft

$r =$ _____ in

$d =$ _____ in

You can describe a cylinder by giving these dimensions: the height (h) of the cylinder and the radius (r) or diameter (d) of the base.

Examples:

2 cm

5 cm

The cylinder has $r = 2$ cm and $h = 5$ cm.

10 in

12 in

The cylinder has $d = 10$ in and $h = 12$ in.

3. Identify the dimensions of the cylinder.

a)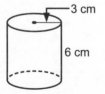

3 cm

6 cm

$r =$ _____

$d =$ _____

$h =$ _____

b)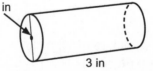

1 in

3 in

$r =$ _____

$d =$ _____

$h =$ _____

c)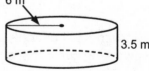

6 m

3.5 m

$r =$ _____

$d =$ _____

$h =$ _____

REMINDER: The area A of a circle with radius r is $A = \pi r^2$. Use 3.14 for π.

4. Find the area of a circle with the given radius. Round to the nearest tenth.

a)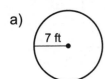

$A \approx$ ___(3.14)(7)²___

$\approx$ ___153.9 ft²___

b)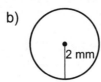

$A \approx$ _____

$\approx$ _____

5. Find the radius of the circle. Then find the area. Round to the nearest tenth.

a)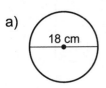

$r =$ _____

$A \approx$ _____

$\approx$ _____

b)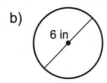

$r =$ _____

$A \approx$ _____

$\approx$ _____

6. Find the area of the circle. Round to the nearest tenth. Hint: Are you given the radius or the diameter?

a)

$A \approx$ _____

$=$ _____

b)

$A \approx$ _____

$\approx$ _____

c)

$A \approx$ _____

$\approx$ _____

d)

$A \approx$ _____

$\approx$ _____

Cylinders and prisms are alike. The volume of a cylinder = area of base × height, or $V = Bh$.

Since the area of a circle $= \pi r^2$, the volume of a cylinder $= \pi r^2 h$.

7. Find the volume of the cylinder. Round to the nearest tenth.

a)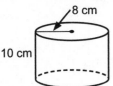

$V =$ ___$\pi r^2 h$___

$\approx$ ___3.14(8)²(10)___

$=$ ___2,009.6 cm³___

b)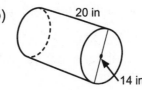

$V =$ _____

$\approx$ _____

$=$ _____

c) 1.5 m

8 m

$V =$ _____

$\approx$ _____

$\approx$ _____

d)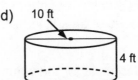

$V =$ _____

$\approx$ _____

$=$ _____

Bonus ▶ Cylinder A has radius 5 inches and height 8 inches. Cylinder B has radius 10 inches and height 8 inches. Write the ratio Volume A : Volume B. Reduce to lowest terms.

8. Two cans of chicken soup have different sizes. Can A has diameter 3 inches and height 5 inches. Can B has diameter 4 inches and height 3 inches.

a) Find the volume of each can to two decimal places. Which can holds more soup?

b) If Can A costs $1.98 and Can B costs $2.29, which soup costs less per in³?

9. a) The water bottle in the picture is filled to the very top. Find the volume of the bottle to one decimal place.

b) One gram of flavored drink powder is mixed with 250 cm³ of water. How many grams of drink powder should be added to the water bottle if it is filled to the very top? Round your answer to one decimal place.

c) There are 4 calories per gram of flavored drink powder. How many calories are in the drink from part b)?

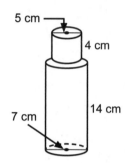

5 cm

4 cm

14 cm

7 cm

10. a) A concrete pipe is a large cylinder with a smaller cylinder removed from its middle. The outer diameter of the pipe is 254 cm and the diameter of the opening is 210 cm. Find the volume of concrete required to make the pipe, to the nearest tenth of a cubic meter.

b) One cubic meter of concrete weighs about 2,406 kg. To the nearest kilogram, how much does the pipe weigh?

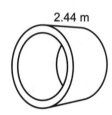

2.44 m

If you know the volume (*V*) and the radius (*r*) of the base, you can find the height (*h*) of a cylinder.

Example:

5 ft

h ft

$V = 785 \text{ ft}^3$

$$V = \pi r^2 h$$
$$785 \approx (3.14)(5)^2 h$$
$$785 \approx 78.5h$$
$$785 \div 78.5 \approx h$$
$$10 \approx h$$

The height of the prism is about 10 ft.

---

11. The volume of a cylinder is about 1,962.5 in³ and the height is 25 in. Write and solve an equation to find the area of the base.

12. The volume of a cylinder is about 6,805.95 cm³ and the radius is 8.5 cm. Write and solve an equation to find the height.

13. A cylindrical water tank has a volume of about 15 m³ and a diameter of 2.5 m. Grace's shed is 2.7 m high. Will the water tank fit in her shed?

Bonus ▶ Write a simplified formula for the volume of a cylinder that uses the diameter of the base instead of the radius.

G8-51 Pyramids

Pyramids are 3-D shapes that have:

- one base that is a polygon
- side faces that are triangles
- an **apex**—the vertex where all side faces meet

Pyramids are named for the shape of the base.

Examples:

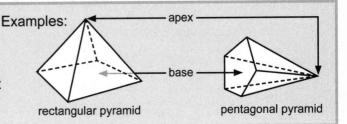

rectangular pyramid   pentagonal pyramid

1. Shade the base of the pyramid. Identify the polygon that makes the base.

a)

b)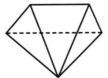

c)

square

_____   _____   _____

When a pyramid stands on its base, its height is the vertical distance from the apex to the base.

In a **right pyramid**, the apex is directly above the center of the base.

In a **skew pyramid**, the apex is not directly above the center of the base.

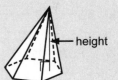

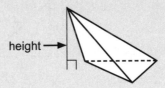

2. Circle the measurement that gives the height of the pyramid.

a)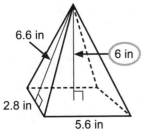

6.6 in   (6 in)

2.8 in

5.6 in

b)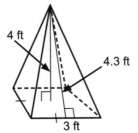

4 ft   4.3 ft

3 ft

c)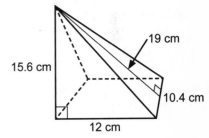

19 cm

15.6 cm

10.4 cm

12 cm

3. a) Sort the 3-D shapes.

A.

B.

C.

D.

E.

F.

Right pyramids _____   Skew pyramids _____   Not pyramids _____

b) Choose one 3-D shape from the last group and explain why it is not a pyramid.

REMINDER: You can use the Pythagorean Theorem to find …

the hypotenuse of a right triangle.

2 cm

z cm

7 cm

$z^2 = 2^2 + 7^2$

$z^2 = 4 + 49$

$z^2 = 53$

$z = \sqrt{53}$

$z \approx 7.3$ cm

the side of a right triangle.

5 in

13 in

x in

$5^2 + x^2 = 13^2$

$25 + x^2 = 169$

$x^2 = 169 - 25$

$x^2 = 144$

$x = \sqrt{144}$

$x = 12$ in

4. Find the hypotenuse. Round to the nearest tenth. All measurements are in cm.

a)

a

6

8

b)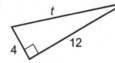

t

4

12

c)

3

b

5

5. Find the unknown side. Round to the nearest tenth. All measurements are in inches.

a)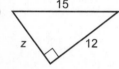

15

z

12

b)

n

4

3

c)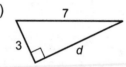

7

3

d

Side faces of a pyramid are also called **lateral faces**.

The height of a lateral face is called the **slant height (s)** or **lateral height**.

slant height (s)

lateral face

6. a) Sketch the triangle shown inside the pyramid.

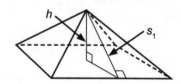

h

s_1

b) Use your sketch to explain why the slant height is always greater than the height of the pyramid.

Bonus ▶ A different triangle from the one you sketched in part a) is shown inside the same pyramid. Compare the triangles. Which measurement(s) would be the same and which measurement(s) would be different? Explain.

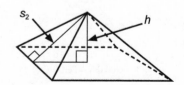

s_2

h

7. Label the length of the line segment drawn from the center of the rectangle.

a)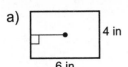
4 in
6 in

b)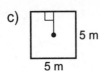
12.5 cm
8.8 cm

c)
5 m
5 m

d)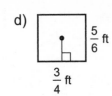
$\frac{5}{6}$ ft
$\frac{3}{4}$ ft

8. Label the sides of the right triangle drawn inside the pyramid.

a)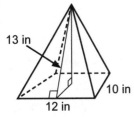
13 in
10 in
12 in

13 in / h
5 in
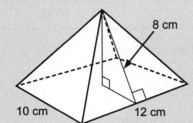

b)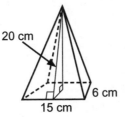
20 cm
6 cm
15 cm

c)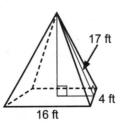
17 ft
4 ft
16 ft

d)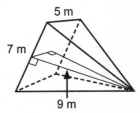
5 m
7 m
9 m

If you know the slant height of a right pyramid, you can use the Pythagorean Theorem to find the height of the pyramid.

Example:

8 cm
10 cm   12 cm

h   8 cm
5 cm

$5^2 + h^2 = 8^2$

$25 + h^2 = 64$

$h^2 = 64 - 25$

$h^2 = 39$

$h = \sqrt{39}$

$h \approx 6.2$

The height of the pyramid is about 6.2 cm.

9. Use the Pythagorean Theorem to find the height of the pyramids in Question 8.
Round to the nearest tenth.

10. The slant height of a right pyramid with a 14 cm square base is 12 cm. What is the height of the pyramid to the nearest tenth?

11. The pyramid in the diagram is a right rectangular pyramid with height *OE*.

a) Sketch triangle *ABC*. Find the length of *AC*.

b) What is the length of *EC*?

c) Find the height (*OE*) of the pyramid to the nearest tenth.

Bonus ▶ Find the slant height of the face of triangle *OBC*.
Hint: *OBC* is isosceles.

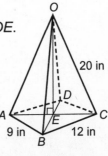

O
20 in
D
A
E
C
9 in   B   12 in

G8-52 Volume of Pyramids

1. The base of the right pyramid is shaded. Find the area of the base (*B*).

a)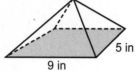

5 in
9 in

B = _____

b)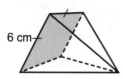

6 cm

B = _____

c)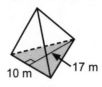

10 m
17 m

B = _____

d)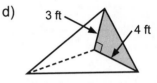

3 ft
4 ft

B = _____

2. The pyramid has the same base and height as the prism.

   a) Fill in the table. All measurements are in inches.

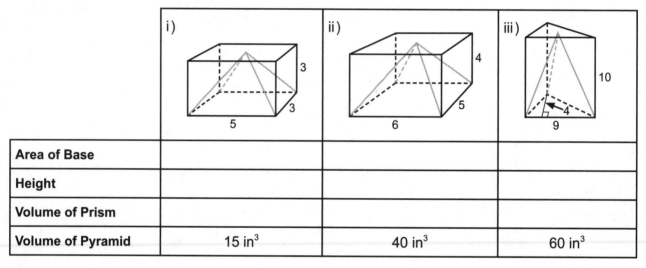

	i)	ii)	iii)
Area of Base			
Height			
Volume of Prism			
Volume of Pyramid	15 in³	40 in³	60 in³

   b) Compare the volumes of the prism and the pyramid with the same base and height. What pattern do you see?

   c) Write a formula for the volume of a pyramid using the area of the base and the height of the pyramid.

3. Use the formula you developed in Question 2 to find the volume of the pyramid.

a)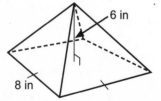

6 in
8 in

V = _____

= _____

= _____

b)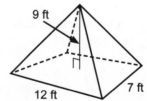

9 ft
12 ft
7 ft

V = _____

= _____

= _____

4. Find the volume of the pyramid. Round to the nearest tenth.

a)

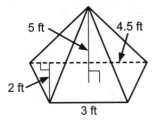

5 ft   4.5 ft

2 ft

3 ft

b)

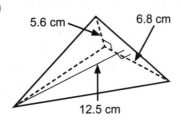

5.6 cm   6.8 cm

12.5 cm

c)

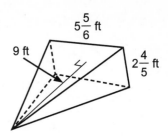

$5\frac{5}{6}$ ft

9 ft

$2\frac{4}{5}$ ft

5. a) Find the volume of a rectangular pyramid with …

   i) a base that is 3 m by 4 m and height 5 m.

   ii) a base that is 6 m by 8 m and height 10 m.

b) When you double each dimension of a rectangular pyramid, how does the volume change? Explain.

If you know the volume (V) and the dimensions of the base, you can find the height (h) of a pyramid.

Example:

7.1 cm   4.8 cm

$V \approx 71.6 \text{ cm}^3$

Area of base: $B = (7.1)(4.8) \div 2 = 17.04$

Height of pyramid: $h = ?$

$V = Bh \div 3$

$71.6 \approx (17.04)h \div 3$

$71.6 \times 3 \div 17.04 \approx h$

$12.6 \approx h$

The height of the pyramid is about 12.6 cm.

---

6. Write and solve an equation to find the height of the pyramid.

a) $V = 420 \text{ m}^3$

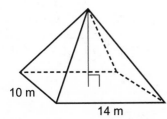

10 m

14 m

b) $V = 1\frac{9}{16} \text{ in}^3$

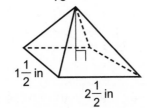

$1\frac{1}{2}$ in

$2\frac{1}{2}$ in

c) $V = 96 \text{ yd}^3$

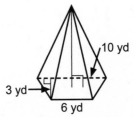

10 yd

3 yd

6 yd

7. a) Find the volume of a cube with edge length 10 cm.

b) A pyramid with a square base has the same base and the same volume as the cube in part a). What is the height? Hint: Compare the formulas.

Bonus ▶ Sketch the cube and the pyramid.

8. Use the Pythagorean Theorem to find the height of the right rectangular pyramid to the nearest tenth. Then find the volume.

a)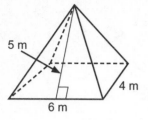

5 m

4 m

6 m

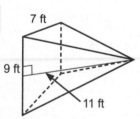

5 m   h

2 m

$2^2 + h^2 = 5^2$

$4 + h^2 = 25$

$h^2 = 25 - 4$

$h^2 = 21$

$h = \sqrt{21}$

$h \approx 4.6\ m$

$V = Bh \div 3$

$\approx (6)(4)(4.6) \div 3$

$= 36.8\ m^3$

b)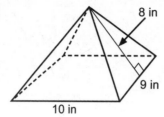

8 in

9 in

10 in

c)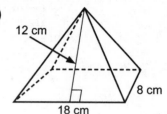

12 cm

8 cm

18 cm

d)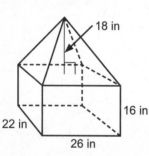

7 ft

9 ft

11 ft

e)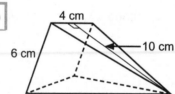

4 cm

10 cm

6 cm

f)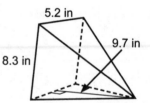

5.2 in

9.7 in

8.3 in

9. Find the volume of the composite solid. Hint: Divide the solid into simpler shapes.

a)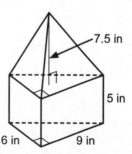

18 in

16 in

22 in

26 in

b)

7.5 in

5 in

6 in   9 in

Bonus ▶

3 ft

0.75 ft→

4 ft

10. When fully open, the canvas on a café umbrella has the shape of a hexagonal pyramid. The base is shown in the far right diagram. The height inside the umbrella is 2 ft. What is the volume of air inside the open umbrella to two decimal places?

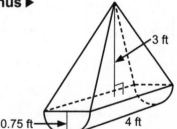

2 ft

9 ft

7.8 ft

4.5 ft

11. An open gold and copper mine has the shape of an upside-down pyramid. It has a 1.2-kilometer square opening and the slant height is 768 meters. What is the depth of the mine to the nearest meter?

G8-53 Volume of Cones

Cones are 3-D shapes that have:

- one base that is a circle
- a curved side surface
- an apex

Examples: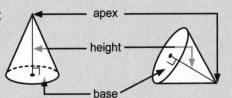

The apex of a **right cone** that stands on its base is directly above the center of the base.

1. Identify the radius (*r*), diameter (*d*), and height (*h*) of the cone.

a)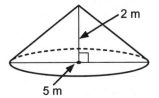

b)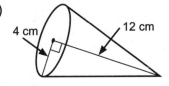

c)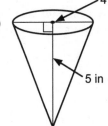

r = ___2.5 m___

d = ___5 m___

h = ___2 m___

r = _____

d = _____

h = _____

r = _____

d = _____

h = _____

2. For each cone in Question 1, find the area of the base. Round to the nearest tenth.
   Hint: Area of a circle $= \pi r^2$. Use 3.14 for π.

a) $A \approx$ _____

  $\approx$ _____

b) $A \approx$ _____

  $\approx$ _____

c) $A \approx$ _____

  $\approx$ _____

Cones and pyramids are alike. The volume of a cone $= \dfrac{1}{3} \times$ area of base $\times$ height, or $V = \dfrac{1}{3} Bh$.

Since the area of a circle $= \pi r^2$, then the volume of a cone $= \dfrac{1}{3} \pi r^2 h$.

3. Replace the variables in $V = \dfrac{1}{3} \pi r^2 h$ with the given dimensions and then evaluate.
   Round to the nearest tenth.

a) *r* = 5 cm, *h* = 9 cm

  $$V = \frac{1}{3}\pi r^2 h$$

  $$\approx \frac{1}{3}(3.14)(5)^2(9)$$

  $$= \frac{1}{3}(3.14)(25)(9)$$

  $$= 235.5 \text{ cm}^3$$

b) *r* = 1 in, *h* = 12 in

c) *d* = 4 ft, *h* = 6 ft

4. Find the volume of a cone with the given dimensions. Round to the nearest tenth.

a) 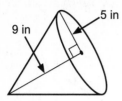 5 in, 9 in

b) 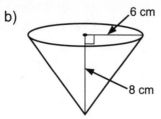 6 cm, 8 cm

c) 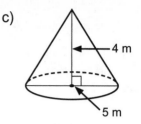 4 m, 5 m

d) $r = 3$ ft, $h = 5$ ft

e) $d = 2.2$ yd, $h = 7.4$ yd

f) $d = 2.9$ m, $h = 6$ m

5. a) At a farm, children can buy a cone of food to feed the goats and sheep. The cone has diameter 10 cm and height 15 cm. What is the volume of the cone?

b) The farmer fills cones using a bag containing 50,000 cm³ of food. How many cones does the bag fill?

c) The farmer fills cones with one bag of food and sells all the filled cones for $1 each. The farmer paid $12 for the bag of food. How much money does the farmer make?

6. Highway workers pile road salt in the shape of a cone. The cone has diameter 40 feet and height 12.5 feet. If salt weighs 72 pounds per cubic foot, what is the total weight of the salt in the pile?

If you know the volume (*V*) and the height (*h*) of the base, you can find the radius (*r*) of a cone.

Example:

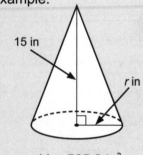

15 in

r in

$V \approx 565.2$ in³

$$V = \frac{1}{3}\pi r^2 h$$

$$565.2 \approx \frac{1}{3}(3.14)r^2(15)$$

$$565.2 \approx 15.7r^2$$

$$565.2 \div 15.7 \approx r^2$$

$$36 \approx r^2$$

$$\sqrt{36} \approx r$$

$$6 \approx r \qquad \text{The radius of the cone is about 6 in.}$$

---

7. The volume of a cone with a 4-inch radius is 177.2 in³. Write and solve an equation to find the height of the cone to the nearest tenth of an inch.

8. A cone has height 9 cm and volume 84.78 cm³. Write and solve an equation to find the radius to the nearest tenth of a centimeter.

9. A cone has height 7.9 ft and volume 152.9 ft³. Write and solve an equation to find the diameter to the nearest tenth of a foot.

If you know the slant height and the radius of a right cone, you can use the Pythagorean Theorem to find the height of the cone.

Example:

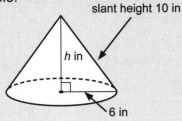
slant height 10 in
h in
6 in

$$6^2 + h^2 = 10^2$$
$$36 + h^2 = 100$$
$$h^2 = 100 - 36$$
$$h^2 = 64$$
$$h = \sqrt{64}$$
$$h = 8 \qquad \text{The height of the cone is 8 in.}$$

10. Use the Pythagorean Theorem to find the height of the cone. Round to the nearest tenth.

a)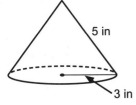
5 in
3 in

b)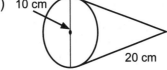
10 cm
20 cm

c)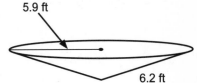
5.9 ft
6.2 ft

11. The Mayon Volcano in the Philippines is cone shaped. The diameter of its base is 20 km and the distance up the curved side, from the base to the apex, is 10.3 km. Find the height of the volcano.

12. Find the height of a cone with the given dimensions. Then find the volume. Round to the nearest tenth.

a)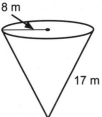
8 m
17 m

b)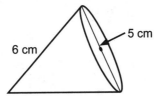
6 cm
5 cm

c)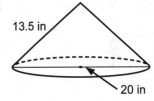
13.5 in
20 in

d) radius = 7 ft
slant height = 25 ft

e) radius = 13 m
slant height = 27 m

f) diameter = 7.2 in
slant height = 8.3 in

13. Find the volume of the composite solid.

a)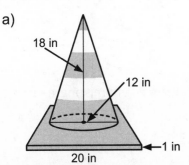
18 in
12 in
20 in
1 in

b)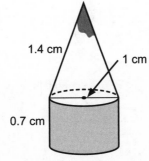
1.4 cm
1 cm
0.7 cm

Bonus ▶ The cone is removed from the cylinder.

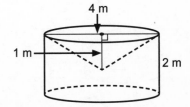
4 m
1 m
2 m

A **sphere** is a 3-D shape where every point on the surface is the same distance from the center.

You can describe a sphere by giving the radius (*r*) or diameter (*d*).

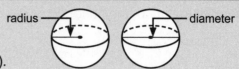

radius   diameter

1. A sphere with a radius of 1 inch will fit exactly inside a cylinder with a radius of 1 inch, as shown in the picture on the right.

a) What is the height of the cylinder? _____

b) What is the volume of the cylinder? Write the symbol π rather than 3.14.

c) Is the volume of the sphere greater than or less than the volume of the cylinder?

d) Use your answer from part b) to write a statement using < or > about the volume of a sphere.

e) The volume of this sphere is $\frac{4}{3}\pi$. Does your answer to part d) agree with this? Explain.

The volume of a sphere $= \frac{4}{3}\pi r^3$. To find the volume of a sphere with a given radius, replace the variable in the formula and evaluate.

Example:

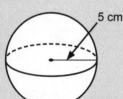

5 cm

$$V = \frac{4}{3}\pi r^3$$

$$\approx \frac{4}{3}(3.14)(5)^3 \longleftarrow \text{Use 3.14 for } \pi$$

$$\approx \frac{4}{3}(3.14)(125)$$

$$\approx 523.3 \qquad \text{The volume of the sphere is about 523.3 cm}^3.$$

2. Find the volume of a sphere with the given dimension. Round to the nearest tenth.

a) 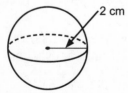 2 cm

b) 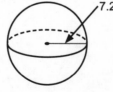 7.2 ft

c) 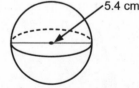 5.4 cm

d) 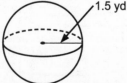 1.5 yd

e) 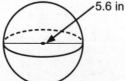 5.6 in

Bonus ▶ A hemisphere is half a sphere.

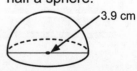 3.9 cm

3. a) An inflated soccer ball has diameter 22 cm. What is the volume of air inside the ball?

b) Kim pumped a bike pump 9 times to inflate the empty soccer ball. How much air did each pump add?

c) There is a small leak in the ball and air is escaping at the rate of 25 cm³ each hour. After how many hours will the ball be half-full of air?

4. Find the volume of the composite solid.

a)

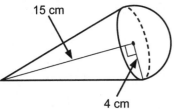

15 cm

4 cm

b)

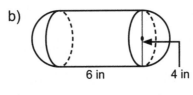

6 in   4 in

c) A hemisphere is removed from a cylinder.

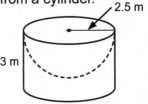

2.5 m

3 m

5. A golf ball has diameter 1.7 inches. One dozen golf balls are packed in a box with dimensions 7.3 inches by 5.5 inches by 1.9 inches. How much space is there around the golf balls?

If you know the volume (V), you can find the radius (r) of a sphere.

Example:

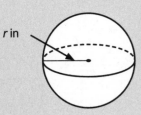

$V \approx 267.9 \text{ in}^3$

r in

$$V = \frac{4}{3}\pi r^3$$

$$267.9 \approx \frac{4}{3}(3.14)r^3$$

$$267.9 \approx 4.2r^3$$

$$267.9 \div 4.2 \approx r^3$$

$$63.8 \approx r^3$$

$\sqrt[3]{63.8} \approx r$ ◀——— Use the $\boxed{\sqrt[3]{x}}$ button on your calculator.

$4 \approx r$ The radius of the sphere is about 4 in.

6. Find the radius of a sphere with the given volume.

a) $V \approx 2{,}143.6 \text{ in}^3$ **b)** $V \approx 65.4 \text{ cm}^3$ **c)** $V \approx 492.6 \text{ ft}^3$

7. The volume of an exercise ball is about 14,130 in³. What is its diameter?

8. The radius of a sphere is 5 cm. Fred cut off the bottom 2 cm to give the shape a flat face to sit on. What is the radius of the base of the shape he cut off? Hint: Label the cross section of the sphere with the information from the question.

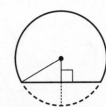

1. Complete the table.

	3-D Shape	3-D Shape Name	Two Real-World Examples	Formula for Volume
a)				
b)				
c)				
d)				
e)				

2. a) A cylinder, a cone, and a sphere each have a radius of 1 inch. The cylinder and the cone each have a height equal to the radius. Write an expression using the symbol π for the volume of each shape.

    i) Volume of the cylinder = _____

    ii) Volume of the cone = _____

    iii) Volume of the sphere = _____

b) A cylinder has a volume of 372 cm³. Its height is equal to its radius.

    i) A cone has the same radius and height as the cylinder. What is the cone's volume?

    ii) A sphere has the same radius as the cylinder. What is the sphere's volume?

3. Find the volume of the shape. Round to the nearest tenth. Use 3.14 for π.

a)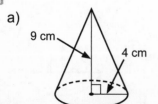

9 cm   4 cm

b)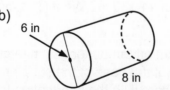

6 in   8 in

c)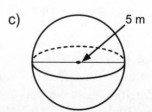

5 m

4. Complete the sentence. Write "two," "four," or "eight."

a) When you double each dimension of a rectangular prism, the volume is multiplied by _____.

b) When you double the height of a pyramid, the volume is multiplied by _____.

c) When you double the radius of a cylinder, the volume is multiplied by _____.

d) When you double the radius of a sphere, the volume is multiplied by _____.

5. Use the Pythagorean Theorem to find h. Then find the volume. Round to the nearest tenth.

a)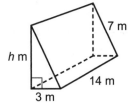

b)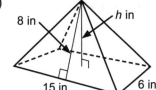

c)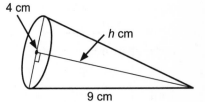

6. Find the volume of the composite solid. Round to the nearest tenth.

a)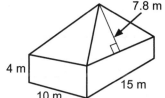

b)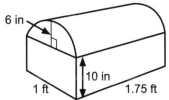

Hint: 1 ft = 12 in

c)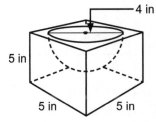

Hint: The hemisphere is removed from the prism.

7. Sketch and label 3 different shapes that each have a volume of 300 in³.

8. a) The diameter of a gumball is 1 inch. Max has a spherical gumball machine with diameter 8 inches. He calculates the volume of the gumball machine and the volume of 1 gumball, and divides to find the number of gumballs the machine can hold. What answer does he get?

b) In reality, will the number of gumballs in the machine be equal to, more than, or less than the answer that Max found in part a)? Explain.

9. Write and solve an equation to find the unknown measurement.

a) $V = 90$ cm³

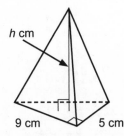

b) $V \approx 100.48$ in³

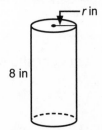

c) $V \approx 67.5$ ft³

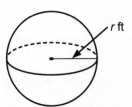

Scatter Plots with Linear Associations

REMINDER:

If the values in the sets of data increase together, there is a positive association.	If the values increase in one set of data as they decrease in the other set of data, there is a negative association.	If there is neither a positive nor negative association, there is no association.
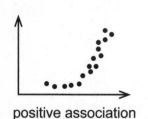	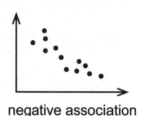	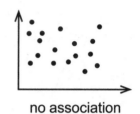
positive association	negative association	no association

1. Write the type of association shown by the scatter plot.

a)

b)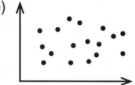

c)

_____negative association_____   _____   _____

REMINDER: A cluster is a group of dots that are close to each other.

An outlier is a data point that is very different from the others in the data set. On a scatter plot, the outliers are far from other dots.

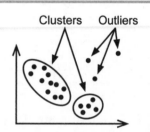

2. a) Circle the clusters and cross out the outliers.

i) 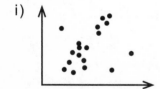   ii)    iii)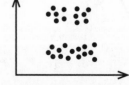

b) What type of association does each scatter plot in part a) show?

i) _____   ii) _____   iii) _____

c) What type of association does the scatter plot at right show?

_____

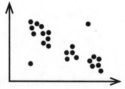

3. The table shows the test marks and final marks of 15 students.

Test Marks (%)	83	68	72	85	68	69	84	87	67	70	72	81	79	71	72
Final Marks (%)	85	67	69	84	77	71	82	78	70	68	69	82	80	70	72

a) Write the data as ordered pairs. Then draw a scatter plot
for the data.

(83 , 85), (,), (,), (,), (,),

(,), (,), (,), (,), (,),

(,), (,), (,), (,), (,)

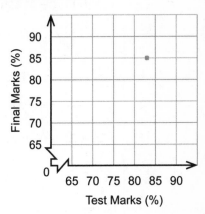

b) Circle the clusters and cross out the outliers.

c) Is there a positive association, a negative association,
or no association between test marks and final marks?

_____

If data shown on a scatter plot generally match a straight line, then there is a **linear association**
between the two sets of data.

Examples:

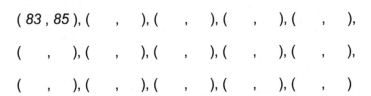

         linear   linear   nonlinear

---

4. a) Is there an association? If so, describe the association as positive or negative and
linear or nonlinear.

i) 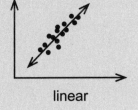   ii) 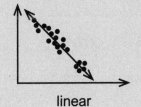   iii)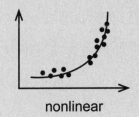

   negative, linear   _____   _____

b) Is there any association in the scatter plot for part iii)? _____

c) When there is no association, is it meaningful to talk about positive and negative,

or linear and nonlinear? _____

d) Describe the association for the scatter plot at right as linear

or nonlinear. _____

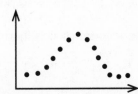

> REMINDER: A line on a graph is increasing if it goes from bottom left to top right.
> A line on a graph is decreasing if it goes from top left to bottom right.

5. a) Describe the type of association.

i)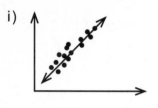

positive, linear

ii)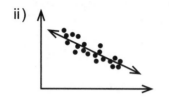

_____

iii)

_____

iv)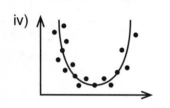

_____

v)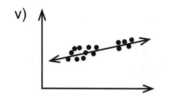

_____

vi)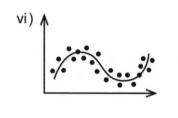

_____

b) Which scatter plots in part a) are linear? _____

c) Which lines in part a) are increasing? _____

d) Which lines in part a) have a positive slope? _____

e) How can you tell from the slope if an association is positive or negative?

_____

_____

6. The table shows the Internet use per week and the math marks of 15 students.

Internet Use per Week (h)	15	20	10	15	15	5	20	15	10	25	15	20	10	15	40
Math Mark (%)	75	72	84	70	60	82	74	76	75	69	70	73	79	81	73

a) Draw a scatter plot for the data.

b) Cross out the outliers. Does the graph show an association between hours of Internet use and math marks? _____

c) If so, is it positive or negative? _____

Is it linear or nonlinear? _____

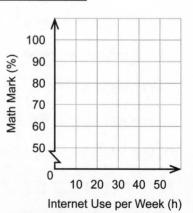

Statistics and Probability 8-4

1. The scatter plot shows the daily temperatures in Portland, OR, and the number of heaters sold.

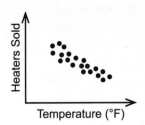

   a) Would you describe the association as positive or negative?

   _____

   b) Would you describe the association as linear or nonlinear?

   _____

   c) Which line below is closest to the data points and best shows the association? _____

   A.   **B.**   **C.**

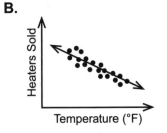 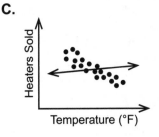

   d) Which line has a negative slope? _____

   e) Which line has a slope equal to zero? _____

In a **strong linear association**, most of the data points are very close to a straight line.

strong linear   strong linear   weak linear   weak linear

---

2. The line on each scatter plot below shows the general direction of the data.

   A.   **B.**   **C.**   **D.**

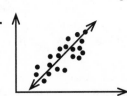 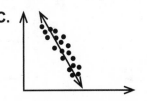 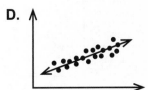

   a) Which linear associations are positive? _____

   b) Which linear associations are negative? _____

   c) Which positive linear association is strongest? _____

   d) Which negative linear association is strongest? _____

A **line of best fit** is a straight line that passes through the center of the data points to show the **trend**. The points in a scatter plot are closely packed around the line of best fit.

Examples:

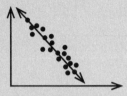

A line of best fit

Not a line of best fit

Not a line of best fit

Not a line of best fit

3. The scatter plot at right shows the relationship between the heights of 12 students and their shoe sizes.

a) Which lines pass through the center of the data points? _____

A.

B.

C.

b) Which lines show the trend of the data? _____

c) Which line shows the line of best fit? _____

4. The scatter plot at right shows the science marks and math marks of 15 students.

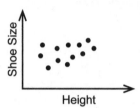

a) Which lines show the trend of the data? _____

A.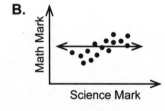

B.

C.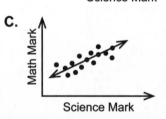

b) Count the number of points on each side of the line.

    A. Points above: ___1___   **B.** Points above: _____   **C.** Points above: _____

         Points below: __14__   Points below: _____   Points below: _____

c) Which line shows the line of best fit? _____

An outlier has an effect on the line of best fit. For example, when an outlier with a relatively high *x*-value and relatively low *y*-value is added, it makes the association less positive or more negative. The line of best fit rotates clockwise.

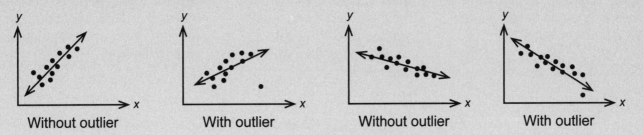

Without outlier   With outlier   Without outlier   With outlier

5. The scatter plot at right shows the relationship between the weights of 10 cars and the braking distance each car needs to make a complete stop.

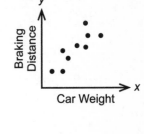

a) Which is the line of best fit for the scatter plot? _____

A. 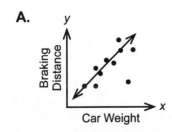   **B.** 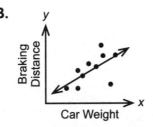   **C.**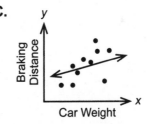

b) The same scatter plot is shown below but with an outlier added. Which

is the line of best fit for the revised scatter plot? _____

A.   **B.**   **C.**

c) Does the outlier affect the line of best fit? _____

6. a) The graph shows the line of best fit for the data set. Would the line rotate clockwise or counter-clockwise if you added an outlier with …

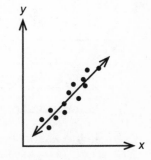

i) a low *x*-value and high *y*-value? _____

ii) a high *x*-value and low *y*-value? _____

b) Add a point far from the others, but on the line of best fit.

Will it change the line of best fit? _____

SP8-6 Drawing the Line of Best Fit Informally

To draw the line of best fit for a scatter plot:

Step 1: Look at the trend shown by the data and determine the type of association.

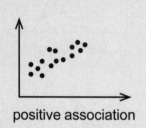

positive association

Step 2: Draw a line through the center of all data points, starting where the data begins and ending where the data ends.

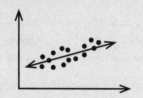

Step 3: Check the line you drew. There should be about the same number of data points on each side of the line.

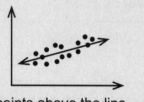

7 points above the line
6 points below the line ✓

1. Draw the line of best fit for the scatter plot. Count the number of points on each side of the line.

a)

Points above: ___5___

Points below: ___6___

b)

Points above: _____

Points below: _____

c)

Points above: _____

Points below: _____

d)

Points above: _____

Points below: _____

e)

Points above: _____

Points below: _____

f)

Points above: _____

Points below: _____

2. The table shows the number of gold medals won by American athletes at the Olympic Summer Games from 1956 to 1968.

Year	1956	1960	1964	1968
Number of Gold Medals	32	34	36	45

a) Draw a scatter plot for the data.

b) Is the association positive or negative? _____

c) Draw the line of best fit for the scatter plot.

Olympic Gold Medals Won by US Athletes by Year

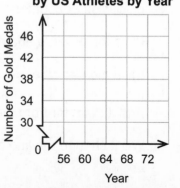

3. The table shows data for ten students.

Height (cm)	163	170	180	154	164	181	140	160	170	143
Foot Length (cm)	23	23	27	23	24	25	21	22	24	24

a) Draw a scatter plot for the data.

b) Is the association positive or negative? _____

c) Draw the line of best fit for the scatter plot.

d) How many points are above the line? _____

e) How many points are below the line? _____

Height and Foot Length

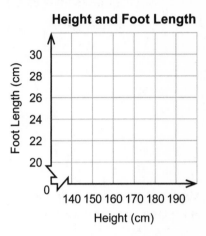

4. Joe researched some of his ancestors and recorded this data:

Years of Education	less than 12	exactly 12	13 to 15	16 or more
Age at Death	74	78	83	84

a) Draw a scatter plot for the data.

b) Is the association positive or negative? _____

c) Draw the line of best fit for the scatter plot.

Years of Education and Age at Death

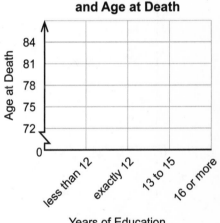

5. Circle any outliers on the scatter plot. Then draw the line of best fit for the scatter plot. Count the number of points on each side of the line.

a)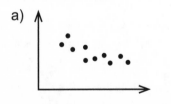

b)

c)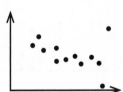

Points above: _____   Points above: _____   Points above: _____

Points below: _____   Points below: _____   Points below: _____

d) What do you notice by comparing the lines of best fit in parts a) and c)?

_____

SP8-7 Writing Equations for the Line of Best Fit

REMINDER: You can find the slope of a straight line using any two points on the line.

Choose two points. Label the point to the left *A* and label the other point *B*. Find the slope from *A* to *B* so that the run will be positive.

Example: *A* (1, 3) and *B* (4, 1)

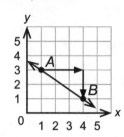

$$\text{run} = 4 - 1 = +3$$
$$\text{rise} = 1 - 3 = -2$$
$$\frac{\text{rise}}{\text{run}} = \frac{-2}{+3} = -\frac{2}{3}$$
$$\text{slope} = -\frac{2}{3}$$

1. Mark points *A* and *B* on the line and then find the slope. Label the point to the left *A*.
   Hint: Use integer coordinates if possible.

a)

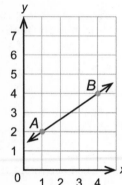

run = _____   rise = _____

$$\text{slope} = \frac{\text{rise}}{\text{run}} = \text{____}$$

b)

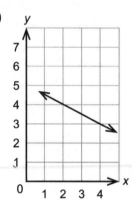

run = _____   rise = _____

$$\text{slope} = \frac{\text{rise}}{\text{run}} = \text{____}$$

c)

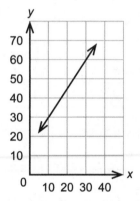

run = _____   rise = _____

$$\text{slope} = \frac{\text{rise}}{\text{run}} = \text{____}$$

2. The table shows data for seven students.

Height and Arm Span

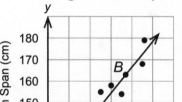

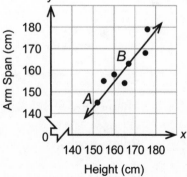

Height (cm)	165	152	176	175	167	155	160
Arm Span (cm)	154	145	179	168	163	156	158

a) The scatter plot shows the data in the table.

   Is the association positive or negative? _____

b) Circle points *A* and *B* in the table.

c) Use points *A* and *B* to find the slope of the line of best fit.

REMINDER: The *y*-intercept is where the line crosses the *y*-axis. When we express a line in
slope-intercept form, $y = mx + b$, m is the slope and b is the *y*-intercept of the line.

3. a) Extend the line to find the *y*-intercept.

i)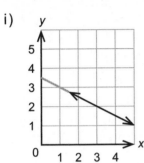

y-intercept: __3.5__

ii)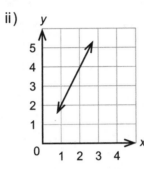

y-intercept: _____

iii)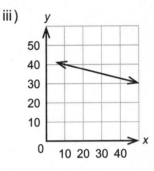

y-intercept: _____

b) Mark two points *A* and *B* on each line and label the left point *A*. Then find the slope.

c) Write the equation for each line in slope-intercept form: $y = mx + b$.

To find the *y*-intercept of a line with slope $= \dfrac{3}{4}$ that passes through point *A* (2, 5) using algebra:

Step 1: Write the equation for the slope-intercept
form of a line, then substitute the given
slope and coordinates of point *A*.

$$y = mx + b$$
$$5 = \frac{3}{4}(2) + b$$

Step 2: Solve the equation to find *b*.

$$5 = \frac{3}{4}(2) + b$$
$$5 = \frac{3}{2} + b$$
$$b = 5 - \frac{3}{2} = 5 - 1.5, \text{ so } b = 3.5$$

4. Find the *y*-intercept of a line with the given slope that passes through the given point *A*.

a) slope $= 3$, *A* (1, 2)

$$y = mx + b$$
$$2 = 3(1) + b$$
$$2 = 3 + b$$
$$b = -1$$

b) slope $= -2$, *A* (1, 5)

c) slope $= 0.4$, *A* (1, 1)

d) slope $= \dfrac{1}{2}$, *A* (2, 1)

e) slope $= \dfrac{2}{3}$, *A* (5, 9)

f) slope $= -\dfrac{1}{2}$, *A* (2, 7)

5. Write the equation of each line from Question 4 in slope-intercept form. Check your answers by substituting the coordinates of point *A*.

a) $y = 3x - 1$

    $2 = 3(1) - 1$

    $2 = 2$ ✓

b) $y =$

c) $y =$

d) $y =$

e) $y =$

f) $y =$

6. The table shows the amount of sugar that dissolves in 100 grams of water at different temperatures.

Temperature (°C)	20	40	60	80	100
Amount of Sugar Dissolved (g)	204	238	287	362	482

Water Temperature and Sugar Dissolved

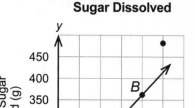
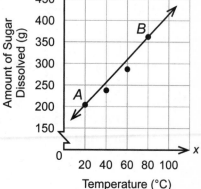

a) Is there any association in the scatter plot at right? _____

    If so, is it positive or negative? _____

b) Use points *A* (20, 204) and *B* (80, 362) to find the slope of the line of best fit.

c) Use the slope and point *A* (20, 204) to predict the *y*-intercept of the line of best fit.

d) The *y*-intercept of the line of best fit is the amount of sugar that dissolves in water

    at _____°C. Write an equation for the line of best fit in slope-intercept form.

    $y =$ _____

e) You can dissolve 179 grams of sugar in 100 grams of 0°C water. How much is your

    prediction from part c) off by?   _179_ − _____ = _____

f) Add point (0, 179) to the scatter plot. Do the points represent a linear or nonlinear

    association? _____

SP8-8 Applications of the Line of Best Fit

1. The graph is linear. Join the points with a straight line to find the missing values in the table.

a)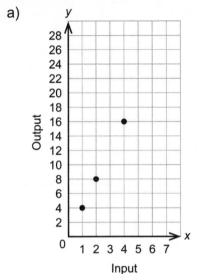

Input	Output
1	4
2	
	16
5.5	
7	

b)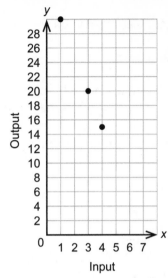

Input	Output
1	30
	20
	15
	7.5
7	

> When there is a strong linear association between two variables, you can use the line of best fit and the value of one variable to predict the value of the second variable.

2. The scatter plot shows the data for seven students.

Height and Arm Span

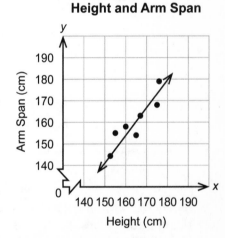

a) Use the line of best fit to estimate …

   i) the arm span of a student who is 170 cm tall. _____

   ii) the height of a student with an arm span of 170 cm. _____

b) Extend the line of best fit to predict …

   i) the arm span of a student who is 190 cm tall. _____

   ii) the height of a student with an arm span of 190 cm. _____

3. Find the value of y for each value of x.

a)

x	$y = 2x - 1$
1	$2(1) - 1$ $= 1$
2	
1.5	
3.2	

b)

x	$y = 0.75x + 2$
1	$0.75(1) + 2$ $= 2.75$
2	
1.5	
3.2	

c)

x	$y = -0.55x + 8.1$
1	$-0.55(1) + 8.1$ $= 7.55$
2	
1.5	
3.2	

4. A math test was graded out of 20 and a science test was graded out of 40. The scatter plot shows the marks of 12 students.

a) Describe the association between the test marks in math and science. _____

b) The equation of the line of best fit is $y = 2.09x + 0.82$, where x is the math mark and y is the science mark. Use this equation to find the science mark of a student whose math mark was 9.

Student Test Results

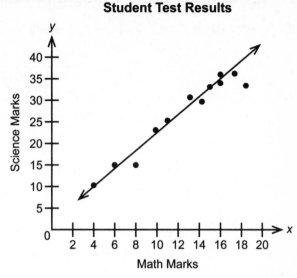

Math Marks

5. Solve the equation to find the value of x for each value of y.

a)

y	$y = 2x - 1$
5	$5 = 2x - 1$ $6 = 2x$ $3 = x$
2	
1.5	

b)

y	$y = 0.75x + 2$
5	$5 = 0.75x + 2$ $3 = 0.75x$ $4 = x$
2	
1.5	

c)

y	$y = -0.55x + 8.1$
5	$5 = -0.55x + 8.1$ $-3.1 = -0.55x$ $5.64 = x$
2	
1.5	

6. The scatter plot shows the fuel efficiency (miles per gallon, or mpg) of cars with different engine sizes (described in liters, or L). The equation of the line of best fit is $y = -8.18x + 53.18$, where x is the engine size and y is the fuel efficiency.

a) Describe the association between engine size

and fuel efficiency. _____

b) Use the equation of the line of best fit to estimate the fuel efficiency of a car with engine size 2.6 L.

c) Use the equation to estimate the engine size of a car with a fuel efficiency of 37 mpg.

Engine Size and Fuel Efficiency

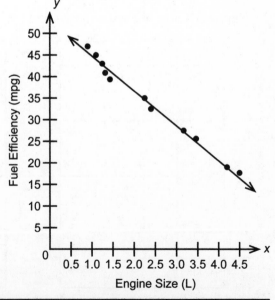

Engine Size (L)

7. **a)** In the graph at right, how much would you expect Nina's test mark to increase by if she studied for

1 extra hour? _____ Where do you see this in

the equation? _____

b) What mark would you expect Nina to get if she doesn't

study for the test at all? _____ Where do you see

this in the equation? _____

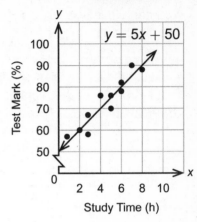

Study Time and Test Marks

$y = 5x + 50$

8. The table shows the marks of 10 students on two tests.

Test A Marks (%)	68	74	81	89	66	55	75	73	76	68
Test B Marks (%)	71	69	85	84	68	62	77	73	79	74

a) Draw a scatter plot for the data.

b) Describe the type of association. _____

c) Draw the line of best fit for the scatter plot.

d) How many points are above your line? _____

e) How many points are below your line? _____

f) Use the line of best fit to estimate …

   i) the mark of a student on Test B who got 70% on Test A. _____

   ii) the mark of a student on Test A who got 82% on Test B. _____

g) Extend the line of best fit and predict …

   i) the mark of a student on Test B who got 95% on Test A. _____

   ii) the mark of a student on Test A who got 90% on Test B. _____

h) Use two points on the line of best fit to find the slope.

i) Use the slope and one point on the line of best fit to find the *y*-intercept.

j) Write an equation for the line of best fit in slope-intercept form. $y =$ _____

k) Use the equation from part j) to calculate the answers to parts f) and g).

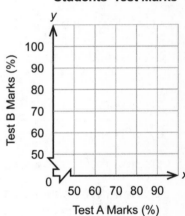

Students' Test Marks

SP8-9 Venn Diagrams and Two-Way Tables

You can visually organize information in categories so
that each category has some common fact.

A Venn diagram uses an oval for each category and
shows if the categories overlap. Example: Information
that is true for both dolphins and fish is shown where
the ovals overlap.

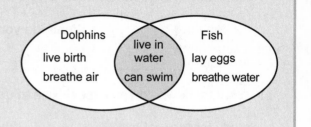

1. a) Organize the numbers in the Venn diagram: 7, $\sqrt{2}$, $\sqrt{9}$, $\sqrt[3]{16}$, 12, $5\frac{2}{3}$

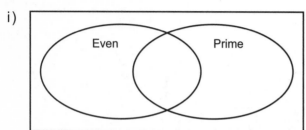 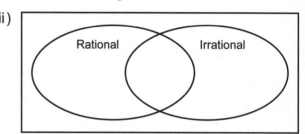

   i) Even   Prime

   ii) Rational   Irrational

   b) Shade the empty region(s) in the Venn diagrams above.

   c) Can you add a number to the overlapping region in part i), above? Explain.

   d) Can you add a number to the overlapping region in part ii), above? Explain.

2. a) Organize the numbers in the Venn diagram: $4\frac{2}{5}$, -3, 13, $\sqrt{75}$, $\frac{41}{4}$, $\sqrt{5}$, $\frac{25}{2}$, $\sqrt[3]{-8}$, $12.\overline{1}$

   b) Shade the empty region in the Venn diagram.

   c) How many numbers are greater than 3? _____

   d) How many numbers are less than 10? _____

   e) How many numbers are greater than 3 and
       less than 10? _____

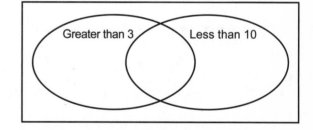

   f) How many numbers are greater than 3 and
       not less than 10? _____

   g) How many numbers are less than 10 and not greater than 3? _____

   h) Complete the table using the numbers in part a) and your answers to parts b) to g).

	Less than 10	Not less than 10	Total
Greater than 3			
Not greater than 3			
Total			

Statistics and Probability 8-9

A **two-way table** shows data for two different categories. Usually, the final row and the final column in the table show totals.

Example: Students in a class were asked if they have a bike and if they have skates.

The table shows the numbers of students in each category.

	Skates	No Skates	Total
Bike	7 (Have skates and bikes)	15 (Have bike only)	22
No Bike	6 (Have only skates)	2 (Have no skates, no bike)	8
Total	13 (Total with skates)	17 (Total with no skates)	**30** (Total number asked)

3. Use the two-way table above to answer the question.

   a) How many students have a bike and skates? _____

   b) How many students only have a bike, but no skates? _____

   c) How many students have skates, but no bike? _____

   d) How many students have no bike and no skates? _____

   e) What is the sum of students with a bike and without a bike? _22 + 8 = 30_

   f) What is the sum of students with skates and without skates? _____

   g) How many students were asked? _____

   Bonus ▶ How many students have a bike or skates? _____

In a **row two-way table**, there is a totals column but there is not a totals row.

4. Find the missing terms in the two-way table or row two-way table.

a)

	Skateboard	No Skateboard	Total
Scooter	15	7	
No Scooter		8	28
Total	35		

b)

	Phone	No Phone	Total
TV		20	73
No TV	12		
Total	65		100

c)

	Soccer	No Soccer	Total
Tennis		8	19
No Tennis	15		31

d)

	Travel Outside US	No Travel Outside US	Total
Camping	13		23
No Camping	7	19	

You can use a Venn diagram to summarize information from a two-way table.

Example: The left oval shows total students with bikes. The right oval shows total students with skates.

Have no bike, no skates →

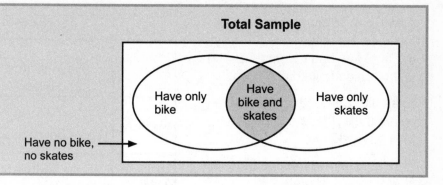

Total Sample

Have only bike | Have bike and skates | Have only skates

5. The two-way table shows the results of surveying 100 students about playing a musical instrument and a sport. Complete the Venn diagram using the two-way table. Don't forget to write a number outside the two ovals.

	Play an Instrument	Play No Instrument	Total
Play a Sport	9	56	65
Play No Sport	15	20	35
Total	24	76	100

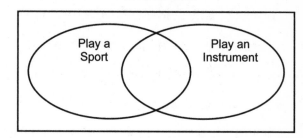

100 Students

Play a Sport | Play an Instrument

6. People in 100 households were asked if they had a television and a landline phone. The Venn diagram shows the results.

a) How many households …

   i) have just a landline phone? __16__

   ii) have just a TV? _____

   iii) have both a landline phone and a TV? _____

   iv) have a landline phone? __16 + 49 = 65__

   v) have no landline phone? __100 − 65 = 35__

   vi) have a TV? _____

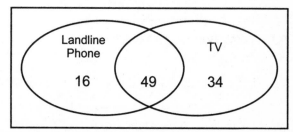

100 Households

Landline Phone — 16 | 49 | TV — 34

b) Complete the two-way table using your answers to part a).

	Landline Phone	No Landline Phone	Total
TV			
No TV	16		
Total	65	35	100

c) Use the table to say how many households have no TV and no landline phone. _____

SP8-10 Two-Way Relative Frequency Tables

A **frequency table** shows how many times a value occurs in a set of data. A **relative frequency table** shows how many times each value occurs as a percent.

Example: For the word "Cincinnati," the table shows the frequency and the relative frequency of the letters in the word.

Letter	Frequency	Relative Frequency
C	2	20%
I	3	30%
N	3	30%
A	1	10%
T	1	10%

1. In a survey of 75 students:

   • 23 students are interested in football,

   • 14 students are interested in basketball,

   • 11 students are interested in baseball,

   • 8 students are interested in soccer, and

   • 19 students are interested in other sports.

   Complete the table.

Sport	Frequency	Relative Frequency
Football	23	$23 \div 75 \approx 31\%$
Basketball		
Baseball		
Soccer		
Other		

2. The Enhanced Fujita Scale (EF-Scale) is used to rate the strength of tornadoes based on the damage they cause. The ratings range from EF0, with light damage, to EF5, with incredible damage or total destruction of buildings.

   The table shows the frequency (freq.) of tornadoes in the United States and Canada in 2014.

   a) Complete the table.

   b) Which country had more EF1 tornadoes? _____

   c) Which country had a greater relative frequency of EF1 tornadoes? _____

   d) EF0 and EF1 cause minor to moderate damage. Is it correct to say that Canada has a greater relative frequency of tornados with minor or moderate damage?

   _____ Explain why. _____

   _____

   _____

Enhanced Fujita Scale	US		Canada	
	Freq.	Relative Freq.	Freq.	Relative Freq.
EF0	476	54%	12	48%
EF1	315		10	
EF2	70		3	
EF3	20		0	
EF4	7		0	
EF5	0		0	
Total	888		25	

To make a **two-way relative frequency table**, divide each value in the two-way table by the total sample size.

Example:

Two-way table

	Skates	No Skates	Total
Bike	7	15	22
No Bike	6	2	8
Total	13	17	30

Two-way relative frequency table

	Skates	No Skates	**Total**
Bike	$\frac{7}{30} \approx 23\%$	$\frac{15}{30} = 50\%$	$\frac{22}{30} \approx 73\%$
No Bike	$\frac{6}{30} = 20\%$	$\frac{2}{30} \approx 7\%$	$\frac{8}{30} \approx 27\%$
Total	$\frac{13}{30} \approx 43\%$	$\frac{17}{30} \approx 57\%$	$\frac{30}{30} = 100\%$

(this table shows the calculations)

3. Use the two-way table to complete the two-way relative frequency table.

a)

	Phone	No Phone	Total
TV	32	5	37
No TV	11	2	13
Total	43	7	50

	Phone	No Phone	Total
TV	$\frac{32}{50} = 64\%$		
No TV			
Total			

b)

	Soccer	No Soccer	Total
Tennis	17	11	28
No Tennis	19	16	35
Total	36	27	63

	Soccer	No Soccer	Total
Tennis			
No Tennis			
Total			

4. Alex surveyed 50 students randomly at his school about being fans of sci-fi movies and thrillers. The table shows the results.

a) Use the two-way table to complete the two-way relative frequency table.

b) Based on the relative frequency table, in which group can you find the most sci-fi fans, among students who like thrillers or students who don't like thrillers? _____

Why? _____

_____

	Sci-fi Fans	Not Sci-fi Fans	Total
Thriller Fans	19	7	26
Not Thriller Fans	8	16	24
Total	27	23	50

	Sci-fi Fans	Not Sci-fi Fans	Total
Thriller Fans			
Not Thriller Fans			
Total			

Statistics and Probability 8-10

1. The row two-way relative frequency table shows the results of a survey.

	Been Camping	Never Been Camping	Total
Live in Country	70%	30%	100%
Live in City	40%	60%	100%

Cathy says 70% of the people surveyed who live in the country have been camping. Mike says 70% of the people surveyed who have been camping live in the country.

Who is right, Cathy or Mike? _____

2. a) Use the row two-way table to complete the row two-way relative frequency table.

	Left-Handed	Right-Handed	Total
Live in Country	32	268	300
Live in City	53	447	500

	Left-Handed	Right-Handed	Total
Live in Country	$\frac{32}{300} \approx 11\%$		100%
Live in City			100%

b) Who is more likely to be left-handed, someone who lives in the country or someone

who lives in the city, or is the likelihood about the same? _____

c) If the number of people who live in the city increases, would you expect the percent of left-handed people to increase, decrease, or stay the same? Why?

_____

d) Is there an association between living in the city and being left handed? _____

3. Kim surveyed 119 students randomly to find any association between being soccer fans and hockey fans. The row two-way table shows the results.

	Soccer Fans	Not Soccer Fans	Total
Hockey Fans	18	56	74
Not Hockey Fans	11	34	45

a) Use the row two-way table to complete the row two-way relative frequency table.

b) Based on the row relative frequency table, can you say hockey fans are more likely to be soccer fans than people who are not hockey fans?

_____ Why? _____

	Soccer Fans	Not Soccer Fans	Total
Hockey Fans			
Not Hockey Fans			

_____

If the relative frequencies are about the same for the rows of data, you can say there is no association between the two variables. Examples:

	Have a Bike	Have No Bike	Total
9 Year Old	70%	30%	100%
13 Year Old	71%	29%	100%

Based on the data, there is no association between having a bike and age.

	Reading Novels	Not Reading Novels	Total
9 Year Old	12%	88%	100%
13 Year Old	23%	77%	100%

Based on the data, there is a positive association between reading novels and age.

4. a) Complete the row two-way relative frequency table for the two-way table.

	Have Ridden a Horse	Have Not Ridden a Horse
Live in Country	25	75
Live in City	30	275

	Have Ridden a Horse	Have Not Ridden a Horse	Total
Live in Country	$\frac{25}{100} = 25\%$		100%
Live in City			100%

b) Who is more likely to have ridden a horse, someone who lives in the country or

someone who lives in the city? _____

c) If the number of people who live in the city increases, would you expect the percent of people who have ridden a horse to increase, decrease, or not be affected?

_____ Why? _____

_____

_____

d) Is there any association between living in the city and having ridden a horse? _____

If so, is it a positive association or a negative association? _____

e) Complete the Venn diagram using the two-way table.

f) How many people were surveyed in total? _____

g) How can you answer part a) using the Venn diagram?

_____

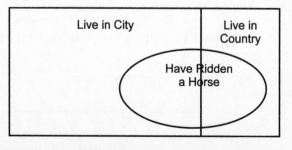

5. The row two-way table shows the results of a survey of Grade 6 and Grade 8 students about what they read.

	Novels	Comics	Other	Total
Grade 6	7	24	8	39
Grade 8	21	17	19	57

a) Complete the two-way relative frequency table for the two-way table.

	Novels	Comics	Other	Total
Grade 6				
Grade 8				

b) Based on the relative frequency table …

   i) from Grade 6 to 8, the rate of reading

   _____ decreases.

   ii) from Grade 6 to 8, the rate of reading

   _____ books increases.

   iii) As students in a middle school get older, do they read more variety of books? _____

6. The Venn diagram shows the results of a survey of 100 households about whether they have televisions and landline phones.

   a) Complete the row two-way table and the row two-way relative frequency table using the Venn diagram.

100 Households

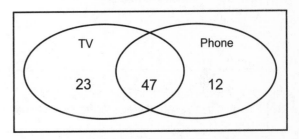

	Phone	No Phone	Total
TV	47		70
No TV			

	Phone	No Phone	Total
TV			
No TV			

b) Is there an association between having a landline phone and having a TV? _____

   If so, is it a positive or negative association? _____ Explain why.

   _____

c) Switch the rows with the columns of the two-way table in part a) and complete the row two-way relative frequency table.

	TV	No TV	Total
Phone	47		59
No Phone			

	TV	No TV	Total
Phone			
No Phone			

Bonus ▶ Can you say that households with landline phones are more likely to have TVs than households with TVs are to have landline phones? Why?

_____

_____

1. Match the scatter plots to the descriptions.

A. 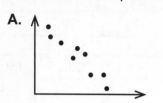   **B.**    **C.**    **D.**

a) a positive association _____

b) a negative association _____

c) a linear association _____

d) a nonlinear association _____

e) a strong linear association _____

f) a weak linear association _____

2. A scatter plot in Question 1 shows the association between the distance a student lives from school and the time it takes the student to walk to school. Which scatter plot is it? Explain.

_____

_____

3. Predict the relationship. Write "increases," "decreases," or "stays the same."

a) As age increases from 8 years to 18 years, the length of hair _____.

b) As age increases from 8 years to 18 years, the arm span _____.

c) As age increases from 8 years to 18 years, the number of toys _____.

4. The table shows the average number of hours per week spent playing sports and watching TV for 8 students.

Playing Sports (Hours per Week)	9	15	12	2	10	4	4	7
Watching TV (Hours per Week)	0	1	10	1	14	13	2	8

a) Use the grid to draw a scatter plot to represent the data. Remember to include a title, labels on the axes, and an appropriate scale.

b) Is there any association between how much time students spend playing sports and how much time students spend watching TV? Explain.

_____

_____

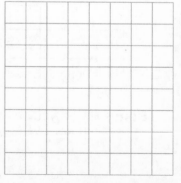

5. The table shows the hours of exercise per week and resting heart rate (in beats per minute, or bpm) of 10 students.

Exercise per Week (h)	4	2	1	3	2	7	4	9	6	1
Resting Heart Rate (bpm)	69	75	83	70	68	60	65	54	57	79

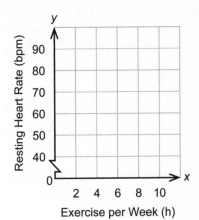

a) Draw a scatter plot for the data.

b) Is there a positive association, negative association, or no association between time spent exercising and

   resting heart rate? _____

c) Draw the line of best fit for the scatter plot.

d) How many points are above your line? _____

e) How many points are below your line? _____

f) Use the graph to estimate …

   i) the resting heart rate of a student who exercises 5 hours per week. _____

   ii) the hours of exercise per week for a student with a resting heart rate of 72. _____

g) Extend the line of best fit and predict …

   i) the resting heart rate of a student who doesn't exercise at all. _____

   ii) the resting heart rate of a student who exercises 10 hours per week. _____

h) Use two points on the line to find the slope of the line of best fit.

i) Find the *y*-intercept of the line of best fit.

j) Write the equation of the line of best fit in slope-intercept form. $y =$ _____

k) Use the equation of the line to calculate the answers to parts f) and g).

6. a) Find the missing terms in the two-way table.

i)

	Hike	Do Not Hike	Total
Swim	19	13	
Do Not Swim		7	23
Total	35		

ii)

	Guitar	No Guitar	Total
Drums		9	36
No Drums	25		
Total	52		69

iii)

	Passed	Failed	Total
Test 1			23
Test 2	28	6	
Total	41		

iv)

	Basketball	No Basketball	Total
Grade 6	14		31
Grade 8		17	
Total			59

b) Make a two-way relative frequency table for each table in part a).

c) Is there any association between the two variables of each two-way relative frequency table in part b)?

7. The Venn diagram shows the results from a survey of a random sample of 43 men and 28 women. The survey asks if they bike to work or not.

a) How many women bike to work? __13__

b) How many women don't bike to work? _____

c) How many men don't bike to work? _____

d) Complete the row two-way table using your answers in parts a) to c).

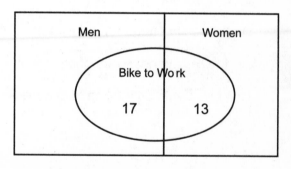

e) Complete the row two-way relative frequency table using the row two-way table.

f) Sam says men bike to work more than women because 17 men bike to work, compared to 13 women. Is Sam correct? Explain why.

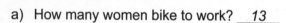

_____

_____

	Bike	No Bike	Total
Men			43
Women	13		28

	Bike	No Bike	Total
Men			43
Women	$\frac{13}{28} \approx 46\%$		28